John Burroughs' America

Selections from the Writings
of the Naturalist

JOHN BURROUGHS

Edited with an Introduction by
Farida A. Wiley

Foreword by
Julian Burroughs

Illustrated by
Francis Lee Jaques

DOVER PUBLICATIONS, INC.
Mineola, New York

Published in Canada by General Publishing Company,
Ltd., 30 Lesmill Road, Don Mills, Toronto, Ontario.
Published in the United Kingdom by Constable and Com-
pany, Ltd., 3 The Lanchesters, 162–164 Fulham Palace Road,
London W6 9ER.

Bibliographical Note

This Dover edition, first published in 1997, is a slightly
rearranged but otherwise complete and unabridged republication of *John Burroughs' America: Selections from the Writings of the Hudson River Naturalist*, originally published by
The Devin-Adair Company, New York, 1951. Original credits
for editing, the foreword and illustrations are retained in the
present publication.

For clearer references, the Dover edition prints the lists
"Books by John Burroughs" and "Sources of Quotations . . ."
in that order (see pp. 295–8); the lists were reversed in the
original publication. Two typographical errors in the Contents have been corrected.

Library of Congress Cataloging-in-Publication Data

Burroughs, John, 1837–1921.
    John Burroughs' America : selections from the writings
of the naturalist / John Burroughs ; edited and with an
introduction by Farida A. Wiley ; foreword by Julian Burroughs ; illustrated by Francis Lee Jaques.
        p.   cm.
    Originally published: New York : Devin-Adair Com-
pany, 1951.
    Includes bibliographical references and index.
    ISBN 0-486-29746-2 (pbk.)
    1. Natural history—Outdoor books. 2. Natural
history—United States. I. Wiley, Farida A. (Farida Anna)
II. Title.
QH81.B936   1997
508.73—dc21   96-44551
                                     CIP

Manufactured in the United States of America
Dover Publications, Inc., 31 East 2nd Street
Mineola, N.Y. 11501

FOREWORD

When sap runs, there is no joy like writing," my father used to say. This well illustrates two characteristics of his life. First, he found his greatest satisfaction in turning nature observations into literature. Second, he nearly always turned to his farm boyhood for his comparisons. He often spoke of the honey bee — the bee, he said, did not get honey from flowers, but got nectar, which was converted into honey. Just so, he felt he made literature from nectar, so to speak, that he gathered in the woods and fields.

Father said of himself, when I once spoke of writing his biography, that all of his life was in his books: "everything that came to fruit and flower in my life," as he expressed it. It was indeed one of the strange things that nature does, giving this farm boy such an urge, such determination to study and to create. He certainly got no encouragement at home. I have heard him say that none of his immediate family ever read a single one of his books!

At one of the Academies he attended he picked up an essay of Emerson's and was instantly thrilled and excited. Soon he was reading everything of Emerson's that he could lay his hands on. And this marked the beginning of his own literary career. Emerson was to have a great influence on his work.

Father wrote about twenty-five books, and on many subjects besides nature: religion, philosophy, literature, criticism, travel, geology, and so on. The purpose of this present volume is to gather into one book selections from a variety of his works. Miss Wiley is well fitted for this task. She is not only an expert ornithologist and botanist herself but also has a wide knowledge of the literature of natural history, and knew Father and much of the country he roamed. She was one of the few guests invited to attend his burial services and went with the group up to Slabsides afterwards, where the organization of a John Burroughs Association was discussed. This group was formed in 1921. Miss Wiley has been a director for many years and is Secretary-Treasurer at the present time.

JULIAN BURROUGHS

West Park, N.Y.

CONTENTS

ACKNOWLEDGMENTS

Except for the encouragement and suggestions of such friends as Helen and Allan Cruickshank, Edwin Way Teale, Fred G. Mason, Catherine Pessino, Lois Hussey, and especially Julian Burroughs, the publishing of the book would not have been attempted.

Publisher and Editor are most grateful to Houghton Mifflin Company for granting permission to use quotations from books on which they still hold copyright.

F. A. W.

INTRODUCTION

John Burroughs was born April 3, 1837, on a farm at the foot of Old Clump in the Catskill Mountains, near what is now the small town of Roxbury, Delaware County, New York. He was one of a family of ten children, whose ancestors had lived in the area for several generations. Although he was to travel widely in England, Hawaii, the West Indies, and Alaska, and was to make excursions to Yellowstone with Theodore Roosevelt, to Yosemite with John Muir, and through the South with Thomas A. Edison, Henry Ford, and Harvey Firestone, most of his eighty-five years were spent in the rural areas near the scene of his birth.

John started to school at the age of five, dressed in a white-striped cotton suit of material woven by his mother. The schoolhouse, known as the Stone Jug, was about a mile from home. By the time he was twelve he was allowed to attend school during the winter months only; at other seasons he was needed on the farm to help with haying, building stone fences, taking cows to pasture, and other chores. This schedule continued through his sixteenth or seventeenth year.

Throughout his childhood, whenever John wished to read during the evening, he would pull his stool up next to his mother's chair, from which a candle hung. Helping to make these candles was one of the many duties required of the Burroughs boys. A candle was made by dipping twisted cords, about sixteen inches long, into melted beef fat. It had to be dipped and hung up to harden many times before it reached the desired size.

The Burroughs family churned its butter in a dog churn, operated by a dog (or boy) treading a large wheel. The cogs of the wheel turned a crank, which worked the dasher of the churn. It was a slow process, taking usually half a day to complete. Old Cuff, the dog, sometimes managed to be elsewhere, and the boys of the family would then have to tread the wheel. The butter which was in excess of summer requirements was packed into fifty-pound firkins and taken late in the fall to the town of Catskill, fifty miles away. It was a momentous day for John when his turn first came to make this trip; it was his first real journey and provided sight of a Hudson River steamboat. A ton of butter was taken on that occasion, for which some fifteen cents a pound was paid — more than $300.00 worth.

Dr. Clara Barrus, the biographer of Burroughs, tells us of an experience that had a great influence on the rest of his life. One Sunday in May, when he was seven or eight, he and his brothers were in the Beacon woods looking for wintergreen. As John lay idly on the ground, gazing into the branches above him, he spied a small bluish bird, with a white spot on each wing, flitting among the trees. Excited, he asked his brothers what it was. They neither knew nor cared; but it was a great event to John. Right here in these woods come strange birds from distant lands! His imagination was fired. There were no bird books to help boys in those days, and it was not till nearly twenty years later that he learned the name of this particular bird — the black-throated blue warbler.

In those days, passenger pigeons were so plentiful that at times they darkened the sky as would a cloud passing over.

One day when some passenger pigeons began pouring down onto the ground in the beech forest next to John's home, looking for beechnuts to feed on, he seized his musket, thinking to bag some for food. He crept behind a stone fence to within a few feet of the fluttering mass; but he became so fascinated by the spectacle that he forgot to shoot.

This was not the last time he "forgot to shoot." One day he heard a pack of hounds baying as they followed the tracks of a fox, and again he reached for his musket. He waited quietly on the hillside, and so still was he that the fox, not seeing him, came close and stopped to look back toward the dogs. John again forgot to shoot and this time gave as his excuse the fact that he had his mittens on. For years thereafter, whenever he failed to perform a task, he would be asked if he was wearing his mittens.

John Burroughs started his teaching career April 11, 1854, in the little country school at Tongore, New York. For part of his salary, he "boarded 'round" in the area. During that time he attended the Hedding Literary Institute at Ashland, New York. His study there, and three months spent at Cooperstown Seminary, completed his formal schooling.

In the fall of 1857, at the age of twenty, he married Ursula North. He was teaching then at High Falls, New York.

Later John Burroughs taught near West Point, and he made frequent use of the Military Academy library. It was there that he saw Audubon's bird paintings and, to his great delight, identified the black-throated blue warbler of twenty years before. Here too he met his much-esteemed mentor, Ralph Waldo Emerson, who provided him with added impetus to keep on with his literary studies.

Burroughs was twenty-seven when, in 1863, he went to Washington, D.C., to work in the Quartermaster General's

Department.   Shortly after arriving, he met Walt Whitman, who became his close friend and adviser.   In 1867 his first book, *Notes on Walt Whitman, Poet and Person,* was published.   Four years later his first nature book, *Wake-Robin,* appeared, the title for which was selected by Whitman.

Leaving Washington in 1873, Burroughs settled on a small fruit farm at West Park, New York, where he planned and helped build the stone house that was to be home for many years.   This farm later became known as "Riverby," in reference to its situation overlooking the Hudson.   It was here that Burroughs wrote several books about the activities that took place in the natural world around him.   His essay on the house wren, *Fuss and Feathers,* recorded observations made in his own yard, where he provided many a box for them to nest in.

But Burroughs' interest was not in birds alone; he took in the whole universe.   When people came to see him, he made them so welcome that he soon needed a place to which he could retire for observation and writing.   He chose a spot about two miles from Riverby, a section of the woods he and his only son Julian were fond of exploring together.   The high point of land next to the site of the cabin, he named "Julian's Rock."   He built this cabin with the help of Julian, his own brother Hiram, and a carpenter.   It was a rustic house of two stories, covered by slabs.   "Slabsides," as it came to be called, still is in good condition.   It is maintained, just as Burroughs left it, by the John Burroughs Association, with headquarters at the American Museum of Natural History, New York City.

Burroughs entertained many noted persons at Slabsides.   He would cook for them over an open fireplace, using water from a nearby spring.   John Muir — "John-o'-Mountains" to Burroughs — was one of the earliest to come.   Theodore Roosevelt vied with Burroughs to see who could find more birds in the vicinity of the cabin. Dr. Frank M. Chapman, the ornithologist, was a frequent visitor, as were the students from nearby Vassar College, authors, teachers, and a host of others who came to enjoy the naturalist's hospitality.

It was my own good fortune to spend many delightful days at Slabsides, together with my sister and her family. We were with John Burroughs on one of the very last days he ever spent there. On this particular occasion he cooked a "brigand steak" for us over an outdoor fire. Here is how he did it: he would find a green twig of sugar maple or black birch, remove the bark, and sharpen one end so meat and onions could be easily pierced. He would alternate on the stick a piece of steak about one inch square with a piece of bacon and a slice of young onion, repeating the process. Resting the end of the stick on the rocks, back of the bed of coals, he would turn it slowly over the fire till done. Then he would serve it between slices of bread or in a roll. He would usually observe, as he slowly revolved the skewer, "It takes all the conceit out of the onion when you cook it."

The brigand steak that John Burroughs cooked for us that day was his last at Slabsides. A few days later, in September 1920, he left for California. He passed away during the return journey on March 29, 1921.

From 1909 to the end of his life he spent his summers on the farm which adjoined the old home farm, and his winters either in California or at Riverby. The summer home became known as "Woodchuck Lodge"; woodchucks were numerous in the neighborhood, and they would come to visit Burroughs' garden. He tried to keep their numbers down by shooting them; in fact he even had a coat made of their skins. But his shooting seemed to have little effect: he would remark that when he "killed one, seven came to the funeral."

From 1900 to 1906 Burroughs had many articles and poems published in *The Century, Harper's, Scribner's, Outlook, Atlantic Monthly,* and other magazines. He had first appeared in the *Atlantic* in 1865. These writings were incorporated, for the most part, into his books.

John Burroughs has left us a rich heritage in these books about adventurous days in the fields; along trout streams; climbing mountains; getting lost while looking for a lake; watching the strange inhabitants of a pond; exploring in deep forests; digging into the den of a weasel; reading the pages of decades in the rocks of the Hudson River Valley or the Catskill Mountains; speculating on the weather, or solving the riddles he found in the vast host of living things that were his neighbors.

Next-door neighbors, to Burroughs, were of more interest than those "faraway places" that have such allure for so many people. In his philosophy, "the most precious things of life are near at hand, without money and without price." This is well worth pondering in a time of turmoil, especially when we remember how much Burroughs was able to add to our knowledge of the field of natural sciences by studying his own backyard.

Burroughs was an accurate observer. He kept a diary and recorded what he saw with such well-chosen words that his writings are just as fresh and inspiring today as when they were written half a century ago. A prolific writer, he turned out twenty-five books. More than a million and a half copies of these were sold before they were allowed to go out of print. Once he remarked to a friend that if he had received one dollar for every *set* of his books that was sold, he would have been a wealthy man. But book royalties in those days were not what they are now.

Trying to choose the "best" of Burroughs' writings for a single volume would have been almost impossible, had not Burroughs himself, unknowingly perhaps, set down a standard for selection: "I am certain," he wrote, "that the majority of my readers would have me stick to natural history themes. I sympathize with them. I am myself never so well pleased as when I can bring them a fresh bit of natural history, or give them a day in the fields and woods or along the murmuring streams."

Burroughs' field of study was among the so-called commonplace things of life. They ceased to be commonplace when they left the tip of his pen. It is hoped that among the quotations in this book you will find a number of your favorite passages. Let John Burroughs, our poet-naturalist, take you afield and show you the wonders at your very door. I found the choosing a very thrilling experience.

FARIDA A. WILEY

American Museum of Natural History
New York

John Burroughs' America

1. The Philosophy of John Burroughs

THE MOST precious things of life are near at hand, without money and without price.* Each of you has the whole wealth of the universe at your very door. All that I ever had, and still have, may be yours by stretching forth your hand and taking it.[1]

One has only to sit down in the woods or fields or by the shore of the river or lake, and nearly everything of interest will come round to him — the birds, the animals, the insects; and presently, after his eye has got accustomed to the place and to the light and shade, he will probably see some plant or flower that he has sought in vain for, and that is a pleasant surprise to him. So, on a large scale, the student and lover of nature has this advantage over people who gad up and down the world seeking some novelty or excitement: he has only to stay at home and see the procession pass. The great globe swings around to him like a revolving showcase; the change of the seasons is like the passage of strange and new countries; the zones of the earth, with all their beauties and marvels, pass one's door and linger long in the passing.

What a voyage is this we make without leaving for a night our own fireside! St. Pierre well says that a sense of the power and mystery of nature shall spring up as fully in one's heart after he has made the circuit of his own field as after returning

* The sources of all material in this book are indicated in the Appendix, to which the numbers, as at the end of this paragraph, refer. [Ed.]

from a voyage round the world. I sit here amid the junipers of the Hudson, with purpose every year to go to Florida or to the West Indies or to the Pacific coast, yet the seasons pass and I am still loitering, with a half-defined suspicion, perhaps, that, if I remain quiet and keep a sharp lookout, these countries will come to me. I may stick it out yet and not miss much after all. The great trouble is for Mohammed to know when the mountain really comes to him. Sometimes a rabbit or a jay or a little warbler brings the woods to my door. A loon on the river, and the Canada lakes are here; the sea gulls and the fish hawk bring the sea; the call of the wild gander at night, what does it suggest? and the eagle flapping by, or floating along on a raft of ice, does not he bring the mountain?

One spring morning five swans flew above my barn in single file, going northward — an express train bound for Labrador. It was a more exhilarating sight than if I had seen them in their native haunts. They made a breeze in my mind, like a noble passage in a poem. How gently their great wings flapped; how easy to fly when spring gives the impulse! On another occasion I saw a line of fowls, probably swans, going northward at such a height that they appeared like a faint, waving black line against the sky. They must have been at an altitude of two or three miles. I was looking intently at the clouds to see which way they moved, when the birds came into my field of vision. I should never have seen them had they not crossed the precise spot upon which my eye was fixed. As it was near sundown, they were probably launched for an all-night pull. They were going with great speed, and as they swayed a little this way and that, they suggested a slender, all-but-invisible aerial serpent cleaving the ether. What a highway was pointed out up there! — an easy grade from the Gulf to Hudson's Bay.

Then the typical spring and summer and autumn days, of all shades and complexions — one cannot afford to miss any of them; and when looked out upon from one's own spot of earth, how much more beautiful and significant they are! Nature comes home to one most when he is at home; the stranger and traveler finds her a stranger and a traveler also. One's own landscape comes in time to be a sort of outlying part of himself; he has sowed himself broadcast upon it, and it reflects his own moods and feelings; he is sensitive to the verge of the horizon: cut those trees, and he bleeds; mar those hills, and he suffers. How has the farmer planted himself in his fields; builded himself into his stone walls, and evoked the sympathy of the hills by his struggle! This home feeling, this domestication of nature, is important to the observer. This is the birdlime with which he catches the bird; this is the private door that admits him behind the scenes.

The fields and woods and waters about one are a book from which he may draw exhaustless entertainment, if he will. One must not only learn the writing, he must translate the language, the signs, and the hieroglyphics. It is a very quaint and elliptical writing, and much must be supplied by the wit of the translator. At any rate, the lesson is to be well conned. Gilbert White said that that locality would be found the richest in zoological or botanical specimens which was most thoroughly examined. For more than forty years he studied the ornithology of his district without exhausting the subject.

I thought I knew my own tramping ground pretty well, but one April day, when I looked a little closer than usual into a small semi-stagnant lakelet where I had peered a hundred times before, I suddenly discovered scores of little creatures that were as new to me as so many nymphs would have been. They were partly fish shaped, from an inch to an inch and a half long, semitransparent, with a dark brownish line visible the entire length of them (apparently the thread upon which the life of the animal hung, and by which its all-but-impalpable frame was held together), and suspending themselves in the water or impelling themselves swiftly forward by means of a double row of fine, waving, hairlike appendages that arose from what appeared to be the back — a kind of undulating, pappus-like wings. What was it? I did not know. None of my friends or scientific acquaintances knew. I wrote to a learned man,* an authority upon fish, describing the creature as well as I could. He replied that it was only a familiar species of phyllopodous crustacean, known as *Eubranchipus vernalis*.

I remember that our guide in the Maine woods, seeing I had names of my own for some of the plants, would often ask me the name of this and that flower for which he had no word; and when I could recall the full Latin term, it seemed overwhelmingly convincing and satisfying to him. It was evidently a relief to know that these obscure plants of his native heath had been found worthy of a learned name, and that the Maine woods were not so uncivil and outlandish as they might at first seem: it was a comfort to him to know that he did not live beyond the reach of botany. In like manner I found satisfaction in knowing that my novel fish had been recognized and worthily named; the title conferred a new dignity at once; but when the learned man added that it was familiarly called the "fairy shrimp," I felt a deeper pleasure. Fairylike it certainly was, in its aerial, unsubstantial look and in its delicate, downlike means of locomotion; but the large head, with its curious folds and its eyes standing out in relief, as if on the heads of two pins, was gnomelike. Probably the fairy wore a mask and wanted to appear terrible to human eyes. Then the creatures had sprung out of the earth as by magic. I found some in a furrow

* John Treadwell Nichols. [Ed.]

in a plowed field that had encroached upon a swamp. In the
fall the plow had been there and had turned up only the moist
earth; now a little water was standing there, from which the
April sunbeams had invoked these airy, fairy creatures.

Dogmatism about nature or about anything else very often
turns out to be an ungrateful cur that bites the hand that reared
it. I speak from experience. I was once quite certain that the
honeybee did not work upon the blossoms of the trailing arbutus, but while walking in the woods one April day I came upon
a spot of arbutus swarming with honeybees. They were so eager
for it that they crawled under the leaves and the moss to get at
the blossoms, and refused on the instant the hive honey which
I happened to have with me and which I offered them. I had
had this flower under observation more than twenty years and
had never before seen it visited by honeybees. The same season
I saw them for the first time working upon the flower of blood-
root and of adder's-tongue. Hence I would not undertake to
say again what flowers bees do not work upon. Virgil implies
that they work upon the violet, and for aught I know they may.
I have seen them very busy on the blossoms of the white oak,
though this is not considered a honey- or pollen-yielding tree.
From the smooth sumac they reap a harvest in midsummer, and
in March they get a good grist of pollen from the skunk cabbage.

One secret of success in observing nature is capacity to take a
hint; a hair may show where a lion is hid. One must put this
and that together and value bits and shreds. Much alloy exists
with the truth. The gold of nature does not look like gold at
the first glance. It must be smelted and refined in the mind of
the observer. And one must crush mountains of quartz and
wash hills of sand to get it. To know the indications is the main
matter. People who do not know the secret are eager to take a
walk with the observer to find where the mine is that contains

such nuggets, little knowing that his ore bed is but a gravel
heap to them. How insignificant appear most of the facts which
one sees in his walks, in the life of the birds, the flowers, the
animals, or in the phases of the landscape or the look of the
sky! — insignificant until they are put through some mental or
emotional process and their true value appears. The diamond
looks like a pebble until it is cut. One goes to Nature only for
hints and half truths. Her facts are crude until you have absorbed them or translated them. Then the ideal steals in and
lends a charm in spite of one. It is not so much what we see as
what the thing seen suggests. We all see about the same; to one
it means much, to another little. A fact that has passed through
the mind of man, like lime or iron that has passed through his
blood, has some quality or property super-added or brought
out that it did not possess before. You may go to the fields and
the woods and gather fruit that is ripe for the palate without
any aid of yours, but you cannot do this in science or in art.
Here, truth must be disentangled and interpreted — must be
made in the image of man. Hence all good observation is more
or less a refining and transmuting process, and the secret is to
know the crude material when you see it.[2]

Unadulterated, unsweetened observations are what the real
nature lover craves. No man can invent incidents and traits
as interesting as the reality. Then, to know that a thing is true
gives it such a savor! The truth — how we do crave the truth!
We cannot feed our minds on simulacra any more than we can
our bodies. Do assure us that the thing you tell is true. If you
must counterfeit the truth, do it so deftly that we shall never
detect you. But in natural history there is no need to counterfeit the truth; the reality always suffices, if you have eyes to see
it and ears to hear it. Behold what Maeterlinck makes out of

the life of the bee simply by getting at and portraying the facts — a true wonder book, the enchantment of poetry wedded to the authority of science.[3]

When I see the discomforts that able-bodied American men will put up with rather than go a mile or half a mile on foot, the abuses they will tolerate and encourage, crowding the street-car on a little fall in the temperature or the appearance of an inch or two of snow, packing up to overflowing, dangling to the straps, treading on each other's toes, breathing each other's breaths, crushing the women and children, hanging by tooth and nail to a square inch of the platform, imperiling their limbs and killing the horses — I think the commonest tramp in the street has good reason to felicitate himself on his rare privilege of going afoot. Indeed, a race that neglects or despises this primitive gift, that fears the touch of the soil, that has no footpaths, no community of ownership in the land which they imply, that warns off the walker as a trespasser, that knows no way but the highway, the carriage way, that forgets the stile, the footbridge, that even ignores the rights of the pedestrian in the public road, providing no escape for him but in the ditch or up the bank, is in a fair way to far more serious degeneracy.

The human body is a steed that goes freest and longest under a light rider, and the lightest of all riders is a cheerful heart. Your sad or morose or embittered or preoccupied heart settles heavily into the saddle, and the poor beast, the body, breaks down the first mile. Indeed, the heaviest thing in the world is a heavy heart. Next to that, the most burdensome to the walker is a heart not in perfect sympathy and accord with the body — a reluctant or unwilling heart. The horse and rider must not only both be willing to go the same way, but the rider must lead the way and infuse his own lightness and eagerness into

the steed. Herein is no doubt our trouble, and one reason of
the decay of the noble art in this country. We are unwilling
walkers. We are not innocent and simple hearted enough to
enjoy a walk. We have fallen from that state of grace which
capacity to enjoy a walk implies. It cannot be said that as a
people we are so positively sad or morose or melancholic as that
we are vacant of that sportiveness and surplusage of animal
spirits that characterized our ancestors, and that springs from
full and harmonious life — a sound heart in accord with a
a sound body. A man must invest himself near at hand and in
common things, and be content with a steady and moderate
return, if he would know the blessedness of a cheerful heart and
the sweetness of a walk over the round earth. This is a lesson
the American has yet to learn — capability of amusement on a
low key. He expects rapid and extraordinary returns. He
would make the very elemental laws pay usury. He has nothing
to invest in a walk; it is too slow, too cheap. We crave the astonishing, the exciting, the far away, and do not know the highways of the gods when we see them — always a sign of the decay
of the faith and simplicity of man.

If I say to my neighbor, "Come with me, I have great wonders to show you," he pricks up his ears and comes forthwith;
but when I take him on the hills under the full blaze of the sun,
or along the country road, our footsteps lighted by the moon
and stars, and say to him, "Behold, these are the wonders, these
are the circuits of the gods, this we now tread is a morning star,"
he feels defrauded and as if I had played him a trick. And yet
nothing less than dilatation and enthusiasm like this is the badge
of the master walker.

If we are not sad, we are careworn, hurried, discontented,
mortgaging the present for the promise of the future. If we
take a walk, it is as we take a prescription, with about the same

relish and with about the same purpose; and the more the fatigue the greater our faith in the virtue of the medicine.

Of these gleesome saunters over the hills in spring, or those sallies of the body in winter, those excursions into space when the foot strikes fire at every step, when the air tastes like a new and finer mixture, when we accumulate force and gladness as we go along, when the sight of objects by the roadside and of the fields and woods pleases more than pictures or than all the art in the world — those ten- or twelve-mile dashes that are but the wit and effluence of the corporeal powers — of such diversion and open-road entertainment, I say, most of us know very little.

I notice with astonishment that at our fashionable watering places nobody walks; that, of all those vast crowds of health seekers and lovers of country air, you can never catch one in the fields or woods, or guilty of trudging along the country road with dust on his shoes and sun tan on his hands and face. The sole amusement seems to be to eat and dress and sit about the hotels and glare at each other. The men look bored, the women look tired, and all seem to sigh, "O Lord! what shall we do to be happy and not be vulgar?"[4]

I have been a seeker of trout from my boyhood, and on all the expeditions in which this fish has been the ostensible purpose, I have brought home more game than my creel showed. In fact, in my mature years I find I got more of nature into me, more of the woods, the wild, nearer to bird and beast, while threading my native streams for trout, than in almost any other way. It furnished a good excuse to go forth; it pitched one in the right key; it sent one through the fat and marrowy places of field and wood. Then the fisherman has a harmless, preoccupied look; he is a kind of vagrant that nothing fears. He blends himself with the trees and the shadows. All his approaches are gentle and indirect. He times himself to the meandering, soliloquizing stream; its impulse bears him along. At the foot of the waterfall he sits sequestered and hidden in its volume of sound. The birds know he has no designs upon them, and the animals see that his mind is in the creek. His enthusiasm anneals him and makes him pliable to the scenes and influences he moves among.

I am sure I run no risk of overpraising the charm and attractiveness of a well-fed trout stream, every drop of water in it as bright and pure as if the nymphs had brought it all the way from its source in crystal goblets, and as cool as if it had been hatched beneath a glacier. When the heated and soiled and jaded refugee from the city first sees one, he feels as if he would like to turn it into his bosom and let it flow through him a few hours, it suggests such healing freshness and newness. How his roily thoughts would run clear; how the sediment would go downstream! Could he ever have an impure or an unwholesome wish afterward? The next best thing he can do is to tramp along its banks and surrender himself to its influence. If he reads it intently enough, he will, in a measure, be taking it into his mind and heart and experiencing its salutary ministrations.[5]

In studying nature, the important thing is not so much what we see as how we interpret what we see. Do we get at the true meaning of the facts? Do we draw the right inference? The fossils in the rocks were long observed before men drew the right inference from them. So with a hundred other things in nature and life.[6]

A great many observers and nature students at the present time are possessed of the notion that the birds and beasts instruct their young, train them and tutor them, much after the human manner. In the familiar sight of a pair of crows for-aging with their young about a field in summer, one of our nature writers sees the old birds giving their young a lesson in flying. She says that the most important thing that the elders had to do was to teach the youngsters how to fly. This they did by circling about the pasture, giving a peculiar call while they were followed by their flock — all but one. This was a bob-tailed crow, and he did not obey the word of command. His mother took note of his disobedience and proceeded to disci-pline him. He stood upon a big stone, and she came down upon him and knocked him off his perch. "He squawked and flutter-ed his wings to keep from falling, but the blow came so sud-denly that he had not time to save himself, and fell flat on the ground. In a minute he clambered back upon his stone, and I watched him closely. The next time the call came to fly he did not linger, but went with the rest, and so long as I could watch him he never disobeyed again."

I should interpret this fact of the old and young crows flying about a field in summer quite differently. The young are fully fledged and are already strong flyers when this occurs. They do not leave the nest until they can fly well and need no tutor-ing. What the writer really saw was what anyone may see on the farm in June and July: she saw the parent crows foraging with their young in a field. The old birds flew about, followed by their brood, clamorous for the food which their parents found. The bobtailed bird, which had probably met with some accident, did not follow, and the mother returned to feed it; the young crow lifted its wings and flapped them and in its eagerness probably fell off its perch; then, when its parent flew away, it followed.

The power to see straight is the rarest of gifts: to see no more

and no less than is actually before you; to be able to detach
yourself and see the thing as it actually is, uncolored or un-
modified by your own sentiments or prepossessions. In short,
to see with your reason as well as with your perceptions, that is
to be an observer and to read the book of nature aright.[7]

If I were to name the three most precious resources of life,
I should say books, friends, and nature; and the greatest of
these, at least the most constant and always at hand, is nature.
Nature we have always with us, an inexhaustible storehouse of
that which moves the heart, appeals to the mind, and fires the
imagination — health to the body, a stimulus to the intellect,
and joy to the soul. To the scientist, nature is a storehouse of
facts, laws, processes; to the artist she is a storehouse of pictures;
to the poet she is a storehouse of images, fancies, a source of
inspiration; to the moralist she is a storehouse of precepts and
parables; to all, she may be a source of knowledge and joy.[8]

For ten or more years past I have been in the habit of jotting
down, among other things in my notebook, observations upon
the seasons as they passed — the complexion of the day, the aspects of nature, the arrival of the birds, the opening of the
flowers, or any characteristic feature of the passing moment or
hour which the great open-air panorama presented. Some of
these notes and observations touching the opening and the
progress of the spring season follow herewith.

But before I give these extracts, let me say a word or two in
favor of the habit of keeping a journal of one's thoughts and
days. To a countryman, especially of a meditative turn, who
likes to preserve the flavor of the passing moment, or to a person
of leisure anywhere who wants to make the most of life, a journal will be found a great help. It is a sort of deposit account

wherein one saves up bits and fragments of his life that would otherwise be lost to him.

What seemed so insignificant in the passing, or as it lay in embryo in his mind, becomes a valuable part of his experiences when it is fully unfolded and recorded in black and white. The process of writing develops it; the bud becomes the leaf or flower; the one is disentangled from the many and takes definite form and hue.

The pleasure and value of every walk or journey we take may be doubled to us by carefully noting down the impressions it makes upon us. There is hardly anything that does not become much more in the telling than in the thinking or in the feeling.

I see the fishermen floating up and down the river above their nets, which are suspended far out of sight in the water beneath them. They do not know what fish they have got, if any, till after a while they lift the nets up and examine them. In all of us there is a region of subconsciousness above which our ostensible lives go forward, and in which much comes to us or is slowly developed, of which we are quite ignorant until we lift up our nets and inspect them.

Then the charm and significance of a day are so subtle and fleeting! Before we know it, it is gone past all recovery. I find that each spring, each summer and fall and winter of my life, has a hue and quality of its own, given by some prevailing mood, a train of thought, an event, an experience — a color or quality of which I am quite unconscious at the time, being too near to it and too completely enveloped by it. But afterward some mood or circumstance, an odor, or fragment of a tune, brings it back as by a flash; for one brief second the adamantine door of the past swings open and gives me a glimpse of my former life. One's journal, dashed off without any secondary motive, may often preserve and renew the past for him in this way.

These leaves from my own journal are not very good samples of this sort of thing, but they preserve for me the image of many a day which memory alone could never have kept.

March 3, 1879. The sun is getting strong, but winter still holds his own. No hint of spring in the earth or air. No sparrow or sparrow song yet. But on the 5th there was a hint of spring. The day warm and the snow melting. The first bluebird note this morning. How sweetly it dropped down from the blue overhead!

March 10. A real spring day at last, and a rouser! Thermometer between fifty and sixty degrees in the coolest spot; bees very lively about the hives and working on the sawdust in the woodyard; how they dig and wallow in the woody meal, apparently squeezing it, as if forcing it to yield up something to them! Here they get their first substitute for pollen. The sawdust of hickory and maple is preferred. The inner milky substance between the bark and the wood, called the cambium layer, is probably the source of their supplies.

In the growing tree it is in this layer or secretion that the vital processes are the most active and potent. It has been found by experiment that this tender, milky substance is capable of exerting a very great force; a growing tree exerts a lifting and pushing force of more than thirty pounds to the square inch, and the force is thought to reside in the soft, fragile cells that make up the cambium layer. It is like the strength of Samson residing in his hair. Saw one bee enter the hive with pollen on his back, which he must have got from some open greenhouse; or had he found the skunk cabbage in bloom ahead of me?

The bluebirds! It seemed as if they must have been waiting somewhere close by for the first warm day, like actors behind the scenes, for they were here in numbers early in the morning; they rushed upon the stage very promptly when their parts were called. No robins yet. Sap runs, but not briskly. It is too warm and still; it wants a brisk day for sap, with a certain sharpness in the air, a certain crispness and tension.

March 12. A change to more crispness and coolness, but a delicious spring morning. Hundreds of snowbirds, with a sprinkling of song, and Canada sparrows are all about the house, chirping and lisping and chattering in a very animated manner. The air is full of bird voices; through this maze of fine sounds come the strong note and warble of the robin and the soft call of the bluebird. A few days ago, not a bird, not a sound; everything rigid and severe; then in a day the barriers of winter give way, and spring comes like an inundation. In a twinkling all is changed.

April 1. Welcome to April, my natal month; the month of the swelling buds, the springing grass, the first nests, the first plantings, the first flowers, and, last but not least, the first shad! The door of the seasons first stands ajar this month and gives us a peep beyond. The month in which to begin the world, in which to begin your house, in which to begin your courtship, in which to enter upon any new enterprise. The bees usually get their first pollen this month and their first honey. All hibernating creatures are out before April is past. The coon, the chipmunk, the bear, the turtles, the frogs, the snakes, come forth beneath April skies.

March 12, 1891. Had positive proof this morning that at least one song sparrow has come back to his haunts of a year ago. One year ago today my attention was attracted, while walking over to the post office, by an unfamiliar bird song. It caught my ear while I was a long way off. I followed it up and found that it proceeded from a song sparrow. Its chief feature was one long, clear high note, very strong, sweet, and plaintive. It sprang out of the trills and quavers of the first part of the bird

song, like a long arc or parabola of sound. To my mental vision
it rose far up against the blue and turned sharply downward
again and finished in more trills and quavers. I had never before heard anything like it. It was the usual long, silvery note
in the sparrow's song greatly increased; indeed, the whole
breath and force of the bird were put in this note, so that you
caught little else than this silver loop of sound. The bird remained in one locality — the bushy corner of a field — the whole
season. He indulged in the ordinary sparrow song, also. I had
repeatedly had my eye upon him when he changed from one
to the other.

And now here he is again, just a year after, in the same place,
singing the same remarkable song, capturing my ear with the
same exquisite lasso of sound. What would I not give to know
just where he passed the winter and what adventures by flood
and field befell him![9]

Man can have but one interest in nature, namely, to see himself reflected or interpreted there, and we quickly neglect both
poet and philosopher who fail to satisfy, in some measure, this
feeling.[10]

2. Exhilaration of the Trail

AN INTELLIGENT English woman, spending a few years in this country with her family, says that one of her serious disappointments is that she finds it utterly impossible to enjoy nature here as she can at home — so much nature as we have and yet no way of getting at it; no paths or byways or stiles or footbridges, no provision for the pedestrian outside of the public road. One would think the people had no feet and legs in this country, or else did not know how to use them.

It is not the walking merely, it is keeping yourself in tune for a walk, in the spiritual and bodily condition in which you can find entertainment and exhilaration in so simple and natural a pastime. You are eligible to any good fortune when you are in the condition to enjoy a walk. When the air and the water taste sweet to you, how much else will taste sweet! When the exercise of your limbs affords you pleasure, and the play of your senses upon the various objects and shows of nature quickens and stimulates your spirit, your relation to the world and to yourself is what it should be — simple and direct and wholesome. The mood in which you set out on a spring or autumn ramble or a sturdy winter walk, and your greedy feet have to be restrained from devouring the distances too fast, is the mood in which your best thoughts and impulses come to you, or in which you might embark upon any noble and heroic

enterprise. Life is sweet in such moods, the universe is complete, and there is no failure or imperfection anywhere.[1]

The born naturalist is one of the most lucky men in the
world. Winter or summer, rain or shine, at home or abroad,
walking or riding, his pleasures are always near at hand. The
great book of nature is open before him and he has only to
turn its leaves.[2]

Slide Mountain* had been a summons and a challenge to
me for many years. I had fished every stream that it nourished
and had camped in the wilderness on all sides of it, and whenever I had caught a glimpse of its summit I had promised myself to set foot there before another season should pass. But
the seasons came and went, and my feet got no nimbler, and
Slide Mountain no lower, until finally, one July, seconded by
an energetic friend, we thought to bring Slide to terms by approaching him through the mountains on the east.

Three hours from the forks brought us out on the broad level
back of the mountain upon which Slide, considered as an iso-
lated peak, is reared. After a time we entered a dense growth
of spruce which covered a slight depression in the table of the
mountain. The moss was deep, the ground spongy, the light
dim, the air hushed. The transition from the open, leafy woods
to this dim, silent, weird grove was very marked. It was like the
passage from the street into the temple. Here we paused awhile
and ate our lunch, and refreshed ourselves with water gathered
from a little well sunk in the moss.

The quiet and repose of this spruce grove proved to be the
calm that goes before the storm. As we passed out of it, we came
plump upon the almost perpendicular battlements of Slide.
The mountain rose like a huge, rock-bound fortress from this

* In the Catskill Mountains in New York State. [Ed.]

plainlike expanse. It was ledge upon ledge, precipice upon precipice, up which and over which we made our way slowly and with great labor, now pulling ourselves up by our hands, then cautiously finding niches for our feet and zigzagging right and left from shelf to shelf. This northern side of the mountain was thickly covered with moss and lichens, like the north side of a tree. This made it soft to the foot and broke many a slip and fall. Everywhere a stunted growth of yellow birch, mountain ash, and spruce and fir opposed our progress. The ascent at such an angle with a roll of blankets on your back is not unlike climbing a tree: every limb resists your progress and pushes you back; so that when we at last reached the summit, after twelve or fifteen hundred feet of this sort of work, the fight was about all out of the best of us. It was then nearly two o'clock, so that we had been about seven hours in coming seven miles.

Here on the top of the mountain we overtook spring, which had been gone from the valley nearly a month. Red clover was opening in the valley below, and wild strawberries just ripening; on the summit the yellow birch was just hanging out its catkins, and the claytonia, or spring beauty, was in bloom. The leaf buds of the trees were just bursting, making a faint mist of green which, as the eye swept downward, gradually deepened until it became a dense, massive cloud in the valleys. At the foot of the mountain the clintonia, or northern green lily, and the low shadbush were showing their berries, but long before the top was reached they were found in bloom. I had never before stood amid blooming claytonia, a flower of April, and looked down upon a field that held ripening strawberries. Every thousand feet elevation seemed to make about ten days' difference in the vegetation, so that the season was a month or more later on the top of the mountain than at its base. A very pretty flower which we began to meet with well up on the mountainside was the painted trillium, the petals white, veined with pink.

The low, stunted growth of spruce and fir which clothes the top of Slide has been cut away over a small space on the highest point, laying open the view on nearly all sides. Here we sat down and enjoyed our triumph. We saw the world as the hawk or the balloonist sees it when he is three thousand feet in the air. How soft and flowing all the outlines of the hills and mountains beneath us looked! The forests dropped down and undulated away over them, covering them like a carpet. To the east we looked over the nearby Wittenberg range to the Hudson and beyond; to the south, Peak-o'-Moose, with its sharp crest, and Table Mountain, with its long, level top, were the two conspicuous objects; in the west, Mt. Graham and Double Top, about three thousand eight hundred feet each, arrested the eye; while in our front to the north we looked over the top of Panther Mountain to the multitudinous peaks of the northern Catskills. All was mountain and forest on every hand. Civilization seemed to have done little more than to have scratched this rough, shaggy surface of the earth here and there. In any such view, the wild, the aboriginal, the geographical greatly predominate. The works of man dwindle, and the original features of the huge globe come out. Every single object or point is dwarfed; the valley of the Hudson is only a wrinkle in the earth's surface. You discover with a feeling of surprise that the great thing is the earth itself, which stretches away on every hand so far beyond your ken.

Slide Mountain enjoys a distinction which no other mountain in the State, so far as is known, does — it has a thrush peculiar to itself. This thrush was discovered and described by Eugene P. Bicknell, of New York, in 1880, and has been named Bicknell's thrush. In its appearance to the eye among the trees, one would not distinguish it from the gray-cheeked thrush of Baird, or the olive-backed thrush, but its song is totally different. The moment I heard it I said, "There is a new bird, a new thrush," for the quality of all thrush songs is the same. A moment more, and I knew it was Bicknell's thrush. The song is in a minor key, finer, more attenuated, and more under the breath than that of any other thrush. It seemed as if the bird was blowing in a delicate, slender golden tube, so fine and yet so flutelike and resonant the song appeared. At times it was like a musical whisper of great sweetness and power. The birds were numerous about the summit, but we saw them nowhere else.

A pleasant task we had in reflooring and reroofing the log hut with balsam boughs against the night. Plenty of small balsams grew all about, and we soon had a huge pile of their branches in the old hut. What a transformation, this fresh green carpet and our fragrant bed, like the deep-furred robe of some huge animal, wrought in that dingy interior!

With the first appearance of the dawn I had heard the new thrush in the scattered trees near the hut — a strain as fine as if blown upon a fairy flute, a suppressed musical whisper from out the tops of the dark spruces. Probably never did there go up from the top of a great mountain a smaller song to greet the day, albeit it was of the purest harmony. It seemed to have in a more marked degree the quality of interior reverberation than any other thrush song I had ever heard. Would the altitude or the situation account for its minor key? Loudness would avail little in such a place. Sounds are not far heard on a mountaintop; they are lost in the abyss of vacant air. But amid these low, dense, dark spruces, which make a sort of canopied privacy of every square rod of ground, what could be more in keeping than this delicate musical whisper? It was but the soft hum of the balsams, interpreted and embodied in a bird's voice.

We were now not long in squaring an account with Slide and making ready to leave. Round pellets of snow began to fall, and we came off the mountain on the 10th of June in a November storm and temperature. Our purpose was to return by the same valley we had come. A well-defined trail led off the summit to the north; to this we committed ourselves. In a few minutes we emerged at the head of the slide that had given the mountain its name. This was the path made by visitors to the scene; when it ended, the track of the avalanche began; no bigger than your hand, apparently, had it been at first, but it rapidly grew, until it became several rods in width. It dropped down from our feet straight as an arrow until it was lost in the fog, and looked perilously steep. The dark forms of the spruce were clinging to the edge of it, as if reaching out to their fellows to save them. We hesitated on the brink, but finally cautiously began the descent. The rock was quite naked and slippery, and only on the margin of the slide were there any boulders to stay the foot or bushy growths to aid the hand. As we paused after some minutes to select our course, one of the finest surprises of the trip awaited us: the fog in our front was swiftly whirled up by the breeze, like the drop curtain at the theatre, only much more rapidly, and in a twinkling the vast gulf opened before us. It was so sudden as to be almost bewildering. The world opened like a book, and there were the pictures; the spaces were without a film, the forests and mountains looked surprisingly near; in the heart of the northern Catskills a wild valley was seen flooded with sunlight. Then the curtain ran down again, and nothing was left but the gray strip of rock to which we clung, plunging down into the obscurity, Down and down we made our way. Then the fog lifted again. It was Jack and his beanstalk renewed; new wonders, new views, awaited us every few moments, till at last the whole valley below us stood in the clear sunshine.

We passed down a precipice, and there was a rill of water, the beginning of the creek that wound through the valley below; farther on, in a deep depression, lay the remains of an old snowbank; Winter had made his last stand here, and April flowers were springing up almost amid his very bones. We did not find a palace and a hungry giant and a princess at the end of our beanstalk, but we found a humble roof and the hospitable heart of Mrs. Larkins, which answered our purpose better. And we were in the mood, too, to have undertaken an eating bout with any giant Jack ever discovered.[3]

The region of which I am about to speak lies in the southern part of the State of New York and comprises parts of three counties — Ulster, Sullivan, and Delaware. It is drained by tributaries of both the Hudson and Delaware and, next to the Adirondack section, contains more wild land than any other tract in the State. The mountains which traverse it and impart to it its severe northern climate belong properly to the Catskill range. On some maps of the State they are called the Pine Mountains, though with obvious local impropriety, as pine, so far as I have observed, is nowhere found upon them. "Birch Mountains" would be a more characteristic name, as on their summits birch is the prevailing tree. They are the natural home of the black and yellow birch, which grow here to unusual size. On their sides beech and maple abound; while, mantling their lower slopes and darkening the valleys, hemlock formerly enticed the lumberman and tanner.

In 1868 a party of three of us set out for a brief trouting excursion to a body of water called Thomas's Lake, situated in the same chain of mountains. On this excursion, more particularly than on any other I have ever undertaken, I was taught how poor an Indian I should make, and what a ridiculous figure a party of men may cut in the woods when the way is uncertain and the mountains high.

We left our team at a farmhouse near the head of the Mill Brook, one June afternoon, and with knapsacks on our shoulders struck into the woods at the base of the mountain, hoping to cross the range that intervened between us and the lake by sunset. We engaged a good-natured but rather indolent young man who happened to be stopping at the house, and who had carried a knapsack in the Union armies, to pilot us a couple of miles into the woods so as to guard against any mistakes at the outset. It seemed the easiest thing in the world to find the lake. The lay of the land was so simple, according to accounts, that I felt sure I could go to it in the dark. "Go up this little brook to its source on the side of the mountain," they said. "The valley that contains the lake heads directly on the other side." What could be easier! But on a little further inquiry, they said we should "bear well to the left" when we reached the top of the mountain. This opened the doors again; "bearing well to the left" was an uncertain performance in strange woods. We might bear so well to the left that it would bring us ill. But why bear to the left at all, if the lake was directly opposite? Well, not quite opposite; a little to the left. There were two or three other valleys that headed in near there. We could easily find the right one. But to make assurance doubly sure, we engaged a guide, as stated, to give us a good start and go with us beyond the bearing-to-the-left point. He had been to the lake the winter before and knew the way.

Our course, the first half hour, was along an obscure wood road which had been used for drawing ash logs off the mountain in winter. There was some hemlock, but more maple and birch. The woods were dense and free from underbrush, the ascent gradual. Most of the way we kept the voice of the creek in our ear on the right. I approached it once and found it swarming with trout. The water was as cold as one ever need wish. After a while the ascent grew steeper, the creek became a mere rill that issued from beneath loose, moss-covered rocks and stones, and with much labor and puffing we drew ourselves up the rugged declivity. Every mountain has its steepest point, which is usually near the summit, in keeping, I suppose, with the providence that makes the darkest hour just before day. It is steep, steeper, steepest, till you emerge on the smooth level or gently rounded space at the top, which the old ice gods polished off so long ago.

We found this mountain had a hollow in its back where the ground was soft and swampy. Some gigantic ferns, which we passed through, came nearly to our shoulders. We passed also several patches of swamp honeysuckles, red with blossoms.

Our guide at length paused on a big rock where the land began to dip down the other way, and concluded that he had gone far enough and that we would now have no difficulty in finding the lake. "It must lie right down there," he said, pointing with his hand. But it was plain that he was not quite sure in his own mind. He had several times wavered in his course and had shown considerable embarrassment when bearing to the left across the summit. Still we thought little of it. We were full of confidence and, bidding him adieu, plunged down the mountainside, following a spring run that we had no doubt led to the lake.

In these woods, which had a southeastern exposure, I first began to notice the wood thrush. In coming up the other side I had not seen a feather of any kind, or heard a note. Now the golden *trillide-de* of the wood thrush sounded through the silent woods. While looking for a fish pole about half way down the mountain, I saw a thrush's nest in a little sapling about ten feet from the ground.

After continuing our descent till our only guide, the spring run, became quite a trout brook and its tiny murmur a loud brawl, we began to peer anxiously through the trees for a glimpse of the lake or for some conformation of the land that would indicate its proximity. An object which we vaguely discerned in looking under the near trees and over the more distant ones proved, on further inspection, to be a patch of plowed ground. Presently we made out a burnt fallow near it. This was a wet blanket to our enthusiasm. No lake, no sport, no trout for supper that night. The rather indolent young man had either played us a trick or, as seemed more likely, had missed the way. We were particularly anxious to be at the lake between sundown and dark, as at that time the trout jump most freely.

Pushing on, we soon emerged into a stumpy field at the head of a steep valley, which swept around toward the west. About two hundred rods below us was a rude log house, with smoke issuing from the chimney. A boy came out and moved toward the spring with a pail in his hand. We shouted to him, when he turned and ran back into the house without pausing to reply. In a moment the whole family hastily rushed into the yard, and turned their faces toward us. If we had come down their chimney, they could not have seemed more astonished. Not making out what they said, I went down to the house and learned to my chagrin that we were still on the Mill Brook side, having crossed only a spur of the mountain. We had not borne sufficiently to the left, so that the main range, which at the point of crossing suddenly breaks off to the southeast, still intervened between us and the lake. We were about five miles, as the water runs, from the point of starting, and over two from the lake. We must go directly back to the top of the range where the guide had left us, and then, by keeping well to the left, we would soon come to a line of marked trees, which would lead us to the lake. So, turning upon our trail, we doggedly began the work of undoing what we had just done — in all cases a disagreeable task, in this case a very laborious one also. It was after sunset when we turned back, and before we had got half way up the mountain it began to be quite dark. We were often obliged to rest our packs against trees and take breath, which made our progress slow. Finally a halt was called beside an immense flat rock which had paused in its slide down the mountain, and we prepared to encamp for the night. A fire was built, the rock cleared off, a small ration of bread served out, our accoutrements hung up out of the way of the hedge-hogs that were supposed to infest the locality, and then we disposed ourselves for sleep. If the owls or porcupines (and I think I heard one of the latter in the middle of the night) reconnoitred our camp, they saw a buffalo robe spread upon a rock, with three old felt hats arranged on one side and three pairs of sorry-looking cowhide boots protruding from the other.

When we lay down, there was apparently not a mosquito in the woods; but the "no-see-ems," as Thoreau's Indian aptly named the midges, soon found us out and, after the fire had gone down, annoyed us much. My hands and wrists suddenly began to smart and itch in a most unaccountable manner. My first thought was that they had been poisoned in some way. Then the smarting extended to my neck and face, even to my scalp, when I began to suspect what was the matter. So, wrapping myself up more thoroughly and stowing my hands away as best I could, I tried to sleep, being some time behind my companions, who appeared not to mind the "no-see-ems." I was further annoyed by some little irregularity on my side of the couch. The chambermaid had not beaten it up well. One huge lump refused to be mollified, and each attempt to adapt it to some natural hollow in my own body brought only a moment's relief. But at last I got the better of this also and slept. Late in the night I woke up, just in time to hear a golden-crowned thrush* sing in a tree nearby. It sang as loud and cheerily as at midday, and I thought myself, after all, quite in luck. Birds occasionally sing at night, just as the cock crows. I have heard the hairbird† and the note of the kingbird; and the ruffed grouse frequently drums at night.

At the first faint signs of day a wood thrush sang, a few rods below us. Then after a little delay, as the gray light began to grow around, thrushes broke out in full song in all parts of the woods. I thought I had never before heard them sing so sweetly. Such a leisurely, golden chant! — it consoled us for all we had undergone. It was the first thing in order — the worms were safe till after this morning chorus. I judged that the birds roosted but a few feet from the ground. In fact, a bird in all cases roosts where it builds, and the wood thrush occupies, as it were, the first story of the woods.

There is something singular about the distribution of the wood thrushes. At an earlier stage of my observations I should have been much surprised at finding them in these woods. Indeed, I had stated in print on two occasions that the wood thrush was not found in the higher lands of the Catskills but that the hermit thrush and the veery, or Wilson's thrush, were common. It turns out that this statement is only half true. The wood thrush is found also, but is much more rare and secluded in its habits than either of the others, being seen only during

* Ovenbird. [Ed.]   † Chipping sparrow. [Ed.]

the breeding season on remote mountains, and then only on their eastern and southern slopes. I have never yet in this region found the bird spending the season in the near and familiar woods, which is directly contrary to observations I have made in other parts of the State. So different are the habits of birds in different localities.

As soon as it was fairly light we were up and ready to resume our march. A small bit of bread and butter and a swallow or two of whiskey was all we had for breakfast that morning. Our supply of each was very limited, and we were anxious to save a little of both, to relieve the diet of trout to which we looked forward.

At an early hour we reached the rock where we had parted with the guide, and looked around us into the dense, trackless woods with many misgivings. To strike out now on our own hook, where the way was so blind and after the experience we had just had, was a step not to be carelessly taken. The tops of these mountains are so broad, and a short distance in the woods seems so far that one is by no means master of the situation after reaching the summit. And then there are so many spurs and offshoots and changes of direction, added to the impossibility of making any generalization by the aid of the eye, that before one is aware of it he is very wide of his mark.

After looking in vain for the line of marked trees, we moved off to the left in a doubtful, hesitating manner, keeping on the highest ground and blazing the trees as we went. We were afraid to go downhill, lest we should descend too soon; our vantage ground was high ground. A thick fog coming on, we were more bewildered than ever. Still we pressed forward, climbing up ledges and wading through ferns for about two hours, when we paused by a spring that issued from beneath an immense wall of rock that belted the highest part of the mountain. There was quite a broad plateau here, and the birch wood was very dense, and the trees of unusual size.

After resting and exchanging opinions, we all concluded that it was best not to continue our search incumbered as we were; but we were not willing to abandon it altogether, and I proposed to my companions to leave them beside the spring with our traps while I made one thorough and final effort to find the lake. If I succeeded and desired them to come forward, I was to fire my gun three times; if I failed and wished to return, I would fire it twice, they of course responding.

So, filling my canteen from the spring, I set out again, taking the spring run for my guide. Before I had followed it two hundred yards it sank into the ground at my feet. I had half a mind to be superstitious and to believe that we were under a spell, since our guides played us such tricks. However, I determined to put the matter to a further test and struck out boldly to the left. This seemed to be the key word — to the left, to the left. The fog had now lifted, so that I could form a better idea of the lay of the land. Twice I looked down the steep sides of the mountain, sorely tempted to risk a plunge. Still I hesitated and kept along on the brink.

I now found myself gradually edging down the side of the mountain, keeping around it in a spiral manner and scanning the woods and the shape of the ground for some encouraging hint or sign. Finally the woods became more open and the descent less rapid. The trees were remarkably straight and uniform in size. Black birches, the first I had seen, were very numerous. I felt encouraged. Listening attentively, I caught, from a breeze just lifting the drooping leaves, a sound that I willingly believed was made by a bullfrog. On this hint, I tore down through the woods at my highest speed. Then I paused and listened again. This time there was no mistaking it; it was the sound of frogs. Much elated, I rushed on. By and by I could hear them as I ran. *Pthrung, pthrung,* croaked the old ones; *pug, pug,* shrilly joined in the smaller fry.

Then I caught, through the lower trees, a gleam of blue which I first thought was distant sky. A second look and I knew it to be water, and in a moment more I stepped from the woods and stood upon the shore of the lake. I exulted silently. There it was at last, sparkling in the morning sun and as beautiful as a dream. It was so good to come upon such open space and such bright hues, after wandering in the dim, dense woods! The eye is as delighted as an escaped bird and darts gleefully from point to point.

The lake was a long oval, scarcely more than a mile in circumference, with evenly wooded shores which rose gradually on all sides. After contemplating the scene for a moment, I stepped back into the woods and, loading my gun as heavily as I dared, discharged it three times. The reports seemed to fill all the mountains with sound. The frogs quickly hushed, and I listened for the response. But no response came. Then I tried again and again, but without evoking an answer. One of my companions, however, who had climbed to the top of the high rocks in the rear of the spring, thought he heard faintly one report. It seemed an immense distance below him and far around under the mountain. I knew I had come a long way, and hardly expected to be able to communicate with my companions in the manner agreed upon. I therefore started back, choosing my course without any reference to the circuitous route by which I had come, and loading heavily and firing at intervals. I must have aroused many long-dormant echoes from a Rip Van Winkle sleep. As my powder got low, I fired and halloed alternately, till I came near splitting both my throat and gun. Finally, after I had begun to have a very ugly feeling of alarm and disappointment and to cast about vaguely for some course to pursue in the emergency that seemed near at hand — namely, the loss of my companions now I had found the lake — a favoring breeze brought me the last echo of a response. I rejoined with spirit and hastened with all speed in the direction whence the sound had come but, after repeated trials, failed to elicit another answering sound. This filled me with apprehension again. I feared that my friends had been misled by the reverberations, and I pictured them to myself hastening in the opposite direction. Paying little attention to my course, but paying dearly for my carelessness afterward, I rushed forward to undeceive them. But they had not been deceived, and in a few moments an answering shout revealed them near at hand. I heard their tramp, the bushes parted, and we three met again.

In answer to their eager inquiries, I assured them that I had seen the lake, that it was at the foot of the mountain, and that we could not miss it if we kept straight down from where we then were.

My clothes were soaked with perspiration, but I shouldered my knapsack with alacrity, and we began the descent. I noticed that the woods were much thicker and had quite a different look from those I had passed through, but thought nothing of it, as I expected to strike the lake near its head, whereas I had before come out at its foot. We had not gone far when we crossed a line of marked trees, which my companions were disposed to follow. It intersected our course nearly at right angles and kept along and up the side of the mountain. My impression was that it led up from the lake and that by keeping our own course we should reach the lake sooner than if we followed this line.

About halfway down the mountain we could see through

the interstices the opposite slope. I encouraged my comrades by telling them that the lake was between us and that, and not more than half a mile distant. We soon reached the bottom, where we found a small stream and quite an extensive alder swamp, evidently the ancient bed of a lake. I explained to my half-vexed and half-incredulous companions that we were probably above the lake and that this stream must lead to it. "Follow it," they said; "we will wait here till we hear from you."

So I went on, more than ever disposed to believe that we were under a spell and that the lake had slipped from my grasp after all. Seeing no favorable sign as I went forward, I laid down my accoutrements and climbed a decayed beech that leaned out over the swamp and promised a good view from the top. As I stretched myself up to look around from the highest attainable branch, there was suddenly a loud crack at the root. With a celerity that would at least have done credit to a bear, I regained the ground, having caught but a momentary glimpse of the country but enough to convince me no lake was near. Leaving all incumbrances here but my gun, I still pressed on, loath to be thus baffled. After floundering through another alder swamp for nearly half a mile, I flattered myself that I was close on to the lake. I caught sight of a low spur of the mountain sweeping around like a half-extended arm, and I fondly imagined that within its clasp was the object of my search. But I found only more alder swamp. After this region was cleared, the creek began to descend the mountain very rapidly. Its banks became high and narrow, and it went whirling away with a sound that seemed to my ears like a burst of ironical laughter. I turned back with a feeling of mingled disgust, shame, and vexation. In fact I was almost sick, and when I reached my companions, after an absence of nearly two hours, hungry, fatigued, and disheartened, I would have sold my

interest in Thomas's Lake at a very low figure. For the first
time I heartily wished myself well out of the woods. Thomas
might keep his lake, and the enchanters guard his possession!
I doubted if he had ever found it the second time or if anyone
else ever had.

My companions, who were quite fresh and who had not
felt the strain of baffled purpose as I had, assumed a more
encouraging tone. After I had rested a while and partaken
sparingly of the bread and whiskey, which in such an emergency is a great improvement on bread and water, I agreed to
their proposition that we should make another attempt. As
if to reassure us, a robin sounded his cheery call nearby, and
the winter wren, the first I had heard in these woods, set his
music box going, which fairly ran over with fine, gushing,
lyrical sounds. There can be no doubt but this bird is one of
our finest songsters. If it would only thrive and sing well when
caged, like the canary, how far it would surpass that bird! It
has all the vivacity and versatility of the canary, without any
of its shrillness. Its song is indeed a little cascade of melody.

We again retraced our steps, rolling the stone, as it were,
back up the mountain, determined to commit ourselves to the
line of marked trees. These we finally reached and, after exploring the country to the right, saw that bearing to the left
was still the order. The trail led up over a gentle rise of
ground, and in less than twenty minutes we were in the woods
I had passed through when I found the lake. The error I had
made was then plain; we had come off the mountain a few
paces too far to the right and so had passed down on the wrong
side of the ridge, into what we afterwards learned was the valley of Alder Creek.

We now made good time, and before many minutes I saw
the mimic sky glance through the trees. As we approached the

lake, a solitary woodchuck, the first wild animal we had seen since entering the woods, sat crouched upon the root of a tree a few feet from the water, apparently completely nonplussed by the unexpected appearance of danger on the land side. All retreat was cut off, and he looked his fate in the face without flinching. I slaughtered him just as a savage would have done, and from the same motive — I wanted his carcass to eat.

The midafternoon sun was now shining upon the lake, and a low, steady breeze drove the little waves rocking to the shore. A herd of cattle were browsing on the other side, and the bell of the leader sounded across the water. In these solitudes its clang was wild and musical.

To try the trout was the first thing in order. On a rude raft of logs which we found moored at the shore and which with two aboard shipped about a foot of water, we floated out and wet our first fly in Thomas's Lake; but the trout refused to jump, and, to be frank, not more than a dozen and a half were caught during our stay.

Much refreshed, I set out with the sun low in the west to explore the outlet of the lake and try for trout there, while my companions made further trials in the lake itself. The outlet, as is usual in bodies of water of this kind, was very gentle and private. The stream, six or eight feet wide, flowed silently and evenly along for a distance of three or four rods, when it suddenly, as if conscious of its freedom, took a leap down some rocks. Thence, as far as I followed it, its descent was very rapid through a continuous succession of brief falls like so many steps down the mountain. Its appearance promised more trout than I found, though I returned to camp with a very respectable string.

At sunset the grouse began to drum in all parts of the woods about the lake. I could hear five at one time, *thump, thump,*

thump, thump, thr-r-r-r-rr. It was a homely, welcome sound. As I returned to camp at twilight, along the shore of the lake, the frogs also were in full chorus. The older ones ripped out their responses to each other with terrific force and volume. I know of no other animal capable of giving forth so much sound in proportion to its size as a frog. Some of these seemed to bellow as loud as a two-year-old bull. They were of immense size, and very abundant. No frog eater had ever been there. Near the shore we felled a tree which reached far out in the lake. Upon the trunk and branches the frogs had soon collected in large numbers and gamboled and splashed about the half-submerged top like a parcel of schoolboys, making nearly as much noise.

We lodged that night on a brush heap and slept soundly. The green, yielding beech twigs, covered with a buffalo robe, were equal to a hair mattress. The heat and smoke from a large fire kindled in the afternoon had banished every "no-see-em" from the locality, and in the morning the sun was above the mountain before we awoke.

We finished our bread that morning and ate every fish we could catch, and about ten o'clock prepared to leave the lake. The weather had been admirable, and the lake was a gem, and I would gladly have spent a week in the neighborhood; but the question of supplies was a serious one and would brook no delay.

When we reached, on our return, the point where we had crossed the line of marked trees the day before, the question arose whether we should still trust ourselves to this line or follow our own trail back to the spring and the battlement of rocks on the top of the mountain, and thence to the rock where the guide had left us. We decided in favor of the former course. After a march of three quarters of an hour the blazed trees ceased, and we concluded we were near the point at which we

had parted with the guide. So we built a fire, laid down our loads, and cast about on all sides for some clew as to our exact locality. Nearly an hour was consumed in this manner and without any result. I came upon a brood of young grouse, which diverted me for a moment. The old one blustered about at a furious rate, trying to draw all attention to herself, while the young ones, which were unable to fly, hid themselves. She whined like a dog in great distress and dragged herself along apparently with the greatest difficulty. As I pursued her, she ran very nimbly and presently flew a few yards. Then, as I went on, she flew farther and farther each time, till at last she got up and went humming through the woods as if she had no interest in them. I went back and caught one of the young, which had simply squatted close to the leaves. I took it up and set it on the palm of my hand, which it hugged as closely as if still upon the ground. I then put it in my coat sleeve, when it ran and nestled in my arm pit.

When we met at the sign of the smoke, opinions differed as to the most feasible course. There was no doubt but that we could get out of the woods; but we wished to get out speedily and as near as possible to the point where we had entered. Half ashamed of our timidity and indecision, we finally tramped away back to where we had crossed the line of blazed trees, followed our old trail to the spring on the top of the range, and after much searching and scouring to the right and left found ourselves at the very place we had left two hours before.

Another deliberation and a divided council. But something must be done. It was then midafternoon, and the prospect of spending another night on the mountains without food or drink was not pleasant. So we moved down the ridge. Here another line of marked trees was found, the course of which formed an obtuse angle with the one we had followed. It kept on the top of the ridge for perhaps a mile, when it entirely disappeared, and we were as much adrift as ever.   Then one of the party swore an oath and said he was going out of those woods, hit or miss, and, wheeling to the right, instantly plunged over the brink of the mountain.   The rest followed but would fain have paused and ciphered away at their own uncertainties, to see if a certainty could not be arrived at as to where we would come out.   But our bold leader was solving the problem in the right way.   Down and down and still down we went, as if we were to bring up in the bowels of the earth.   It was by far the steepest descent we had made, and we felt a grim satisfaction in knowing that we could not retrace our steps this time, be the issue what it might.   As we paused on the brink of a ledge of rocks, we chanced to see, through the trees, distant cleared land.   A house or barn also was dimly descried.   This was encouraging; but we could not make out whether it was on Beaver Kill or Mill Brook or Dry Brook, and did not long stop to consider where it was.   We at last brought up at the bottom of a deep gorge, through which flowed a rapid creek that literally swarmed with trout.   But we were in no mood to catch them and pushed on along the channel of the stream, sometimes leaping from rock to rock and sometimes splashing heedlessly through the water and speculating the while as to where we should probably come out. On the Beaver Kill, my companions thought; but, from the position of the sun, I said, on the Mill Brook, about six miles below our team; for I remembered having seen, in coming up this stream, a deep, wild valley that led up into the mountains, like this one.   Soon the banks of the stream became lower, and we moved into the woods.   Here we entered upon an obscure wood road which presently conducted us into the midst of a vast hemlock forest.   The land had a gentle slope, and we wondered why the lumbermen and barkmen who prowl through these woods had left this fine tract untouched. Beyond this the forest was mostly birch and maple.

We were now close to the settlement and began to hear human sounds. One rod more, and we were out of the woods. It took us a moment to comprehend the scene. Things looked very strange at first; but quickly they began to change and to put on familiar features. Some magic scene shifting seemed to take place before my eyes till, instead of the unknown settlement which I at first seemed to look upon, there stood the farmhouse at which we had stopped two days before, and at the same moment we heard the stamping of our team in the barn. We sat down and laughed heartily over our good luck. Our desperate venture had resulted better than we had dared to hope and had shamed our wisest plans. At the house our arrival had been anticipated about this time, and dinner was being put upon the table.

It was then five o'clock, so that we had been in the woods just forty-eight hours; but if time is only phenomenal, as the philosophers say, and life only in feeling, as the poets aver, we were some months, if not years, older at that moment than we had been two days before. Yet younger, too — though this be a paradox — for the birches had infused into us some of their own suppleness and strength.[4]

If there ever was a stream cradled in the rocks, detained lovingly by them, held and fondled in a rocky lap or tossed in rocky arms, that stream is the Rondout.* Its course for several miles from its head is over the stratified rock, and into this it has worn a channel that presents most striking and peculiar features. Now it comes silently along on the top of the rock, spread out and flowing over that thick, dark green moss that is found only

* In the Catskills. [Ed.]

in the coldest streams; then drawn into a narrow canal only four or five feet wide, through which it shoots, black and rigid, to be presently caught in a deep basin with shelving, overhanging rocks, beneath which the phoebe bird builds in security and upon which the fisherman stands and casts his twenty or thirty feet of line without fear of being thwarted by the brush; then into a black, well-like pool, ten or fifteen feet deep, with a smooth, circular wall of rock on one side worn by the water through long ages; or else into a deep, oblong pocket, into which and out of which the water glides without a ripple.

The surface rock is a coarse sandstone superincumbent upon a lighter colored conglomerate that looked like Shawangunk grits, and when this latter is reached by the water it seems to be rapidly disintegrated by it, thus forming the deep excavations alluded to.

My eyes had never before beheld such beauty in a mountain stream. The water was almost as transparent as the air — was, indeed, like liquid air; and as it lay in these wells and pits enveloped in shadow, or lit up by a chance ray of the vertical sun, it was a perpetual feast to the eye — so cool, so deep, so pure; every reach and pool like a vast spring. You lay down and drank or dipped the water up in your cup and found it just the right degree of refreshing coldness. One is never prepared for the clearness of the water in these streams. It is always a surprise. See them every year for a dozen years, and yet, when you first come upon one, you will utter an exclamation. I saw nothing like it in the Adirondacks or in Canada. Absolutely without stain or hint of impurity, it seems to magnify like a lens, so that the bed of the stream and the fish in it appear deceptively near. It is rare to find even a trout stream that is not a little "off color," as they say of diamonds, but the waters in the section of which I am writing have the genuine ray; it is the undimmed and untarnished diamond.

If I were a trout, I should ascend every stream till I found the Rondout. It is the ideal brook. What homes these fish have, what retreats under the rocks, what paved or flagged courts and areas, what crystal depths where no net or snare can reach them! — no mud, no sediment, but here and there in the clefts and seams of the rock, patches of white gravel — spawning beds ready-made.

The finishing touch is given by the moss with which the rock is everywhere carpeted. Even in the narrow grooves or channels where the water runs the swiftest, the green lining is unbroken. It sweeps down under the stream and up again on the other side, like some firmly woven texture. It softens every outline and cushions every stone. At a certain depth in the great basins and wells it of course ceases, and only the smooth-swept flagging of the place rock is visible.

The trees are kept well back from the margin of the stream by the want of soil, and the large ones unite their branches far above it, thus forming a high winding gallery along which the fisherman passes and makes his long casts with scarcely an interruption from branch or twig. In a few places he makes no cast but sees from his rocky perch the water twenty feet below him and drops his hook into it as into a well.

The fish are small in these streams, seldom weighing over a few ounces. Occasionally a large one is seen of a pound or pound and a half weight. I remember one such, as black as night, that ran under a black rock. But I remember much more distinctly a still larger one that I caught and lost one eventful day.

I had him on my hook ten minutes and actually got my thumb in his mouth, and yet he escaped.

It was only the overeagerness of the sportsman. I imagined I could hold him by the teeth.

The place where I struck him was a deep wellhole, and I was

perched upon a log that spanned it ten or twelve feet above the water. The situation was all the more interesting because I saw no possible way to land my fish. I could not lead him ashore, and my frail tackle could not be trusted to lift him sheer from that pit to my precarious perch. What should I do? call for help? but no help was near. I had a revolver in my pocket and might have shot him through and through, but that novel proceeding did not occur to me until it was too late. I would have taken a Sam Patch leap into the water and have wrestled with my antagonist in his own element, but I knew the slack, thus sure to occur, would probably free him; so I peered down upon the beautiful creature and enjoyed my triumph as far as it went. He was caught very lightly through his upper jaw, and I expected every struggle and somersault would break the hold.

Presently I saw a place in the rocks where I thought it possible, with such an incentive, to get down within reach of the water: by careful manoeuvring I slipped my pole behind me and got hold of the line, which I cut and wound around my finger; then I made my way toward the end of the log and the place in the rocks, leading my fish along much exhausted on the top of the water. By an effort worthy the occasion I got down within reach of the fish and, as I have already confessed, thrust my thumb into his mouth and pinched his cheek; he made a spring and was free from my hand and the hook at the same time; for a moment he lay panting on the top of the water, then, recovering himself slowly, made his way down through the clear, cruel element beyond all hope of recapture. My blind impulse to follow and try to seize him was very strong, but I kept my hold and peered and peered long after the fish was lost to view, then looked my mortification in the face and laughed a bitter laugh.

"But, hang it! I had all the fun of catching the fish and only miss the pleasure of eating him, which at this time would not be great."

Not the least of the charm of camping out is your campfire at night. What an artist! What pictures are boldly thrown or faintly outlined upon the canvas of the night! Every object, every attitude of your companion, is striking and memorable. You see effects and groups every moment that you would give money to be able to carry away with you in enduring form. How the shadows leap and skulk and hover about! Light and darkness are in perpetual tilt and warfare, with first the one un-horsed then the other. The friendly and cheering fire, what acquaintance we make with it! We had almost forgotten there was such an element, we had so long known only its dark off-spring, heat. Now we see the wild beauty uncaged and note its manner and temper. How surely it creates its own draft and sets the currents going, as force and enthuiasm always will! It carves itself a chimney out of the fluid and houseless air. A friend, a ministering angel, in subjection; a fiend, a fury, a mon-ster, ready to devour the world, if ungoverned. By day it bur-rows in the ashes and sleeps; at night it comes forth and sits upon its throne of rude logs and rules the camp, a sovereign queen.[5]

3. Straight Seeing and Thinking

A GREAT MANY intelligent persons tolerate or encourage our fake natural history on the ground that they find it entertaining, and that it interests the schoolchildren in the wild life about them. Is the truth, then, without value for its own sake? What would these good people think of a United States school history that took the same liberties with facts that certain of our nature writers do: that, for instance, made Washington take his army over the Delaware in balloons, or in sleighs on the solid ice with bands playing; or that made Lincoln a victim of the Evil Eye; or that portrayed his slayer as a self-sacrificing hero; or that represented the little Monitor that eventful day on Hampton Roads as diving under the Merrimac and tossing it ashore on its beak?

The nature fakers take just this kind of liberties with the facts of our natural history. The young reader finds it entertaining, no doubt, but is this sufficient justification?

The scientist, the artist, the nature lover, and the like, all look for and find different things in nature, yet there is no contradiction between the different things they find. The truth of one is not the falsehood of another. The field naturalist is interested in the live animal, the laboratory zoölogist in the measuring and dissecting of the dead carcass. What interests one is of little or no interest to the other. So with the field botanist as compared with the mere herbalist. Both are seekers for the truth, but for a different kind of truth. One seeks that kind of truth that appeals to his emotion and to his imagination; the other that kind of truth — truth of structure, relation of parts, family ties — that appeals to his scientific faculties. Does this fact, therefore, give the nature faker warrant to exaggerate or to falsify the things he sees in the fields and woods? Let him make the most of what he sees, embellish it, amplify it, twirl it on the point of his pen like a juggler, but let him beware of adding to it; let him be sure he sees accurately. Let him beware of letting invention take the place of observation. It is one thing to work your gold or silver up into sparkling ornaments, and quite another to manufacture an imitation gold or silver, and this is what the nature fakers do. Their natural history is for the most part a sham, a counterfeit. No one quarrels with them because they are not scientific, or because they deal in something more than dry facts; the ground of quarrel is that they do not start with facts, that they grossly and absurdly misrepresent the wild lives they claim to portray.

The truth of animal life is more interesting than any fiction about it. Can there be any doubt, for instance, that if one knew just how the fur seals find their way back from the vast wilderness of the Pacific Ocean, where there is, apparently, nothing for the eye, or the ear, or the nose to seize upon in guiding them, to the little island in Bering Sea that is their breeding haunt in spring — can there be any doubt, I say, that such knowledge would be vastly more interesting than anything our natural history romancers could invent about it? But it is the way of our romancers to draw upon their invention when their observation fails them. Thus one of them tells how the salmon get up the high falls that they meet with in the rivers they ascend in spring — it is by easy stages; they rest upon shelves or upon niches in the rocks behind the curtain of water, and leap from these upward through the pouring current till the top is gained; and he tells it as if he knew it to be a fact, when, in truth, it is a fiction.

Not till the mind is purged of dread, superstition, and all notions of a partnership between the visible and the occult will the eye see straight. The mind that is athirst for the marvelous and the mysterious will rarely see straight. The mind that believes the wild creatures are half human, that they plot and plan and reason as men do, will not see straight nor report the facts without addition or diminution. There is plenty that is curious and inexplicable in nature, things that astonish or baffle us, but there is no "hocus-pocus," nothing that moves on the borderland between the known and the unknown, or that justifies the curious superstitions of the past. Things of the twilight are more elusive and difficult of verification than things of the noon, but they are no less real, and no less a part of the common day.

I was reminded of this lately on hearing the twilight flight song of the woodcock — one of the most curious and tantalizing yet interesting bird songs we have. I fancy that the persons who hear and recognize it in the April or May twilight are few and far between. I myself have heard it only on three occasions — one season in late March, one season in April, and the last time in the middle of May. It is a voice of ecstatic song coming down from the upper air and through the mist and the darkness — the spirit of the swamp and the marsh climbing heavenward and pouring out its joy in a wild burst of lyric melody; a haunter of the muck and a prober of the mud suddenly transformed into a bird that soars and circles and warbles like a lark hidden or half hidden in the depths of the twilight sky. The passion of the spring has few more pleasing exemplars. The madness of the season, the abandon of the mating instinct, is in every move and note. Ordinarily the woodcock is a very dull, stupid bird, with a look almost idiotic, and is seldom seen except by the sportsman or the tramper along marshy brooks. But for a brief season in his life he is an inspired creature, a winged song that baffles the eye and thrills the ear from the mystic regions of the upper air.

When I last heard it, I was with a companion, and our attention was arrested, as we were skirting the edge of a sloping, rather marshy, boulder-strewn field, by the *zeep, zeep,* which the bird utters on the ground, preliminary to its lark-like flight. We paused and listened. The light of day was fast failing; a faint murmur went up from the fields below us that defined itself now and then in the goodnight song of some bird. Now it was the lullaby of the song sparrow or the swamp sparrow. Once the tender, ringing, infantile voice of the bush sparrow* stood out vividly for a moment on that great background of silence. *Zeep, zeep,* came out of the dimness six or eight rods away. Presently there was a faint, rapid whistling of wings, and my companion said: "There, he is up." The ear could trace his flight, but not the eye. In less than a minute the straining ear failed to catch any sound, and we knew he had reached his climax and was circling. Once we distinctly saw him whirling far above us. Then he was lost in the obscurity, and in a few seconds there rained down upon us the notes of his ecstatic song — a novel kind of hurried, chirping, smacking warble. It was very brief, and when it ceased, we knew the bird was dropping plummet-like to the earth. In half a minute or less his *zeep, zeep,* came up again from the ground. In two or three minutes he repeated his flight and song, and thus kept it up during the half-hour or more that we remained to listen: now a harsh plaint out of the obscurity upon the ground; then a jubilant strain from out the obscurity of the air above. His mate was probably somewhere within earshot, and we wondered just how much interest she took in the performance. Was it all for her

* Field Sparrow. [Ed.]

benefit, or inspired by her presence? I think, rather, it was inspired by the May night, by the springing grass, by the unfolding leaves, by the apple bloom, by the passion of joy and love that thrills through nature at this season.[1]

Nature does nothing merely for beauty; beauty follows as the inevitable result; and the final impression of health and finish which her works make upon the mind is owing as much to those things which are not technically called beautiful as to those which are. The former give identity to the latter. The one is to the other what substance is to form, or bone to flesh. The beauty of nature includes all that is called beautiful, as its flower; and all that is not called beautiful, as its stalk and roots.

Indeed, when I go to the woods or fields or ascend to the hilltop, I do not seem to be gazing upon beauty at all, but to be breathing it like the air. I am not dazzled or astonished; I am in no hurry to look lest it be gone. I would not have the litter and débris removed or the banks trimmed or the ground painted. What I enjoy is commensurate with the earth and sky itself. It clings to the rocks and trees; it is kindred to the roughness and savagery; it rises from every tangle and chasm; it perches on the dry oak stubs with the hawks and buzzards; the crows shed it from their wings and weave it into their nests of coarse sticks; the fox barks it, the cattle low it, and every mountain path leads to its haunts. I am not a spectator of, but a participator in it. It is not an adornment; its roots strike to the centre of the earth.

All true beauty in nature or in art is like the iridescent hue of mother-of-pearl, which is intrinsic and necessary, being the result of the arrangement of the particles — the flowering of the mechanism of the shell; or like the beauty of health which comes out of and reaches back again to the bones and the digestion.

In fact, beauty as a separate and distinct thing does not exist.

Neither can it be reached by any sorting or sifting or clarifying process. It is an experience of the mind, and must be preceded by the conditions, just as light is an experience of the eye, and sound of the ear.

To attempt to manufacture beauty is as vain as to attempt to manufacture truth; and to give it to us in poems or any form of art, without a lion of some sort, a lion of truth or fitness or power, is to emasculate it and destroy its volition.

But current poetry is, for the most part, an attempt to do this very thing, to give us beauty without beauty's antecedents and foil. The poets want to spare us the annoyance of the beast. Since beauty is the chief attraction, why not have this part alone, pure and unadulterated — why not pluck the plumage from the bird, the flower from its stalk, the moss from the rock, the shell from the shore, the honey bag from the bee, and thus have in brief what pleases us? Hence, with rare exceptions, one feels, on opening the latest book of poems, like exclaiming, "Well, here is the beautiful at last divested of everything else — of truth, of power, of utility — and one may add of beauty, too. It charms as color, or flowers, or jewels, or perfume, charms — and that is the end of it."

The perception of cosmical beauty comes by a vital original process. It is in some measure a creative act, and those works that rest upon it make demands — perhaps extraordinary ones — upon the reader or beholder. We regard mere surface glitter, or mere verbal sweetness, in a mood entirely passive and with a pleasure entirely profitless. The beauty of excellent stage scenery seems much more obvious and easy of apprehension than the beauty of trees and hills themselves, inasmuch as the act of association in the mind is much easier and cheaper than the act of original perception.

Only the greatest works in any department afford any explanation of this wonder we call nature, or aid the mind in arriving at correct notions concerning it.   To copy here and there a line or a trait is no explanation; but to translate nature into another language — to bridge it to us, to repeat in some sort the act of creation itself — is the final and crowning triumph of poetic art.

After the critic has enumerated all the stock qualities of the poet, as taste, fancy, melody, etc., it remains to be said that unless there is something in him that is *living identity,* something analogous to the growing, pushing, reproducing forces of nature, all the rest in the end pass for but little.[2]

It might almost be said that the birds are all birds of the poets and of no one else, because it is only the poetical temperament that fully responds to them.   So true is this, that all the great ornithologists — original namers and biographers of the birds — have been poets in deed if not in word.   Audubon is a notable case in point, who, if he had not the tongue or pen of the poet, certainly had the eye and ear and heart — "the fluid and attaching character" — and the singleness of purpose, the enthusiasm, the unworldliness, the love, that characterize the true and divine race of bards.

So had Wilson, though perhaps not in as large a measure; yet he took fire as only a poet can.   While making a journey on foot to Philadelphia, shortly after landing in this country, he caught sight of the red-headed woodpecker flitting among the trees — a bird that shows like a tricolored scarf among the foliage — and it so kindled his enthusiasm that his life was devoted to the pursuit of the birds from that day.   It was a lucky hit.   Wilson had already set up as a poet in Scotland, and was still fermenting when the bird met his eye and suggested to his soul a new outlet for its enthusiasm.

The very idea of a bird is a symbol and a suggestion to the poet. A bird seems to be at the top of the scale, so vehement and intense is his life — large-brained, large-lunged, hot, ecstatic, his frame charged with buoyancy and his heart with song. The beautiful vagabonds, endowed with every grace, masters of all climes, and knowing no bounds — how many human aspirations are realized in their free, holiday lives, and how many suggestions to the poet in their flight and song!

The very oldest poets, the towering antique bards, seem to make little mention of the songbirds. They loved better the soaring, swooping birds of prey, the eagle, the ominous birds, the vultures, the storks and cranes, or the clamorous seabirds and the screaming hawks. These suited better the rugged, war-like character of the times and the simple, powerful souls of the singers themselves. Homer must have heard the twittering of the swallows, the cry of the plover, the voice of the turtle, and the warble of the nightingale; but they were not adequate symbols to express what he felt or to adorn his theme. Æschylus saw in the eagle "the dog of Jove," and his verse cuts like a sword with such a conception.

It is not because the old bards were less as poets, but that they were more as men. To strong, susceptible characters, the music of nature is not confined to sweet sounds. The defiant scream of the hawk circling aloft, the wild whinney of the loon, the whooping of the crane, the booming of the bittern, the vulpine bark of the eagle, the loud trumpeting of the migratory geese sounding down out of the midnight sky; or, by the seashore, the coast of New Jersey or Long Island, the wild crooning of the flocks of gulls, repeated, continued by the hour, swirling sharp and shrill, rising and falling like the wind in a storm, as they circle above the beach or dip to the dash of the waves — are much more welcome in certain moods than any and all mere

bird melodies, in keeping as they are with the shaggy and un-
tamed features of ocean and woods, and suggesting something
like the Richard Wagner music in the ornithological orchestra.

Keats's poem on the nightingale is doubtless more in the
spirit of the bird's strain than any other. It is less a description
of the song and more the song itself.

I mention the nightingale only to point my remarks upon its
American rival, the famous mockingbird of the Southern States,
which is also a nightingale — a night-singer — and which no
doubt excels the Old World bird in the variety and compass of
its powers. The two birds belong to totally distinct families,
there being no American species which answers to the European
nightingale, as there are that answer to the robin, the cuckoo,
the blackbird, and numerous others. Philomel has the color,
manners, and habits of a thrush — our hermit thrush — but it
is not a thrush at all, but a warbler.

Our nightingale has mainly the reputation of the caged bird,
and is famed mostly for its powers of mimicry, which are truly
wonderful, enabling the bird to reproduce exactly and even im-
prove upon the notes of almost any other songster. But in a
state of freedom it has a song of its own which is infinitely rich
and various. It is a garrulous polyglot when it chooses to be,
and there is a dash of the clown and the buffoon in its nature
which too often flavors its whole performance, especially in cap-
tivity; but in its native haunts, and when its love passion is upon
it, the serious and even grand side of its character comes out. In
Alabama and Florida its song may be heard all through the sultry summer night, at times low and plaintive, then full and
strong. A friend of Thoreau and a careful observer who has re-
sided in Florida, tells me that this bird is a much more marvelous singer than it has the credit of being. He describes a habit
it has of singing on the wing on moonlight nights that would be

worth going South to hear. Starting from a low bush, it mounts in the air and continues its flight apparently to an altitude of several hundred feet, remaining on the wing a number of minutes and pouring out its song with the utmost clearness and abandon — a slowly rising musical rocket that fills the night air with harmonious sounds.[3]

There is a feeling in heroic poetry, or in a burst of eloquence, that I sometimes catch in quite different fields. I caught it this morning, for instance, when I saw the belated trains go by and knew how they had been battling with storm, darkness, and distance, and had triumphed. They were due at my place in the night but did not pass till after eight o'clock in the morning. Two trains coupled together — the fast mail and the express — making an immense line of coaches hauled by two engines. They had come from the West, were all covered with snow and ice, like soldiers with the dust of battle upon them. They had massed their forces and were now moving with augmented speed and with a resolution that was epic and grand. Talk about the railroad dispelling the romance from the landscape; if it does, it brings the heroic element in. The moving train is a proud spectacle, especially in stormy and tempestuous nights. When I look out and see its light, steady and unflickering as the planets, and hear the roar of its advancing tread, or its sound diminishing in the distance, I am comforted and made stout of heart. O night, where is thy stay! O space, where is thy victory! Or to see the fast mail pass in the morning is as good as a page of Homer. It quickens one's pulse for all day. It is the Ajax of trains. I hear its defiant, warning whistle, hear it thunder over the bridges, and its sharp, rushing ring among the rocks, and in the winter mornings see its glancing, meteoric lights, or in summer its white form bursting through the silence and the shadows, its plume of smoke lying flat upon its roofs and stretching far behind — a sight better than a battle. It is something of the same feeling one has in witnessing any wild, free careering in storms, and in floods in nature; or in beholding the charge of an army; or in listening to an eloquent man, or to a hundred instruments of music in full blast — it is triumph, victory.   What is eloquence but mass in motion — a flood, a cataract, an express train, a cavalry charge?   We are literally carried away, swept from our feet, and recover our senses again as best we can.[4]

I wonder that Wilson Flagg did not include the cow among his "Picturesque Animals," for that is where she belongs. She has not the classic beauty of the horse, but in picture-making qualities she is far ahead of him. Her shaggy, loose-jointed body; her irregular, sketchy outlines, like those of the landscape — the hollows and ridges, the slopes and prominences; her tossing horns, her bushy tail, her swinging gait, her tranquil, ruminating habits — all tend to make her an object upon which the artist eye loves to dwell. The artists are forever putting her into pictures, too. In rural landscape scenes she is an important feature. Behold her grazing in the pastures and on the hillsides, or along banks of streams, or ruminating under wide-spreading trees, or standing belly-deep in the creek or pond, or lying upon the smooth places in the quiet summer afternoon, the day's grazing done, and waiting to be summoned home to be milked; and again in the twilight lying upon the level summit of the hill, or where the sward is thickest and softest; or in winter a herd of them filing along toward the spring to drink, or being "foddered" from the stack in the field upon the new snow — surely the cow is a picturesque animal, and all her goings and comings are pleasant to behold.

Neither have the poets made much of the cow, but have rather dwelt upon the steer, or the ox yoked to the plow. But the ear is charmed, nevertheless, especially if it be not too near, and the air be still and dense, or hollow, as the farmer says. And again, if it be springtime and she task that powerful bellows of hers to its utmost capacity, how round the sound is, and how far it goes over the hills!

The cow has at least four tones or lows. First, there is her alarmed or distressed low when deprived of her calf, or separated from her mates — her low of affection. Then there is her call of hunger, a petition for food, sometimes full of impatience, or her answer to the farmer's call, full of eagerness. Then there is that peculiar frenzied bawl she utters on smelling blood, which causes every member of the herd to lift its head and hasten to the spot — the native cry of the clan. When she is gored or in great danger she bawls also, but that is different. And lastly, there is the long, sonorous volley she lets off on the hills or in the yard, or along the highway, and which seems to be expressive of a kind of unrest and vague longing — the longing of the imprisoned Io for her lost identity. She sends her voice forth so that every god on Mount Olympus can hear her plaint. She makes this sound in the morning, especially in the spring, as she goes forth to graze.

The cow figures in Grecian mythology, and in the Oriental literature is treated as a sacred animal. "The clouds are cows and the rain milk." I remember what Herodotus says of the Egyptians' worship of heifers and steers; and in the traditions of the Celtic nations the cow is regarded as a divinity. In Norse mythology the milk of the cow Andhumbla afforded nourishment to the Frost giants, and it was she that licked into being and into shape a god, the father of Odin. If anything could lick a god into shape, certainly the cow could do it. You may see her perform this office for young Taurus any spring. She licks him out of the fogs and bewilderments and uncertainties in which he finds himself on first landing upon these shores, and up on to his feet in an incredibly short time. Indeed, that potent tongue of hers can almost make the dead alive any day, and the creative lick of the old Scandinavian mother cow is only a large-lettered rendering of the commonest facts.

The cow belongs more especially to the northern peoples, to the region of the good green grass. She is the true *grazing* animal. That broad, smooth, always dewy nose of hers is just the suggestion of greensward. She caresses the grass; she sweeps off the ends of the leaves; she reaps it with the soft sickle of her tongue. She crops close, but she does not bruise or devour the turf like the horse. She is the sward's best friend, and will make it thick and smooth as a carpet.

What a variety of individualities a herd of cows presents when you have come to know them all, not only in form and color, but in manners and disposition! Some are timid and awkward, and the butt of the whole herd. Some remind you of deer. Some have an expression in the face like certain persons you have known. A petted and well-fed cow has a benevolent and gracious look; an ill-used and poorly fed one, a pitiful and forlorn look. Some cows have a masculine or ox expression; others are extremely feminine. The latter are the ones for milk. Some cows will kick like a horse; some jump fences like deer. Every herd has its ringleader, its unruly spirit — one that plans all the mischief and leads the rest through the fences into the grain or into the orchard. This one is usually quite different from the master spirit, the "boss of the yard." The latter is generally the most peaceful and law-abiding cow in the lot, and the least bullying and quarrelsome. But she is not to be trifled with; her will is law; the whole herd give way before her, those that have crossed horns with her and those that have not, but yielded their allegiance without crossing. I remember such a one among my father's milkers when I was a boy — a slender-horned, deep-shouldered, large-uddered, dewlapped old cow that we always put first in the long stable, so she could not have a cow on each side of her to forage upon; for the master is yielded to no less in the stanchions than in the yard. She always had the first place anywhere. She had her choice of standing room in the milking yard, and when she wanted to lie down there or in the fields the best and softest spot was hers. When the herd were foddered from the stack or barn, or fed with pumpkins in the fall, she was always first served. Her demeanor was quiet but impressive. She never bullied or gored her mates, but literally ruled them with the breath of her nostrils. If any newcomer or ambitious younger cow, however, chafed under her supremacy, she was ever ready to make good her claims. And with what spirit she would fight when openly challenged! She was a whirl-wind of pluck and valor; and not after one defeat or two defeats would she yield the championship. The boss cow, when over-come, seems to brood over her disgrace, and day after day will meet her rival in fierce combat.[5]

We toiled up the long steep hill, where only an occasional mullein stalk or other tall weed stood above the snow. Near the top the hill was girded with a bank of snow that blotted out the stone wall and every vestige of the earth beneath. These hills wear this belt till May, and sometimes the plow pauses beside them. From the top of the ridge an immense landscape in im-maculate white stretches before us. Miles upon miles of farms, smoothed and padded by the stainless element, hang upon the sides of the mountains or repose across the long sloping hills. The fences or stone walls show like half-obliterated black lines. I turn my back to the sun or shade my eyes with my hand. Every object or movement in the landscape is sharply revealed; one could see a fox half a league. The farmer foddering his cattle, or drawing manure afield, or leading his horse to water; the pedestrian crossing the hill below; the children wending their way toward the distant schoolhouse — the eye cannot help but note them: they are black specks upon square miles of luminous white. What a multitude of sins this unstinted charity of the snow covers! How it flatters the ground! Yonder sterile field might be a garden, and you would never suspect that that gentle slope with its pretty dimples and curves was not the smoothest of meadows, yet it is paved with rocks and stone. It is like some conjurer's trick. The very trees have turned to snow. The smallest branch is like a cluster of great white antlers. The eye is bewildered by the soft fleecy labyrinth before it. On the lower ranges the forests were entirely bare, but now we perceive the summit of every mountain about us runs up into a kind of arctic region where the trees are loaded with snow. The beginning of this colder zone is sharply marked all around the horizon; the line runs as level as the shore line of a lake or sea; indeed, a warmer aerial sea fills all the valleys, submerging the lower peaks and making white islands of all the higher ones. The branches bend with the rime. The winds have not shaken it down. It adheres to them like a growth. On examination I find the branches coated with ice from which shoot slender spikes and needles that penetrate and hold the cord of snow. It is a new kind of foliage wrought by the frost and the clouds, and it obscures the sky and fills the vistas of the woods nearly as much as the myriad leaves of summer. The sun blazes, the sky is without a cloud or a film, yet we walk in a soft white shade. A gentle breeze was blowing on the open crest of the mountain, but one could carry a lighted

candle through these snow-curtained and snow-canopied chambers.[6]

Not a little of the sunshine of our Northern winters is surely wrapped up in the apple. How could we winter over without it? How is life sweetened by its mild acids! A cellar well filled with apples is more valuable than a chamber filled with flax and wool. So much sound, ruddy life to draw upon, to strike one's roots down into, as it were.

Especially to those whose soil of life is inclined to be a little clayey and heavy, is the apple a winter necessity. It is the natural antidote of most of the ills the flesh is heir to. Full of vegetable acids and aromatics, qualities which act as refrigerants and antiseptics, what an enemy it is to jaundice, indigestion, torpidity of liver, etc.! It is a gentle spur and tonic to the whole biliary system. Then I have read that it has been found by analysis to contain more phosphorus than any other vegetable. This makes it the proper food of the scholar and the sedentary man; it feeds his brain and it stimulates his liver. Neither is this all. Beside its hygienic properties, the apple is full of sugar and mucilage, which make it highly nutritious. It is said "the operators of Cornwall, England, consider ripe apples nearly as nourishing as bread, and far more so than potatoes. In the year 1801 — which was a year of much scarcity — apples, instead of being converted into cider, were sold to the poor, and the laborers asserted that they could "stand their work" on baked apples without meat; whereas a potato diet required either meat or some other substantial nutriment. The apple is the commonest and yet the most varied and beautiful of fruits. A dish of them is as becoming to the centre table in winter as was the vase of flowers in the summer — a bouquet of spitzenburgs and greenings and northern spies. A rose when it blooms, the apple is a rose when it ripens. It pleases every sense to which it can be addressed, the touch, the smell, the sight, the taste; and when it falls, in the still October days, it pleases the ear. It is a call to a banquet, it is a signal that the feast is ready. The bough would fain hold it, but it can now assert its independence; it can now live a life of its own.

An apple orchard is sure to bear you several crops beside the apple. There is the crop of sweet and tender reminiscences, dating from childhood and spanning the seasons from May to October, and making the orchard a sort of outlying part of the household. You have played there as a child, mused there as a youth or lover, strolled there as a thoughtful, sad-eyed man. Your father, perhaps, planted the trees, or reared them from the seed, and you yourself have pruned and grafted them and worked among them, till every separate tree has a peculiar history and meaning in your mind. Then there is the never-failing crop of birds — robins, goldfinches, kingbirds, cedarbirds, hairbirds, orioles, starlings — all nesting and breeding in its branches, and fitly described by Wilson Flagg as "Birds of the Garden and Orchard." Whether the pippin and sweet bough bear or not, the "punctual birds" can always be depended on. Indeed, there are few better places to study ornithology than in the orchard. Besides its regular occupants, many of the birds of the deeper forest find occasion to visit it during the season. The cuckoo comes for the tent caterpillar, the jay for frozen apples, the ruffed grouse for buds, the crow foraging for birds' eggs, the woodpecker and chickadees for their food, and the high-hole for ants. The redbird comes, too, if only to see what a friendly covert its branches form; and the wood thrush now and then comes out of the grove nearby and nests alongside of its cousin, the robin. The smaller hawks know that this is a most likely spot for their prey, and in spring the shy northern warblers may be studied as they pause to feed on the fine insects amid its branches. The mice love to dwell here also, and hither come from the near woods the squirrel and the rabbit.[7]

I have frequently been surprised, in late fall and early winter, to see how unequal or irregular was the encroachment of the frost upon the earth. If there is suddenly a great fall in the mercury, the frost lays siege to the soil and effects a lodgment here and there, and extends its conquests gradually. At one place in the field you can easily run your staff through into the soft ground, when a few rods farther on it will be as hard as a rock. A little covering of dry grass or leaves is a great protection. The moist places hold out long and the spring runs never freeze. You find the frost has gone several inches into the plowed ground, but on going to the woods and poking away the leaves and débris under the hemlocks and cedars, you find there is no frost at all. The Earth freezes her ears and toes and naked places first, and her body last.

If heat were visible, or if we represent it say by smoke, then the December landscape would present a curious spectacle. We should see the smoke lying low over the meadows, thickest in the hollows and moist places and where the turf was oldest and densest. It would cling to the fences and ravines. Under every evergreen tree we should see the vapor rising and filling the branches, while the woods of pine and hemlock would be blue with it long after it had disappeared from the open country. It would rise from the tops of the trees and be carried this way and that with the wind. The valleys of the great rivers, like the Hudson, would overflow with it. Large bodies of water become regular magazines in which heat is stored during the summer, and they give it out again during the fall and early winter. The early frosts keep well back from the Hudson, skulking behind the ridges, and hardly come over in sight at any point. But they grow bold as the season advances, till the river's fires, too, are put out and Winter covers it with his snows.[8]

One seems to get nearer to nature in the early spring days: all screens are removed, the earth everywhere speaks directly to you; she is not hidden by verdure and foliage; there is a peculiar delight in walking over the brown turf of the fields that one cannot feel later on. How welcome the smell of it, warmed by the sun; the first breath of the reviving earth. How welcome the full, sparkling watercourses, too, everywhere drawing the eye; by and by they will be veiled by the verdure and shrunken by the heat. When March is kind, for how much her slightest favors count! The other evening, as I stood on the slope of a hill in the twilight, I heard a whistling of approaching wings, and presently a woodcock flying low passed near me. I could see his form and his long curved wings dimly against the horizon; his whistling slowly vanished in the gathering night, but his passage made something stir and respond within me. March was on the wing, she was abroad in the soft still twilight searching out the moist, springy places where the worms first come to the surface and where the grass first starts; and her course was up the valley from the south. A day or two later I sat on a hillside in the woods late in the day, amid the pines and the hemlocks, and heard the soft, elusive spring call of the little owl — a curious musical undertone hardly separable from the silence; a bell, muffled in feathers, tolling in the twilight of the woods and discernible only to the most alert ear. But it was the voice of spring, the voice of the same impulse that sent the woodcock winging his way through the dusk, that was just beginning to make the pussywillows swell and the grass to freshen in the spring runs.

Occasionally, of a bright, warm, still day in March, the little flying spider is abroad. It is the most delicate of all March tokens, but very suggestive. Its long, waving threads of gossamer, invisible except when the sunlight falls upon them at a particular angle, stream out here and there upon the air, a filament of life, reaching and reaching as if to catch and detain the most subtle of the skyey influences.

Nature is always new in the spring, and lucky are we if it finds us new also.[9]

4. Weathered Rocks

A SMALL RIVER or stream flowing by one's door has many attractions over a large body of water like the Hudson. One can make a companion of it; he can walk with it and sit with it, or lounge on its banks and feel that it is all his own. It becomes something private and special to him. You cannot have the same kind of attachment and sympathy with a great river; it does not flow through your affections like a lesser stream. The Hudson is a long arm of the sea, and it has something of the sea's austerity and grandeur. I think one might spend a lifetime upon its banks without feeling any sense of ownership in it or becoming at all intimate with it: it keeps one at arm's length. It is a great highway of travel and of commerce; ships from all parts of our seaboard plow its waters.

The river never seems so much a thing of life as in the spring when it first slips off its icy fetters. The dead comes to life before one's very eyes. The rigid, pallid river is resurrected in a twinkling. You look out of your window one moment, and there is that great, white, motionless expanse; you look again, and there in its place is the tender, dimpling, sparkling water. But if your eyes are sharp, you may have noticed the signs all the forenoon; the time was ripe, the river stirred a little in its icy shroud, put forth a little streak or filament of blue water near shore, made breathing holes. Then, after a while, the ice

72

was rent in places, and the edges crushed together or shoved one slightly upon the other; there was apparently something growing more and more alive and restless underneath. Then suddenly the whole mass of the ice from shore to shore begins to move downstream — very gently, almost imperceptibly at first, then with a steady, deliberate pace that soon lays bare a large expanse of bright, dancing water. The island above keeps back the northern ice, and the ebb tide makes a clean sweep from that point south for a few miles until the return of the flood, when the ice comes back.

After the ice is once in motion, a few hours suffice to break it up pretty thoroughly. Then what a wild, chaotic scene the river presents: in one part of the day the great masses hurrying downstream, crowding and jostling each other and struggling for the right of way; in the other, all running upstream again, as if sure of escape in that direction. Thus they race up and down, the sport of the ebb and flow; but the ebb wins each time by some distance.

If the opening of the river is gentle, the closing of it is sometimes attended by scenes exactly the reverse.

A cold wave one December was accompanied by a violent wind, which blew for two days and two nights. The ice formed rapidly in the river, but the wind and waves kept it from uniting and massing. On the second day the scene was indescribably wild and forbidding; the frost and fury of December were never more vividly pictured: vast crumpled, spumy ice-fields interspersed with stretches of wildly agitated water, the heaving waves thick with forming crystals, the shores piled with frozen foam and pulverized floes. After the cold wave had spent itself and the masses had become united and stationary, the scene was scarcely less wild. I fancied the plain looked more like a field of lava and scoria than like a field of ice, an eruption from some huge frost volcano of the north. Or did it suggest that a battle had been fought there and that this wild confusion was the ruin wrought by the contending forces?

No sooner has the river pulled his icy coverlid over him than he begins to snore in his winter sleep. It is a singular sound. Thoreau calls it a "whoop," Emerson a "cannonade" and in "Merlin" speaks of

> *the gasp and moan*
> *Of the ice-imprisoned flood.*

Sometimes it is a well-defined grunt — *e-h-h, e-h-h,* as if some ice god turned uneasily in his bed.

One fancies the sound is like this, when he hears it in the still winter nights seated by his fireside or else when snugly wrapped in his own bed.

One winter the river shut up in a single night, beneath a cold wave of great severity and extent. Zero weather continued nearly a week, with a clear sky and calm, motionless air; and the effect of the brillant sun by day and of the naked skies by night upon this vast area of new black ice, one expanding it, the other contracting, was very marked.

A cannonade indeed! As the morning advanced, out of the sunshine came peal upon peal of soft mimic thunder; occasionally becoming a regular crash, as if all the ice batteries were discharged at once. As noon approached the sound grew to one continuous mellow roar, which lessened and became more intermittent as the day waned, until about sundown it was nearly hushed. Then, as the chill of night came on, the conditions were reversed, and the ice began to thunder under the effects of contraction; cracks opened from shore to shore and grew to be two or three inches broad under the shrinkage of the ice. On the morrow the expansion of the ice often found vent in one of these cracks; the two edges would first crush together and then gradually overlap each other for two feet or more.

This expansive force of the sun upon the ice is sometimes enormous. I have seen the ice explode with a loud noise and a great commotion in the water, and a huge crack shoot like a thunderbolt from shore to shore, with its edges overlapping and shivered into fragments.

When unprotected by a covering of snow, the ice, under the expansive force of the sun, breaks regularly, every two or three miles, from shore to shore. The break appears as a slight ridge, formed by the edges of the overlapping ice.

This icy uproar is like thunder, because it seems to proceed from something in swift motion; you cannot locate it; it is everywhere and yet nowhere. There is something strange and phantomlike about it. To the eye all is still and rigid, but to the ear all is in swift motion.

A fall of snow, and this icy uproar is instantly hushed, the river sleeps in peace. The snow is like a coverlid, which protects the ice from the changes of temperature of the air and brings repose to its uneasy spirit.

When the river is at its wildest, usually in March, the eagles appear. They prowl about amid the ice floes, alighting upon them or flying heavily above them in quest of fish or a wounded duck or other game.

I have counted ten of these noble birds at one time, some seated grim and motionless upon cakes of ice — usually surrounded by crows — others flapping along, sharply scrutinizing the surface beneath. Where the eagles are, there the crows do congregate. The crow follows the eagle, as the jackal follows the lion, in hope of getting the leavings of the royal table. Then I suspect the crow is a real hero worshiper. I have seen a dozen or more of them sitting in a circle about an eagle upon the ice, all with their faces turned toward him and apparently in silent admiration of the dusky king.

Of the Hudson it may be said that it is a very large river for its size — that is, for the quantity of water it discharges into the sea. Its watershed is comparatively small — less, I think, than that of the Connecticut.

It is a huge trough with a very slight incline, through which the current moves very slowly and which would fill from the sea were its supplies from the mountains cut off. Its fall from Albany to the bay is only about five feet. Any object upon it, drifting with the current, progresses southward no more than eight miles in twenty-four hours. The ebb tide will carry it about twelve miles, and the flood set it back from seven to nine. A drop of water at Albany, therefore, will be nearly three weeks in reaching New York, though it will get pretty well pickled some days earlier.

Some rivers by their volume and impetuosity penetrate the sea, but here the sea is the aggressor and sometimes meets the mountain water nearly halfway.

This fact was illustrated a few years ago, when the basin of the Hudson was visited by one of the most severe droughts ever known in this part of the State. In the early winter, after the river was frozen over above Poughkeepsie, it was discovered that immense numbers of fish were retreating upstream before the slow encroachment of the salt water. There was a general exodus of the finny tribes from the whole lower part of the river; it was like the spring and fall migration of the birds or the fleeing of the population of a district before some approaching danger: vast swarms of catfish, white and yellow perch, and striped bass were *en route* for the fresh water farther north. When the people alongshore made the discovery, they turned

out as they do in the rural districts when the pigeons appear, and, with small gill nets let down through holes in the ice, captured them in fabulous numbers. On the heels of the retreating perch and catfish came the denizens of salt water, and codfish were taken ninety miles above New York. When the February thaw came and brought up the volume of fresh water again, the sea brine was beaten back, and the fish, what was left of them, resumed their old feeding grounds.

According to Professor Newberry, that part of our coast that flanks the mouth of the Hudson is still sinking at the rate of a few inches per century, so that in the twinkling of a hundred thousand years or so the sea will completely submerge the city of New York, the top of Trinity Church steeple alone standing above the flood. We who live so far inland and sigh for the salt water need only to have a little patience, and we shall wake up some fine morning and find the surf beating upon our doorsteps.[1]

I find there is enough of the troglodyte in most persons to make them love the rocks and the caves and ledges that the air and the rains have carved out of them.

The rocks are not so close akin to us as the soil; they are one more remove from us; but they lie back of all and are the final source of all. I do not suppose they attract us on this account, but on quite other grounds. Rocks do not recommend the land to the tiller of the soil, but they recommend it to those who reap a harvest of another sort — the artist, the poet, the walker, the student and lover of all primitive open-air things.

Time, geologic time, looks out at us from the rocks as from no other objects in the landscape. Geologic time! How the striking of the great clock, whose hours are millions of years, reverberates out of the abyss of the past! Mountains fall and the foundations of the earth shift as it beats out the moments of terrestrial history. Rocks have literally come down to us from a foreworld. The youth of the earth is in the soil and in the trees and verdure that spring from it; its age is in the rocks; in the great stone book of the geologic strata its history is written. Even if we do not know our geology, there is something in the face of a cliff and in the look of a granite boulder that gives us pause and draws us thitherward in our walk.

The rocks have a history; gray and weatherworn, they are veterans of many battles; they have most of them marched in the ranks of vast stone brigades during the ice age; they have been torn from the hills, recruited from the mountaintops, and marshaled on the plains and in the valleys; and now the elemental war is over, there they lie waging a gentle but incessant warfare with time and slowly, oh, so slowly, yielding to its attacks! I say they lie there, but some of them are still in motion, creeping down the slopes or out from the claybanks, nudged and urged along by the frosts and the rains and the sun. It is hard even for the rocks to keep still in this world of motion, but it takes the hour hand of many years to mark their progress. What in my childhood we called "the old pennyroyal rock," because pennyroyal always grew beside it, has, in my time, crept out of the bank by the roadside three or four feet. When a rock, loosened from its ties in the hills, once becomes a wanderer, it is restless ever after and stirs in its sleep. Heat and cold expand and contract it and make it creep down an incline. Hitch your rock to a sunbeam and come back in a hundred years and see how much it has moved. I know a great platform of rock weighing hundreds of tons and large enough to build a house upon, that has slid down the hill from the ledges above and that is pushing a roll of turf before it as a boat pushes a wave, but stand there till you are gray, and you will see no motion; return in a century and you will doubtless find that the great rock raft has progressed a few inches. What a sense of leisure such things give us hurrying mortals!

In our Northern States there are two classes of rocks: the place rocks and the wanderers, or drift boulders. The boulders are in some ways the more interesting; they have a story to tell which the place rock has not; they have drifted about upon a sea of change, slow and unwilling voyagers from the north many tens of thousands of years ago; now they lie here in the fields and on the hills, shipwrecked mariners, in some cases hundreds of miles from home. But usually they have been plucked from the neighboring ledges or mountains and shoved or transported to where they now lie. In nearly all cases the sharp points and angles have been rubbed down, as with most travelers, and they lie about the fields like cattle ruminating upon the ground.

"The shadow of a great rock in a weary land" is pretty sure to be the shadow of a drift boulder. The rock about which, and on which, we played as children was doubtless a drift boulder; the rocks beneath which the woodchucks and the foxes burrow are drift boulders; the rock under the spreading maples where the picnickers eat their lunch is a drift boulder; the rock that makes the deep pool in the trout stream of your boyhood is a drift boulder; the rocks which you helped your father pry up from the fields and haul to their place for the "rockbottom" of the stone wall, in the old days on the farm, were all drift boulders. How sod bound many of them were, and how the old oxen used to settle into their bows with rigid muscles in pulling them from their beds! If you had looked on their undersides you would have seen how smoothed and worn most of them were. They had been hauled across the land by oxen of another kind long before yours were heard of.

The rocks that give the eyebrows to the faces of the hills are place rocks — the cropping out of the original strata. The place rock gives the contour to the landscape; it forms the ledges and cliffs; it thrusts a huge rocky fist up through the turf here and there, or it exposes a broad smooth surface where you may see the grooves and scratches of the great ice sheet, tens of thousands of years old. The marks of the old ice plane upon the rocks weather out very slowly. When they are covered with a few inches of soil they are as distinct as those we saw in Alaska under the edges of the retreating glaciers.

When you want to read a stirring and heroic chapter in the great rock volume of the earth, the very Iliad or Odyssey of the rocks, go to the Grand Cañon of the Colorado or to Yosemite. As you gaze, a sentence from Job may come to your mind as it did to a friend of mine — "Where wast thou when I laid the foundations of the earth?"

All through the Southwest the great book of geologic Revelation lies open to the traveler in an astonishing manner. Its massive but torn and crumpled leaves of limestone, sandstone, and basalt lie spread out before him all through Colorado, New Mexico, and Arizona, and he may read snatches of the long geologic record from the flying train.

The purity of the strain of the different breeds of rocks is remarkable; about as little crossing or mingling among the different systems as there is among the different species of animals: considering the blind warring and chaos of the elements out of which they came, one can but wonder at the homogeneity of the different kinds. They are usually as uniform as if their production had been carefully watched over by some expert in the business — which is, indeed, the case. This expert is water. Was there ever such a sorter and sifter? See the vast claybanks, as uniform in quality and texture as a snowbank, slowly built up in the privacy of deep, still rivers or lakes during hundreds or thousands of years, implying a kind of secrecy and seclusion of nature. Mountains of granite have been ground down or disintegrated, and the clay washed out and carried in suspension by the currents, till it was impounded in some lake or basin and then slowly dropped.

The great claybanks and snowbanks of the Hudson River Valley doubtless date from the primary rocks of the Adirondack region. Much of the quartz sand is still in the soil of that region, and much of it is piled up along the river banks, but most of the clay has gone downstream and been finally deposited in the great river terraces that are now being uncovered and worked by the brickmakers. The sand and the clay rarely get mixed; the great hydraulic machine turns out a pretty pure product. The occasional mingling of sand and gravel shows that at times the workmen nodded, but the wonder is that, on the whole, the two should be so thoroughly separated and so carefully deposited each by itself. Flowing water drops its coarser material first, the sand next, and the mud and silt last. Hence the coarser grained rocks and conglomerates are built up in shallow water near shore, the sandstones in deeper water, and the slates and argillaceous rocks in deeper still. The limestone rocks, which are of animal origin, also imply deep, calm seas during periods that embrace hundreds and thousands of centuries. It is, then, the long ages of peace and tranquillity in the processes of the earth-building forces that have contributed to the homogeneity of the different systems of secondary rocks. What peace must have brooded over that great inland sea when those vast beds of Indiana limestone and sandstone were being laid down! A depth of thousands of feet of each without a flaw. Vast stretches of Cambrian and Silurian and Devonian time were apparently as free from violent movements and warrings of the elements as in our own day.[2]

5. Spring—Nature's Door Ajar

MARCH 1. The first day of spring and the first spring day!
I felt the change the moment I put my head out of doors in
the morning. A fitful, gusty south wind was blowing, though
the sky was clear. But the sunlight was not the same. There was
an interfusion of a new element. Not ten days before there had
been a day just as bright — even brighter and warmer — a clear,
crystalline day of February, with nothing vernal in it; but this
day was opaline; there was a film, a sentiment in it, a nearer
approach to life. Then there was that fresh, indescribable odor,
a breath from the Gulf or from Florida and the Carolinas — a
subtle, persuasive influence that thrilled the sense. Every root
and rootlet underground must have felt it; the buds of the soft
maple* and silver poplar felt it and swelled perceptibly during
the day. The robins knew it and were here that morning; so
were the crow blackbirds. The shad must have known it, down
deep in their marine retreats, and leaped and sported about the
mouths of the rivers, ready to dart up them if the genial influence continued. The bees in the hive also, or in the old tree in
the woods, no doubt awoke to new life; and the hibernating
animals, the bears and woodchucks, rolled up in their subter-
ranean dens — I imagine the warmth reached even them and
quickened their sluggish circulation.[1]

* Red Maple, *Acer rubrum.* [Ed.]

April is also the month of the new furrow. As soon as the frost is gone and the ground settled, the plow is started upon the hill, and at each bout I see its brightened mouldboard flash in the sun. Where the last remnants of the snowdrift lingered yesterday the plow breaks the sod today. Where the drift was deepest the grass is pressed flat, and there is a deposit of sand and earth blown from the fields to windward. Line upon line the turf is reversed, until there stands out of the neutral landscape a ruddy square visible for miles, or until the breasts of the broad hills glow like the breasts of the robins.

I think April* is the best month to be born in. One is just in time, so to speak, to catch the first train, which is made up in this month. My April chickens always turn out best. They get an early start; they have rugged constitutions. Late chickens cannot stand the heavy dews or withstand the predaceous hawks. In April all nature starts with you. You have not come out of your hibernaculum too early or too late; the time is ripe, and if you do not keep pace with the rest, why, the fault is not in the season.[2]

And yonder bluebird with the earth tinge on his breast and the sky tinge on his back — did he come down out of heaven on that bright March morning when he told us so softly and plaintively that, if we pleased, spring had come?   Indeed, there is nothing in the return of the birds more curious and suggestive than in the first appearance, or rumors of the appearance, of this little bluecoat. The bird at first seems a mere wandering voice in the air: one hears its call or carol on some bright March morning but is uncertain of its source or direction; it falls like a drop of rain when no cloud is visible; one looks and listens, but to no purpose.

* Burroughs' natal month. [Ed.]

When nature made the bluebird she wished to propitiate both the sky and the earth, so she gave him the color of the one on his back and the hue of the other on his breast, and ordained that his appearance in spring should denote that the strife and war between these two elements was at an end. He is the peace harbinger; in him the celestial and terrestrial strike hands and are fast friends. He means the furrow and he means the warmth; he means all the soft, wooing influences of the spring on the one hand, and the retreating footsteps of winter on the other.

It is sure to be a bright March morning when you first hear his note; and it is as if the milder influences up above had found a voice and let a word fall upon your ear, so tender is it and so prophetic, a hope tinged with a regret.

Bermuda! Bermuda! Bermuda! he seems to say, as if both invoking and lamenting, and, behold! Bermuda follows close, though the little pilgrim may be only repeating the tradition of his race, himself having come only from Florida, the Carolinas, or even from Virginia, where he has found his Bermuda on some broad sunny hillside thickly studded with cedars and persimmon trees.

In New York and in New England the sap starts up in the sugar maple the very day the bluebird arrives, and sugar making begins forthwith. The bird is generally a mere disembodied voice; a rumor in the air for two or three days before it takes visible shape before you. The males are the pioneers, and come several days in advance of the females. By the time both are here and the pair have begun to prospect for a place to nest, sugar making is over, the last vestige of snow has disappeared, and the plow is brightening its mouldboard in the new furrow.

The bluebird enjoys the preeminence of being the first bit of color that cheers our northern landscape. The other birds that arrive about the same time — the sparrow, the robin, the phœbe bird — are clad in neutral tints, gray, brown, or russet; but the bluebird brings one of the primary hues and the divinest of them all.[3]

This was a typical March day, clear, dry, and windy, the river rumpled and crumpled, the sky intense, distant objects strangely near; a day full of strong light, unusual; and extraordinary lightness and clearness all along the horizon, as if there were a diurnal aurora streaming up and burning through the sunlight; smoke from the first spring fires rising up in various directions; a day that winnowed the air and left no film in the sky. At night, how the big March bellows did work! Venus was like a great lamp in the sky. The stars all seemed brighter than usual, as if the wind blew them up like burning coals. Venus actually seemed to flare in the wind.

Each day foretells the next, if one could read the signs; today is the progenitor of tomorrow. When the atmosphere is telescopic and distant objects stand out unusually clear and sharp, a storm is near. We are on the crest of the wave, and the depression follows quickly. It often happens that clouds are not so indicative of a storm as the total absence of clouds. In this state of the atmosphere the stars are unusually numerous and bright at night, which is also a bad omen.

There is one redness in the east in the morning that means storm, another that means wind. The former is broad, deep, and angry; the clouds look like a huge bed of burning coals just raked open; the latter is softer, more vapory, and more widely extended. Just at the point where the sun is going to rise, and some minutes in advance of his coming, there sometimes rises straight upward a rosy column; it is like a shaft of deeply dyed vapor, blending with and yet partly separated from the clouds, and the base of which presently comes to glow like the sun itself. The day that follows is pretty certain to be very windy.   At other times the undersides of the eastern clouds are all turned to pink or rose-colored wool; the transformation extends until nearly the whole sky flushes, even the west glowing slightly; the sign is always to be interpreted as meaning fair weather.

The approach of great storms is seldom heralded by any striking or unusual phenomenon. The real weather gods are free from brag and bluster; but the sham gods fill the sky with portentous signs and omens.

To what extent the birds or animals can foretell the weather is uncertain. When the swallows are seen hawking very high it is a good indication: the insects upon which they feed venture up there only in the most auspicious weather. Yet bees will continue to leave the hive when a storm is imminent.

The critical moments of the day as regards the weather are at sunrise and sunset. A clear sunset is always a good sign; an obscured sun, just at the moment of going down after a bright day, bodes storm. There is much truth, too, in the saying that if it rain before seven, it will clear before eleven. Nine times in ten it will turn out thus. The best time for it to begin to rain or snow, if it wants to hold out, is about midforenoon. The great storms usually begin at this time. On all occasions the weather is very sure to declare itself before eleven o'clock. If you are going on a picnic or are going to start on a journey, and the morning is unsettled, wait till ten and one half o'clock and you shall know what the remainder of the day will be. Midday clouds and afternoon clouds, except in the season of thunderstorms, are usually harmless idlers and vagabonds.[4]

From what fact or event shall one really date the beginning of spring? The little piping frogs usually furnish a good start-ing point. One spring I heard the first note on the 6th of April;

the next on the 27th of February; but in reality the latter season was only about two weeks earlier than the former. When the bees carry in their first pollen, one would think spring had come; yet this fact does not always correspond with the real stage of the season. Before there is any bloom anywhere, bees will bring pollen to the hive. Where do they get it?

I have seen them gathering it on the fresh sawdust in the woodyard, especially on that of hickory or maple. They wallow amid the dust, working it over and over and searching it like diamond hunters, and after a time their baskets are filled with the precious flour, which is probably only a certain part of the wood, doubtless the soft, nutritious inner bark.

In fact, all signs and phases of life in the early season are very capricious and are earlier or later just as some local or exceptional circumstance favors or hinders. It is only such birds as arrive after about the 20th of April that are at all "punctual" according to the almanac. I have never known the arrival of the barn swallow to vary much from that date in this latitude, no matter how early or late the season might be.

There are many birds that do not come here till May, be the season never so early. The spring of 1878 was very forward, and on the 27th of April I made this entry in my notebook: "In nature it is the middle of May, and, judging from vegetation alone, one would expect to find many of the later birds, as the oriole, the wood thrush, the kingbird, the catbird, the tanager, the indigo bird, the vireos, and many of the warblers, but they have not arrived. The May birds, it seems, will not come in April, no matter how the season favors."

I have seen the sweet English violet, escaped from the garden and growing wild by the roadside, in bloom on the 25th of March, which is about its date of flowering at home. During the same season, the first of our native flowers to appear was the hepatica, which I found on April 4. The arbutus and the dicentra appeared on the 10th, and the coltsfoot — which, however, is an importation — about the same time. The blood-root, claytonia, saxifrage, and anemone were in bloom on the 17th, and I found the first blue violet and the great spurred violet on the 19th (saw the little violet-colored butterfly dancing about the woods the same day). I plucked my first dandelion on a meadow slope on the 23d, and in the woods, protected by a high ledge, my first trillium. During the month at least twenty native shrubs and wild flowers bloomed in my vicinity, which is an unusual showing for April.

There are many things left for May, but nothing fairer, if as fair as, the first flower, the hepatica. I find I have never admired this little firstling half enough. When at the maturity of its charms, it is certainly the gem of the woods. What an individuality it has! No two clusters alike; all shades and sizes; some are snow-white, some pale pink, with just a tinge of violet, some deep purple, others the purest blue, others blue touched with lilac. A solitary blue-purple one, fully expanded and rising over the brown leaves or the green moss, its cluster of minute anthers showing like a group of pale stars on its little firmament, is enough to arrest and hold the dullest eye. Then, as I have elsewhere stated, there are individual hepaticas, or individual families among them, that are sweet scented. The gift seems as capricious as the gift of genius in families. You cannot tell which the fragrant ones are till you try them. Sometimes it is the large white ones, sometimes the large purple ones, sometimes the small pink ones. The odor is faint and recalls that of the sweet violets.

There is a brief period in our spring when I like more than at any other time to drive along the country roads, or even to be shot along by steam and have the landscape presented to me like a map. It is at that period, usually late in April, when we

behold the first quickening of the earth. The waters have sub-
sided, the roads have become dry, the sunshine has grown
strong and its warmth has penetrated the sod; there is a stir of
preparation about the farm and all through the country. One
does not care to see things very closely; his interest in nature is
not special but general. The earth is coming to life again. All
the genial and more fertile places in the landscape are brought
out; the earth is quickened in spots and streaks; you can see at
a glance where man and nature have dealt the most kindly with
it.

Another pleasant feature of spring, which I have not mentioned, is the full streams. Riding across the country one
bright day in March, I saw and felt, as if for the first time, what
an addition to the satisfaction one has in the open air at this
season are the clear, full watercourses. They come to the front,
as it were, and lure and hold the eye. There are no weeds or
grasses or foliage to hide them; they are full to the brim, and
fuller; they catch and reflect the sunbeams and are about the
only objects of life and motion in nature. The trees stand so
still, the fields are so hushed and naked, the mountains so exposed and rigid, that the eye falls upon the blue, sparkling,
undulating watercourses with a peculiar satisfaction. By and
by the grass and trees will be waving, and the streams will be
shrunken and hidden, and our delight will not be in them.
The still ponds and lakelets will then please us more.[5]

It would not be easy to say which is our finest or most beautiful wild flower, but certainly the most poetic and the best
beloved is the arbutus. So early, so lowly, so secretive there in
the moss and dry leaves, so fragrant, tinged with the hues of
youth and health, so hardy and homelike, it touches the heart
as no other does.

April's flower offers the first honey to the bee and the first fragrance to the breeze. Modest, exquisite, loving the ever-greens, loving the rocks, untamable, it is the very spirit and breath of the woods. Trailing, creeping over the ground, hiding its beauty under withered leaves, stiff and hard in foliage, but in flower like the cheek of a maiden.

One may brush away the April snow and find this finer snow beneath it. Oh, the arbutus days, what memories and longings they awaken! In this latitude they can hardly be looked for before April, and some seasons not till the latter days of the month. The first real warmth, the first tender skies, the first fragrant showers — the woods are flooded with sunlight and the dry leaves and the leafmold emit a pleasant odor.

In wild, delicate beauty we have flowers that far surpass the arbutus: the columbine, for instance, jetting out of a seam in a gray ledge of rock, its many crimson and flame-colored flowers shaking in the breeze; but it is mostly for the eye. The spring beauty, the painted trillium, the fringed polygala, the showy lady's-slipper, are all more striking to look upon, but they do not quite touch the heart; they lack the soul that perfume suggests. Their charms do not abide with you as do those of the arbutus.[6]

In March the door of the seasons first stands ajar a little; in April it is opened much wider; in May the windows go up also; and in June the walls are fairly taken down and the genial currents have free play everywhere.[7]

6. Summer—Nature's Door Wide Open

W<small>HO SHALL</small> say when one season ends and another begins? Only the almanac makers can fix these dates. It is like saying when babyhood ends and childhood begins, or when childhood ends and youth begins.

Summer always comes in the person of June, with a bunch of daisies on her breast and clover blossoms in her hands. A new chapter in the season is opened when these flowers appear. One says to himself, "Well, I have lived to see the daisies again and to smell the red clover." One plucks the first blossoms tenderly and caressingly. What memories are stirred in the mind by the fragrance of the one and the youthful face of the other! There is nothing else like that smell of the clover: it is the maidenly breath of summer; it suggests all fresh, buxom, rural things. A field of ruddy, blooming clover, dashed or sprinkled here and there with the snow-white of the daisies; its breath drifts into the road when you are passing; you hear the boom of bees, the voice of bobolinks, the twitter of swallows, the whistle of woodchucks; you smell wild strawberries; you see the cattle upon the hills; you see your youth, the youth of a happy farm boy, rise before you.

The blooming orchards are the glory of May, the blooming clover fields the distinction of June. Other characteristic June perfumes come from the honey locusts and the blooming grape-

95

vines.   At times and in certain localities the air at night and
morning is heavy with the breath of the former, and along the
lanes and roadsides we inhale the delicate fragrance of the wild
grape.   The early grasses, too, with their frostlike bloom, contribute something very welcome to the breath of June.

Nearly every season I note what I call the bridal day of summer — a white, lucid, shining day, with a delicate veil of mist
softening all outlines.   How the river dances and sparkles; how
the new leaves of all the trees shine under the sun; the air has a
soft lustre; there is a haze, it is not blue, but a kind of shining,
diffused nimbus.   No clouds, the sky a bluish white, very soft
and delicate.   It is the nuptial day of the season; the sun fairly
takes the earth to be his own, for better or for worse, on such a
day, and what marriages there are going on all about us: the
marriages of the flowers, of the bees, of the birds.   Everything
suggests life, love, fruition.   These bridal days are often repeated; the serenity and equipoise of the elements combine.
They were such days as these that the poet Lowell had in mind
when he exclaimed, "What is so rare as a day in June?"   Here is
the record of such a day, June 1, 1883: "Day perfect in temper,
in mood, in everything.   Foliage all out except on buttonballs
and celtis,* and putting on its dark-green summer color, solid
shadows under the trees, and stretching down the slopes.   A
few indolent summer clouds here and there.   A day of gently
rustling and curtsying leaves, when the breeze almost seems to
blow upward.   The fields of full-grown, nodding rye slowly
stir and sway like vast assemblages of people.   How the chimney swallows chipper as they sweep past!   The vireo's cheerful
warble echoes in the leafy maples; the branches of the Norway
spruce and the hemlocks have gotten themselves new light-
green tips; the dandelion's spheres of ethereal down rise above
the grass: and now and then one of them suddenly goes down:

* Hackberry. [Ed.]

the little chippy, or social sparrow, has thrown itself upon the frail stalk and brought it to the ground, to feed upon its seeds; here it gets the first fruits of the season."

Go to the top of the hill on such a morning, say by nine o'clock, and see how unspeakably fresh and full the world looks. The morning shadows yet linger everywhere, even in the sunshine; a kind of blue coolness and freshness, the vapor of dew tinting the air.

Heat and moisture, the father and mother of all that lives, when June has plenty of these, the increase is sure.

Early in June the rye and wheat heads begin to nod; the motionless stalks have a reflective, meditative air. It is one of the most pleasing spectacles of June, a field of rye gently shaken by the wind. How the breezes are defined upon its surface — a surface as sensitive as that of water; how they trip along, little breezes and big breezes together! Just as this glaucous green surface of the rye field bends beneath the light tread of the winds, so, we are told, the crust of the earth itself bends beneath the giant strides of the great atmospheric waves.[1]

The strawberry is always the hope of the invalid and sometime, no doubt, his salvation. It is the first and finest relish among fruits, and well merits Dr. Boteler's memorable saying, that "doubtless God could have made a better berry, but doubtless God never did."

On the threshold of summer, nature proffers us this her virgin fruit; more rich and sumptuous are to follow, but the wild delicacy and fillip of the strawberry are never repeated — that keen feathered edge greets the tongue in nothing else.

Let me not be afraid of overpraising it, but probe and probe for words to hint its surprising virtues. We may well celebrate it with festivals and music. It has that indescribable quality of

all first things — that shy, uncloying, provoking barbed sweetness.   It is eager and sanguine as youth.   It is born of the copious dews, the fragrant nights, the tender skies, the plentiful
rains of the early season.   The singing of birds is in it, and the
health and frolic of lusty nature.   It is the product of liquid
May touched by the June sun.   It has the tartness, the brisk-
ness, the unruliness of spring, and the aroma and intensity of
summer.

Oh the strawberry days! how vividly they come back to one!
The smell of clover in the fields, of blooming rye on the hills,
of the wild grape beside the woods, and of the sweet honey-
suckle and spiræa about the house.   The first hot, moist days.
The daisies and buttercups; the songs of the birds, their first
reckless jollity and love-making over; the full tender foliage of
the trees; the bees swarming and the air strung with resonant
musical chords.   The time of the sweetest and most succulent
grass, when the cows come home with aching udders.   Indeed,
the strawberry belongs to the juiciest time of the year.

What a challenge it is to the taste! how it bites back again!
and is there any other sound like the snap and crackle with
which it salutes the ear on being plucked from the stem?   It is
a threat to one sense that the other is soon to verify.   It snaps
to the ear as it smacks to the tongue.   All other berries are tame
beside it.

The wild strawberry, like the wild apple, is spicy and high
flavored, but, unlike the apple, it is also mild and delicious.   It
has the true rustic sweetness and piquancy.   What it lacks in
size, when compared with the garden berry, it makes up in intensity.   It is never dropsical or overgrown, but firm-fleshed
and hardy.

Of the field strawberry there are a great many varieties —
some growing in meadows, some in pastures, and some upon

mountaintops. Some are round, and stick close to the calyx or hull; some are long and pointed, with long, tapering necks. These usually grow upon tall stems. They are, indeed, of the slim, linear kind. Your corpulent berry keeps close to the ground; its stem and footstalk are short, and neck it has none. Its color is deeper than that of its tall brother, and of course it has more juice. You are more apt to find the tall varieties upon knolls in low, wet meadows and again upon mountaintops, growing in tussocks of wild grass about the open summits. These latter ripen in July and give one his last taste of strawberries for the season.

But the favorite haunt of the wild strawberry is an uplying meadow that has been exempt from the plow for five or six years and that has little timothy and much daisy. When you go a-berrying, turn your steps toward the milk-white meadows. The slightly bitter odor of the daisies is very agreeable to the smell and affords a good background for the perfume of the fruit. The strawberry cannot cope with the rank and deep-rooted clover, and seldom appears in a field till the clover has had its day. But the daisy with its slender stalk does not crowd or obstruct the plant, while its broad white flower is like a light parasol that tempers and softens the too-strong sunlight. Indeed, daisies and strawberries are generally associated. Nature fills her dish with the berries then covers them with the white and yellow of milk and cream, thus suggesting a combination we are quick to follow.

Then the delight of "picking" the wild berries! It is one of the fragrant memories of boyhood. Indeed, for boy or man to go a-berrying in a certain pastoral country I know of, where a passer-by along the highway is often regaled by a breeze loaded with a perfume of the o'erripe fruit, is to get nearer to June than by almost any course I know of. Your errand is so private and confidential! You stoop low. You part away the grass and the daisies and would lay bare the inmost secrets of the meadow Everything is yet tender and succulent; the very air is bright and new; the warm breath of the meadow comes up in your face; to your knees you are in a sea of daisies and clover; from your knees up, you are in a sea of solar light and warmth. Now you are prostrate like a sw'mmer or like a surf bather reaching for pebbles or shells; the white and green spray breaks above you, then, like a devotee before a shrine or naming his beads, your rosary strung with luscious berries; anon you are a grazing Nebuchadnezzar, or an artist taking an inverted view of the landscape.[2]

As I sit here of a midsummer day, in front of the wide-open doors of a big hay barn,* busy with my pen, and look out upon broad meadows where my farmer neighbor is busy with his haymaking, I idly contrast his harvest with mine. I have to admit that he succeeds with his better than I do with mine, though he can make hay only while the sun shines, while I can reap and cure my light fancies nearly as well in the shade as in the sun. Yet his crop is the surer and of more certain value to mankind. But I have this advantage over him — I might make literature out of his haymaking or might reap his fields after him and gather a harvest he never dreamed of. What does Emerson say?

> *One harvest from the field*
> > *Homeward bring the oxen strong;*
> *A second crop thine acres yield,*
> > *Which I gather in a song.*

But the poet, like the farmer, can reap only where he has

* This building was known as the Hay-barn Study. It is near Roxbury, N. Y. [Ed.]

sown, and if Emerson had not scattered his own heart in the fields his Muse would not reap much there. Song is not one of the instruments with which I gather my harvest, but long ago, as a farm boy, in haymaking and in driving the cows to and from the pasture I planted myself there, and whatever comes back to me now from that source is honestly my own. The second crop which I gather is not much more tangible than that which the poet gathers, but the farmer as little suspects its existence as he does that of the poet. I can use what he would gladly reject. His daisies, his buttercups, his orange hawk-weed, his yarrow, his meadow rue, serve my purpose better than they do his. They look better on the printed page than they do in the haymow. Yes, and his timothy and clover have their literary uses, and his new-mown hay may perfume a line in poetry. When one of our poets writes, "wild carrot blooms nod round his quiet bed," he makes better use of this weed than the farmers can.

Certainly a midsummer day in the country, with all its sights and sounds, its singing birds, its skimming swallows, its grazing or ruminating cattle, its drifting cloud shadows, its grassy per-fumes from the meadows and the hillsides, and the farmer with his men and teams busy with the harvest, has material for the literary artist. A good hay day is a good day for the writer and the poet, because it has a certain crispness and pureness; it is positive; it is rich in sunshine; there is a potency in the blue sky which you feel; the high barometer raises your spirits; your thoughts ripen as the hay cures. You can sit in a circle of shade beneath a tree in the fields or in front of the open hay-barn doors, as I do, and feel the fruition and satisfaction of nature all about you. The brimming meadows seem fairly to purr as the breezes stroke them; the trees rustle their myriad leaves as if in gladness; the many-colored butterflies dance by; the

steel blue of the swallows' backs glistens in the sun as they skim
the fields, and the mellow boom of the passing bumblebee but
enhances the sense of repose and contentment that pervades
the air. The hay cures; the oats and corn deepen their hue;
the delicious fragrance of the last wild strawberries is on the
breeze; your mental skies are lucid, and life has the midsummer fullness and charm.

A high barometer is best for the haymakers and it is best for
the human spirits. When the smoke goes straight up, one's
thoughts are more likely to soar also and revel in the higher air.
The persons who do not like to get up in the morning till the
day has been well sunned and aired evidently thrive best on a
high barometer. Such days do seem better ventilated, and our
lungs take in fuller draughts of air. How curious it is that the
air should seem heavy to us when it is light, and light when it
is heavy! On those sultry, muggy days when it is an effort to
move and the grasshopper is a burden, the air is light, and we
are in the trough of the vast atmospheric wave; while we are
on its crest and are buoyed up both in mind and in body, on
the crisp, bright days when the air seems to offer us no resist-
ance. We know that the heavier salt sea water buoys us up
more than the fresh river or pond water, but we do not feel
in the same way the lift of the high barometric wave.

Even the rough, tough-coated maple trees in spring are
quickly susceptible to these atmospheric changes. The farmer
knows that he needs sunshine and crisp air to make maple
sugar as well as to make hay. Let the high blue-domed day
with its dry northwest breezes change to a warmer, overcast,
humid day from the south, and the flow of sap lessens at once.
It would seem as if the trees had nerves on the outside of their
dry bark, they respond to the change so quickly. There is
no sap without warmth, and yet warmth, without any memory
of the frost, stops the flow.

The more the air presses upon us the lighter we feel, and the less it presses upon us the more "logy" we feel. Climb to the top of a mountain ten thousand feet high, and you breathe and move with an effort. The air is light, water boils at a low temperature, and our lungs and muscles seem inadequate to perform their usual functions. There is a kind of pressure that exhilarates us and an absence of pressure that depresses us.

The pressure of congenial tasks, of worthy work, sets one up, while the idle, the unemployed, has a deficiency of hæmoglobin in his blood. The Lord pity the unemployed man and pity the man so overemployed that the pressure upon him is like that upon one who works in a tunnel filled with compressed air.

Haying in this pastoral region is the first act in the drama of the harvest, and one likes to see it well staged, as it is today — the high blue dome, the rank, dark foliage of the trees, the daisies still white in the sun, the buttercups gilding the pastures and hill slopes, the clover shedding its perfume, the timothy shaking out its little clouds of pollen as the sickle bar strikes it, most of the songbirds still vocal, and the tide of summer standing poised at its full. Very soon it will begin to ebb, the stalks of the meadow grasses will become dry and harsh, the clover will fade, the girlish daisies will become coarse and matronly, the birds will sing fitfully or cease altogether, the pastures will turn brown, and the haymakers will find the hay half cured as it stands waiting for them in the meadows.

What a wonderful thing is the grass, so common, so abundant, so various, a green summer snow that softens the outlines of the landscape, that makes a carpet for the foot, that brings a hush to the fields, and that furnishes food to so many and such various creatures! More than the grazing animals live upon the grass. All our cereals — wheat, barley, rye, rice, oats, corn — belong to the great family of the grasses.

Grass is the nap of the fields; it is the undergarment of the hills. It gives us the meadow, a feature in the northern landscape so common that we cease to remark it, but which we miss at once when we enter a tropical or semitropical country. In Cuba and Jamaica and Hawaii I saw no meadows and no pastures, no grazing cattle, none of the genial, mellow look which our landscape presents. Harshness, rawness, aridity are the prevailing notes.

From my barn-door outlook I behold meadows, with their boundary line of stone fences, that are like lakes and reservoirs of timothy and clover. They are full to the brim, they ripple and rock in the breeze, the green inundation seems about to overwhelm its boundaries, all the surface inequalities of the land are wiped out, the small rocks and stones are hidden, the woodchucks make their roads through it, immersed like dolphins in the sea. What a picture of the plenty and the flowing beneficence of our temperate zone it all presents! Nature in her kinder, gentler moods, dreaming of the tranquil herds and the bursting barns. Surely the vast army of the grass hath its victories, for the most part noiseless, peace-yielding victories that gladden the eye and tranquillize the heart.

The meadow presents a pleasing picture before it is invaded by the haymakers, and a varied and animated one after it is thus invaded; the mowing machine sending a shudder ahead of it through the grass, the hay tedder kicking up the green locks like a giant, many-legged grasshopper, the horse rake gathering the cured hay into windrows, the white-sleeved men with their forks pitching it into cocks, and lastly the huge, soft-cheeked loads of hay, towering above the teams that draw them, brushing against the barways and the lower branches of the trees along their course, slowly winding their way toward the barn. Then the great mows of hay, or the shapely stacks in the fields, and the battle is won. Milk and cream are stored up in well-cured hay, and when the snow of winter fills the meadows as grass fills them in summer, the tranquil cow can still rest and ruminate in contentment.

Is not the swallow one of the oldest and dearest of birds? Known to the poets and sages and prophets of all peoples! So infantile, so helpless and awkward upon the earth, so graceful and masterful on the wing, the child and darling of the summer air, reaping its invisible harvest in the fields of space as if it dined on the sunbeams, touching no earthly food, drinking and bathing and mating on the wing, swiftly, tirelessly cours· ing the long day through, a thought on wings, a lyric in the shape of a bird! Only in the free fields of the summer air could it have got that steel blue of the wings and that warm tan of the breast. Of course I refer to the barn swallow. The cliff swallow seems less a child of the sky and sun, probably because its sheen and glow are less and its shape and motions less arrowy. More varied in color, its hues yet lack the intensity and its flight the swiftness of those of its brother of the hay-lofts. The tree swallows and the bank swallows are pleasing, but they are much more local and restricted in their ranges than the barn frequenters. As a farm boy I did not know them at all, but the barn swallows the summer always brought.

After all, there is but one swallow; the others are particular kinds that we specify. How curious that men should ever have got the notion that this airy, fairy creature, this playmate of the sunbeams, spends the winter hibernating in the mud of ponds and marshes, the bedfellow of newts and frogs and turtles! It is an Old World legend, born of the blindness and superstition of earlier times. One knows that the rain of the rainbow may be gathered at one's feet in a mud puddle, but the fleeting spectrum of the bow is not a thing of life. Yet one would as soon think of digging up a rainbow in the mud as a swallow. The swallow follows the sun and in August is off for the equatorial regions, where it hibernates on the wing, buried in tropical sunshine.

Well, this brilliant day is a good day for the swallows, a good day for the haymakers, and a good day for him who sits before his open barn door and weaves his facts and midsummer fancies into this slight literary fabric.[3]

7. Autumn—Nature's Invitation to Rest

THE TIME of the falling of leaves has come again.   Once more in our morning walk we tread upon carpets of gold and crimson, of brown and bronze, woven by the winds or the rains out of these delicate textures while we slept.

How beautifully the leaves grow old! How full of light and color are their last days! There are exceptions, of course. The leaves of most of the fruit trees fade and wither and fall ingloriously. They bequeath their heritage of color to their fruit. Upon it they lavish the hues which other trees lavish upon their leaves. The pear tree is often an exception. I have seen pear orchards in October painting a hillside in hues of mingled bronze and gold. And well may the pear tree do this, it is so chary of color upon its fruit.

But in October what a feast to the eye our woods and groves present! The whole body of the air seems enriched by their calm, slow radiance. They are giving back the light they have been absorbing from the sun all summer.

The carpet of the newly fallen leaves looks so clean and delicate when it first covers the paths and the highways that one almost hesitates to walk upon it. Was it the gallant Raleigh who threw down his cloak for Queen Elizabeth to walk upon? See what a robe the maples have thrown down for you and me to walk upon! How one hesitates to soil it!

The maples perhaps undergo the most complete transformation of all the forest trees. Their leaves fairly become luminous, as if they glowed with inward light. In October a maple tree before your window lights up your room like a great lamp. Even on cloudy days its presence helps to dispel the gloom. The elm, the oak, the beech, possess in a much less degree that quality of luminosity, though certain species of oak at times are rich in shades of red and bronze. The leaves of the trees just named for the most part turn brown before they fall. The great leaves of the sycamore assume a rich tan color like fine leather.[1]

I sally out in the morning with the ostensible purpose of gathering chestnuts or autumn leaves or persimmons or exploring some run or branch. It is, say, the last of October or the first of November. The air is not balmy, but tart and pungent, like the flavor of the red-cheeked apples by the roadside. In the sky not a cloud, not a speck; a vast dome of blue ether lightly suspended above the world. The woods are heaped with color like a painter's palette — great splashes of red and orange and gold. The ponds and streams bear upon their bosoms leaves of all tints, from the deep maroon of the oak to the pale yellow of the chestnut. In the glens and nooks it is so still that the chirp of a solitary cricket is noticeable. The red berries of dogwood and spicebush and other shrubs shine in the sun like rubies and coral. The crows fly high above the earth, as they do only on such days, forms of ebony floating across the azure, and the buzzards look like kingly birds, sailing round and round.[2]

The season is always a little behind the sun in our climate, just as the tide is always a little behind the moon. According to the calendar, the summer ought to culminate about the 21st of June, but in reality it is some weeks later; June is a maiden month all through. It is not high noon in nature till about the first or second week in July. When the chestnut tree blooms, the meridian of the year is reached. By the first of August it is fairly one o'clock. The lustre of the season begins to dim, the foliage of the trees and woods to tarnish, the plumage of the birds to fade, and their songs to cease. The hints of approaching fall are on every hand. How suggestive this thistledown, for instance, which, as I sit by the open window, comes in and brushes softly across my hand! The first snowflake tells of winter not more plainly than this driving down heralds the approach of fall. Come here, my fairy, and tell me whence you come and whither you go? What brings you to port here, you gossamer ship sailing the great sea? How exquisitely frail and delicate! One of the lightest things in nature; so light that in the closed room here it will hardly rest in my open palm. A feather is a clod beside it. Only a spider's web will hold it; coarser objects have no power over it. Caught in the upper currents of the air and rising above the clouds, it might sail perpetually. Indeed, one fancies it might almost traverse the interstellar ether and drive against the stars. And every thistle-head by the roadside holds hundreds of these sky rovers — imprisoned Ariels unable to set themselves free. Their liberation may be by the shock of the wind or the rude contact of cattle, but it is oftener the work of the goldfinch with its complaining brood. The seed of the thistle is the proper food of this bird, and in obtaining it myriads of these winged creatures are scattered to the breeze. Each one is fraught with a seed which it exists to sow, but its wild careering and soaring does not fairly begin till its burden is dropped and its spheral form is complete. The seeds of many plants and trees are disseminated through the agency of birds; but the thistle furnishes its own birds — flocks of them, with wings more ethereal and tireless than were ever given to mortal creature. From the pains nature thus takes to sow the thistle broadcast over the land, it might be expected to be one of the most troublesome and abundant of weeds. But such is not the case, the more pernicious and baffling weeds, like snapdragon or blind nettles, being more local and restricted in their habits and unable to fly at all.

In the fall, the battles of the spring are fought over again, beginning at the other or little end of the series. There is the same advance and retreat, with many feints and alarms, between the contending forces that was witnessed in April and May. The spring comes like a tide running against a strong wind; it is ever beaten back, but ever gaining ground, with now and then a mad "push upon the land" as if to overcome its antagonist at one blow. The cold from the north encroaches upon us in about the same fashion. In September or early in October it usually makes a big stride forward and blackens all the more delicate plants and hastens the "mortal ripening" of the foliage of the trees, but it is presently beaten back again and the genial warmth repossesses the land. Before long, however, the cold returns to the charge with augmented forces and gains much ground.

The course of the seasons never does run smooth, owing to the unequal distribution of land and water, mountain, wood, and plain.

An equilibrium, however, is usually reached in our climate in October, sometimes the most marked in November, forming the delicious Indian summer; a truce is declared, and both forces, heat and cold, meet and mingle in friendly converse on the field. In the earlier season, this poise of the temperature,

this slack water in nature, comes in May and June; but the October calm is most marked. Day after day, and sometimes week after week, you cannot tell which way the current is setting. Indeed, there is no current, but the season seems to drift a little this way or a little that, just as the breeze happens to freshen a little in one quarter or the other. The fall of '74 was the most remarkable in this respect I remember ever to have seen. The equilibrium of the season lasted from the middle of October till near December, with scarcely a break. There were six weeks of Indian summer, all gold by day and, when the moon came, all silver by night. The river was so smooth at times as to be almost invisible, and in its place was the indefinite continuation of the opposite shore down toward the nether world. One seemed to be in an enchanted land and to breathe all day the atmosphere of fable and romance. Not a smoke, but a kind of shining nimbus filled all the spaces. The vessels would drift by as if in mid-air with all their sails set. The gypsy blood in one, as Lowell calls it, could hardly stay between four walls and see such days go by. Living in tents, in groves and on the hills seemed the only natural life.

This halcyon period of our autumn will always in some way be associated with the Indian. It is red and yellow and dusky like him. The smoke of his campfire seems again in the air. The memory of him pervades the woods. His plumes and moccasins and blanket of skins form just the costume the season demands. It was doubtless his chosen period. The gods smiled upon him then if ever. The time of the chase, the season of the buck and the doe and of the ripening of all forest fruits; the time when all men are incipient hunters, when the first frosts have given pungency to the air, when to be abroad on the hills or in the woods is a delight that both

old and young feel — if the red aborigine ever had his summer
of fullness and contentment, it must have been at this season,
and it fitly bears his name.

To return a little, September may be described as the month
of tall weeds. Where they have been suffered to stand, along
fences, by roadsides, and in forgotten corners — redroot, pigweed, ragweed, vervain, goldenrod, burdock, elecampane,
thistles, teasels, nettles, asters, etc. — how they lift themselves
up as if not afraid to be seen now! They are all outlaws; every
man's hand is against them; yet how surely they hold their own!
They love the roadside, because here they are comparatively
safe; and ragged and dusty, like the common tramps that they
are, they form one of the characteristic features of early fall.

I have often noticed in what haste certain weeds are at times
to produce their seeds. Redroot will grow three or four feet
high when it has the whole season before it; but let it get a
late start, let it come up in August, and it scarcely gets above
the ground before it heads out and apparently goes to work
with all its might and main to mature its seed. In the growth
of most plants or weeds, April and May represent their root,
June and July their stalk, and August and September their
flower and seed. Hence, when the stalk months are stricken
out, as in the present case, there is only time for a shallow root
and a foreshortened head. I think most weeds that get a late
start show this curtailment of stalk and this solicitude to reproduce themselves. But I have not observed that any of the
cereals are so worldly wise. They have not had to think and
shift for themselves as the weeds have. It does indeed look like
a kind of forethought in the redroot. It is killed by the first
frost and hence knows the danger of delay.

How rich in color, before the big show of the tree foliage
has commenced, our roadsides are in places in early autumn —

rich to the eye that goes hurriedly by and does not look too closely — with the profusion of goldenrod and blue and purple asters dashed in upon here and there with the crimson leaves of the dwarf sumac; and at intervals, rising out of the fence corner or crowning a ledge of rocks, the dark green of the cedars with the still fire of the woodbine at its heart. I wonder if the waysides of other lands present any analogous spectacles at this season.

Then, when the maples have burst out into color, showing like great bonfires along the hills, there is indeed a feast for the eye. A maple before your windows in October, when the sun shines upon it, will make up for a good deal of the light it has excluded; it fills the room with a soft golden glow.

By mid-October most of the Rip Van Winkles among our brute creatures have lain down for their winter nap. The toads and turtles have buried themselves in the earth. The woodchuck is in his hibernaculum, the skunk in his, the mole in his; and the black bear has his selected and will go in when the snow comes. He does not like the looks of his big tracks in the snow. They publish his goings and comings too plainly. The coon retires about the same time. The provident wood mice and the chipmunk are laying by a winter supply of nuts or grain, the former usually in decayed trees, the latter in the ground. I have observed that any unusual disturbance in the woods, near where the chipmunk has his den, will cause him to shift his quarters. One October, for many successive days, I saw one carrying into his hole buckwheat which he had stolen from a near field. The hole was only a few rods from where we were getting out stone, and as our work progressed and the racket and uproar increased, the chipmunk became alarmed. He ceased carrying in, and after much hesitating and darting about, and some prolonged absences, he began to carry out;

he had determined to move; if the mountain fell, he, at least, would be away in time. So, by mouthfuls or cheekfuls, the grain was transferred to a new place. He did not make a "bee" to get it done, but carried it all himself, occupying several days and making a trip about every ten minutes.

Insects also go into winter quarters by or before this time: the bumblebee, hornet, and wasp. But here only royalty escapes; the queen mother alone foresees the night of winter coming and the morning of spring beyond. The rest of the tribe try gypsying for a while but perish in the first frosts. The present October I surprised the queen of the yellow jackets in the woods looking out for a suitable retreat. The royal dame was house hunting, and on being disturbed by my inquisitive poking among the leaves, she got up and flew away with a slow, deep hum. Her body was unusually distended, whether with fat or eggs I am unable to say. In September I took down the nest of the black hornet and found several large queens in it, but the workers had all gone. The queens were evidently weathering the first frosts and storms here and waiting for the Indian summer to go forth and seek a permanent winter abode. If the covers could be taken off the fields and woods at this season, how many interesting facts of natural history would be revealed! — the crickets, ants, bees, reptiles, animals, and, for aught I know, the spiders and flies asleep or getting ready to sleep in their winter dormitories; the fires of life banked up and burning just enough to keep the spark over till spring.

The fish all run down the stream in the fall except the trout; it runs up or stays up and spawns in November, the male becoming as brilliantly tinted as the deepest-dyed maple leaf. I have often wondered why the trout spawns in the fall, instead of in the spring like other fish. Is it not because a full supply of clear spring water can be counted on at that season more than at any other? The brooks are not so liable to be suddenly muddied by heavy showers and defiled with the washings of the roads and fields, as they are in spring and summer. The artificial breeder finds that absolute purity of water is necessary to hatch the spawn; also that shade and a low temperature are indispensable.

Our northern November day itself is like spring water. It is melted frost, dissolved snow. There is a chill in it and an exhilaration also. The forenoon is all morning and the afternoon all evening. The shadows seem to come forth and to revenge themselves upon the day. The sunlight is diluted with darkness. The colors fade from the landscape, and only the sheen of the river lights up the gray and brown distance.[3]

8. Winter—Nature's Door Closed

DECEMBER IN our climate is the month when nature finally shuts up house and turns the key. She has been slowly packing up and putting away her things and closing a door and a window here and there all the fall. Now she completes the work and puts up the last bar. She is ready for winter. The leaves are all off the trees, except that here and there a beech or an oak or a hickory still clings to a remnant of its withered foliage. Her streams are full, her new growths of wood are ripened, her saps and juices are quiescent. The muskrat has completed his house in the shallow pond or stream, the beaver in the northern woods has completed his. The wild mice and the chipmunk have laid up their winter stores of nuts and grains in their dens in the ground and in the cavities of trees. The woodchuck is rolled up in his burrow in the hillside, sleeping his long winter sleep. The coon has deserted his chamber in the old tree and gone into winter quarters in his den in the rocks. The winter birds have taken on a good coat of fat against the coming cold and a possible scarcity of food. The frogs and toads are all in their hibernaculums in the ground.

Insects in all stages of their growth are creatures of the warmth; the heat is the motive power that makes them go; when this fails, they are still. The katydids rasp away in the fall as long as there is warmth enough to keep them going; as the heat fails, they fail, till from the emphatic "Katy did it" of August they dwindle to a hoarse, dying, "Kate, Kate," in October. Think of the stillness that falls upon the myriad wood borers in the dry trees and stumps in the forest as the chill of autumn comes on. All summer have they worked incessantly in oak and hickory and birch and chestnut and spruce, some of them making a sound exactly like that of the old-fashioned hand auger, others a fine, snapping, and splintering sound; but as the cold comes on, they go slower and slower, till they finally cease to move. A warm day starts them again, slowly or briskly according to the degree of heat, but in December they are finally stilled for the season.

Nature looks ahead and makes ready for the new season in the midst of the old. Cut open the terminal hickory buds in the late fall and you will find the new growth of the coming season all snugly packed away there, many times folded up and wrapped about by protecting scales. The catkins of the birches, alders, and hazel are fully formed and, as in the case of the buds, are like eggs to be hatched by the warmth of spring. The present season is always the mother of the next, and the inception takes place long before the sun loses his power. The eggs that hold the coming crop of insect life are mostly laid in the late summer or early fall, and an analogous start is made in the vegetable world. The egg, the seed, the bud, are all alike in many ways and look to the future. Our earliest spring flower, the skunk cabbage, may be found with its round green spear point an inch or two above the mold in December. It is ready to welcome and make the most of the first fitful March warmth. Look at the elms, too, and see how they swarm with buds. In early April they suggest a swarm of bees.

In all cases, before nature closes her house in the fall, she makes ready for its spring opening.[1]

If the October days were a cordial like the subacids of fruit, these are a tonic like the wine of iron. Drink deep, or be careful how you taste this December vintage. The first sip may chill, but a full draught warms and invigorates. No loitering by the brooks or in the woods now, but spirited, rugged walking along the public highway. The sunbeams are welcome now. They seem like pure electricity — like friendly and recuperating lightning. Are we led to think electricity abounds only in summer when we see in the storm clouds, as it were, the veins and orebeds of it? I imagine it is equally abundant in winter and more equable and better tempered. Who ever breasted a snowstorm without being excited and exhilarated, as if this meteor had come charged with latent auroræ of the North, as doubtless it has? It is like being pelted with sparks from a battery. Behold the frostwork on the pane — the wild, fantastic limnings and etchings! can there be any doubt but this subtle agent has been here? Where is it not? It is the life of the crystal, the architect of the flake, the fire of frost, the soul of the sunbeam. This crisp winter air is full of it. When I come in at night after an all-day tramp I am charged like a Leyden jar; my hair crackles and snaps beneath the comb like a cat's back, and a strange new glow diffuses itself through my system.

It is a spur that one feels at this season more than at any other. How nimbly you step forth! The woods roar, the waters shine, and the hills look invitingly near. You do not miss the flowers and the songsters or wish the trees or the fields any different or the heavens any nearer. Every object pleases. A rail fence, running athwart the hills, now in sunshine and now in shadow — how the eye lingers upon it! Or the straight, light-gray trunks of the trees, where the woods have recently been laid open by a road or a clearing — how curious they look, and as if surprised in undress! Next year they will begin to shoot out branches and make themselves a screen. Or the farm scenes — the winter barnyards littered with husks and straw, the rough-coated horses, the cattle sunning themselves or walking down to the spring to drink, the domestic fowls moving about — there is a touch of sweet, homely life in these things that the winter sun enhances and brings out. Every sign of life is welcome at this season. I love to hear dogs bark, hens cackle, and boys shout; one has no privacy with nature now and does not wish to seek her in nooks and hidden ways. She is not at home if he goes there; her house is shut up and her hearth cold; only the sun and sky and perchance the waters wear the old look, and today we will make love to them, and they shall abundantly return it.[2]

He who marvels at the beauty of the world in summer will find equal cause for wonder and admiration in winter. It is true the pomp and the pageantry are swept away, but the essential elements remain — the day and the night, the mountain and the valley, the elemental play and succession and the perpetual presence of the infinite sky. In winter the stars seem to have rekindled their fires, the moon achieves a fuller triumph, and the heavens wear a look of a more exalted simplicity. Summer is more wooing and seductive, more versatile and human, appeals to the affections and the sentiments, and fosters inquiry and the art impulse. Winter is of a more heroic cast and addresses the intellect. The severe studies and disciplines come easier in winter. One imposes larger tasks upon himself, and is less tolerant of his own weaknesses.

The tendinous part of the mind, so to speak, is more developed in winter; the fleshy, in summer. I should say winter had given the bone and sinew to literature, summer the tissues and blood.

Look up at the miracle of the falling snow — the air a dizzy maze of whirling, eddying flakes, noiselessly transforming the world, the exquisite crystals dropping in ditch and gutter and disguising in the same suit of spotless livery all objects upon which they fall. How novel and fine the first drifts! The old, dilapidated fence is suddenly set off with the most fantastic ruffles, scalloped and fluted after an unheard-of fashion! Looking down a long line of decrepit stone wall, in the trimming of which the wind had fairly run riot, I saw, as for the first time, what a severe yet master artist old Winter is. Ah, a severe artist! How stern the woods look, dark and cold and as rigid against the horizon as iron!

All life and action upon the snow have an added emphasis and significance. Every expression is underscored.

A severe artist! No longer the canvas and the pigments, but the marble and the chisel. When the nights are calm and the moon full, I go out to gaze upon the wonderful purity of the moonlight and the snow. The air is full of latent fire, and the cold warms me — after a different fashion from that of the kitchen stove. The world lies about me in a "trance of snow." The clouds are pearly and iridescent and seem the farthest possible remove from the condition of a storm — the ghosts of clouds, the indwelling beauty freed from all dross. I see the hills, bulging with great drifts, lift themselves up cold and white against the sky, the black lines of fences here and there obliterated by the depth of the snow. Presently a fox barks away up next the mountain, and I imagine I can almost see him sitting there in his furs, upon the illuminated surface, and looking down in my direction. As I listen, one answers him from behind the woods in the valley. What a wild winter sound, wild and weird, up among the ghostly hills!

In what bold relief stand out the lives of all walkers of the

snow! The snow is a great telltale and blabs as effectually as
it obliterates. I go into the woods and know all that has happened. I cross the fields, and if only a mouse has visited his
neighbor the fact is chronicled.

Entering the woods, the number and variety of the tracks
contrast strongly with the rigid, frozen aspect of things. Warm
jets of life still shoot and play amid this snowy desolation. Fox
tracks are far less numerous than in the fields; but those of
hares, skunks, partridges, squirrels, and mice abound. The
mouse tracks are very pretty and look like a sort of fantastic
stitching on the coverlid of the snow. One is curious to know
what brings these tiny creatures from their retreats; they do
not seem to be in quest of food but rather to be traveling about
for pleasure or sociability, though always going posthaste, and
linking stump with stump and tree with tree by fine, hurried
strides. That is when they travel openly; but they have hidden
passages and winding galleries under the snow, which un-
doubtedly are their main avenues of communication. Here
and there these passages rise so near the surface as to be covered
by only a frail arch of snow, and a slight ridge betrays their
course to the eye. I know him well. He is known to the farmer
as the "deer mouse," to the naturalist as the white-footed mouse
— a very beautiful creature, nocturnal in his habits, with large
ears and large, fine eyes full of a wild, harmless look. He is
daintily marked, with white feet and a white belly. When
disturbed by day he is very easily captured, having none of the
cunning or viciousness of the common Old World mouse.

It is he who, high in the hollow trunk of some tree, lays by
a store of beechnuts for winter use. Every nut is carefully
shelled, and the cavity that serves as storehouse lined with
grass and leaves. The woodchopper frequently squanders this
precious store. I have seen half a peck taken from one tree, as

clean and white as if put up by the most delicate hands — as
they were. How long it must have taken the little creature to
collect this quantity, to hull them one by one, and convey them
up to his fifth-story chamber! He is not confined to the woods
but is quite as common in the fields, particularly in the fall,
amid the corn and potatoes.

The snow walkers are mostly night walkers also, and the
record they leave upon the snow is the main clew one has to
their life and doings.

The sharp-rayed track of the partridge adds another figure
to this fantastic embroidery upon the winter snow. Her course
is a clear, strong line, sometimes quite wayward but generally
very direct, steering for the densest, most impenetrable places
— leading you over logs and through brush, alert and expect-
ant, till suddenly she bursts up a few yards from you and goes
humming through the trees — the complete triumph of en-
durance and vigor. Hardy native bird, may your tracks never
be fewer, or your visits to the birch tree less frequent!

Red and gray squirrels are more or less active all winter,
though very shy and, I am inclined to think, partially nocturnal
in their habits. Here a gray one has just passed — came down
that tree and went up this; there he dug for a beechnut and left
the burr on the snow. How did he know where to dig?

His home is in the trunk of some old birch or maple, with an
entrance far up amid the branches.

The track of the red squirrel may be known by its smaller
size. He is more common and less dignified than the gray, and
oftener guilty of petty larceny about the barns and grain fields.
At home, in the woods, he is the most frolicsome and loquacious. The appearance of anything unusual, if after contemplating it a moment he concludes it not dangerous, excites his
unbounded mirth and ridicule, and he snickers and chatters,

hardly able to contain himself; now darting up the trunk of a tree and squealing in derision, then hopping into position on a limb and dancing to the music of his own cackle, and all for your special benefit.

There is something very human in this apparent mirth and mockery of the squirrels. It seems to be a sort of ironical laughter and implies self-conscious pride and exultation in the laughter. "What a ridiculous thing you are, to be sure!" he seems to say; "how clumsy and awkward, and what a poor show for a tail! Look at me, look at me!" — and he capers about in his best style. Again, he would seem to tease you and provoke your attention; then suddenly assumes a tone of good-natured, childlike defiance and derision.[3]

The preparations of a snowstorm are, as a rule, gentle and quiet; a marked hush pervades both the earth and the sky. The movements of the celestial forces are muffled, as if the snow already paved the way of their coming. There is no uproar, no clashing of arms, no blowing of wind trumpets. These soft, feathery, exquisite crystals are formed as if in the silence and privacy of the inner cloud chambers. Rude winds would break the spell and mar the process. The clouds are smoother, and slower in their movements, with less definite outlines than those which bring rain. In fact, everything is prophetic of the gentle and noiseless meteor that is approaching, and of the stillness that is to succeed it, when "all the batteries of sound are spiked," as Lowell says, and "we see the movements of life as a deaf man sees it — a mere wraith of the clamorous existence that inflicts itself on our ears when the ground is bare." After the storm is fairly launched, the winds not infrequently awake and, seeing their opportunity, pipe the flakes a lively dance. I am speaking now of the typical, full-born midwinter storm that comes to us from the North or N. N. E., and that piles the landscape knee-deep with snow.

Such a storm once came to us the last day of January — the master storm of the winter. Previous to that date, we had had but light snow. The spruces had been able to catch it all upon their arms and keep a circle of bare ground beneath them where the birds scratched. But the day following this fall, they stood with their lower branches completely buried. If the Old Man of the North had but sent us his couriers and errand boys before, the old graybeard appeared himself at our doors on this occasion, and we were all his subjects. His flag was upon every tree and roof, his seal upon every door and window, and his embargo upon every path and highway. He slipped down upon us, too, under the cover of such a bright, seraphic day — a day that disarmed suspicion with all but the wise ones, a day without a cloud or a film, a gentle breeze from the west, a dry, bracing air, a blazing sun that brought out the bare ground under the lee of the fences and farm buildings, and at night a spotless moon near her full. The next morning the sky reddened in the east, then became gray, heavy, and silent. A seamless cloud covered it. The smoke from the chimneys went up with a barely perceptible slant toward the north. In the forenoon the cedarbirds, purple finches, yellowbirds, nuthatches, bluebirds, were in flocks or in couples and trios about the trees, more or less noisy and loquacious. About noon a thin white veil began to blur the distant southern mountains. It was like a white dream slowly descending upon them. The first flake or flakelet that reached me was a mere white speck that came idly circling and eddying to the ground. I could not see it after it alighted. It might have been a scale from the feather of some passing bird, or a larger mote in the air that the stillness was allowing to settle. Yet it was the altogether inaudible and infinitesimal trumpeter that announced that coming storm, the grain of sand that heralded the desert. Presently another fell, then another; the white mist was creeping up the river valley. How slowly and loiteringly it came, and how microscopic its first siftings!

This mill is bolting its flour very fine, you think. But wait a little; it gets coarser by and by; you begin to see the flakes; they increase in numbers and in size, and before one o'clock it is snowing steadily. The flakes come straight down, but in a half hour they have a marked slant toward the north; the wind is taking a hand in the game. By midafternoon the storm is coming in regular pulse beats or in vertical waves. The wind is not strong but seems steady; the pines hum, yet there is a sort of rhythmic throb in the meteor, the air toward the wind looks ribbed with steady-moving vertical waves of snow. The impulses travel along like undulations in a vast suspended white curtain, imparted by some invisible hand there in the northeast. As the day declines the storm waxes, the wind increases, the snowfall thickens, and

> *the housemates sit*
> *Around the radiant fireplace, inclosed*
> *In a tumultuous privacy of storm,*

outside as well as in. Out of doors you seem in a vast tent of snow; the distance is shut out, nearby objects are hidden; there are white curtains above you and white screens about you, and you feel housed and secluded in storm. Your friend leaves your door, and he is wrapped away in white obscurity, caught up in a cloud, and his footsteps are obliterated. Travelers meet on the road and do not see or hear each other till they are face to face. The passing train, half a mile away, gives forth a mere wraith of sound. Its whistle is deadened as in a dense wood.

Still the storm rose. At five o'clock I went forth to face it in a two-mile walk. It was exhilarating in the extreme. The snow was lighter than chaff. It had been dried in the Arctic ovens to the last degree. The foot sped through it without hindrance. I fancied the grouse and quail quietly sitting down in the open places and letting it drift over them. With head under wing, and wing snugly folded, they would be softly and tenderly buried in a few moments. The mice and the squirrels were in their dens, but I fancied the fox asleep upon some rock or log and allowing the flakes to cover him. The hare in her form, too, was being warmly sepulchred with the rest. I thought of the young cattle and the sheep huddled together on the lee side of a haystack in some remote field, all enveloped in mantles of white.

As I passed the creek, I noticed the white woolly masses that filled the water. It was as if somebody upstream had been washing his sheep and the water had carried away all the wool, and I thought of the Psalmist's phrase, "He giveth snow like wool." On the river a heavy fall of snow simulates a thin layer of cotton batting. The tide drifts it along, and where it meets with an obstruction alongshore, it folds up and becomes wrinkled or convoluted like a fabric, or like cotton sheeting. Attempt to row a boat through it, and it seems indeed like cotton or wool, every fibre of which resists your progress.

As the sun went down and darkness fell, the storm impulse reached its full. It became a wild conflagration of wind and snow; the world was wrapt in frost flame; it enveloped one and penetrated his lungs and caught away his breath like a blast from a burning city. How it whipped around and under every cover and searched out every crack and crevice, sifting under the shingles in the attic, darting its white tongue under the kitchen door, puffing its breath down the chimney, roaring through the woods, stalking like a sheeted ghost across the hills, bending in white and ever-changing forms above the fences, sweeping across the plains, whirling in eddies behind the buildings, or leaping spitefully up their walls — in short, taking the world entirely to itself and giving a loose rein to its desire.

But in the morning, behold! the world was not consumed; it was not the besom of destruction, after all, but the gentle hand of mercy. How deeply and warmly and spotlessly Earth's nakedness is clothed! — the "wool" of the Psalmist nearly two feet deep. And as far as warmth and protection are concerned, there is a good deal of the virtue of wool in such a snowfall. How it protects the grass, the plants, the roots of the trees, and the worms, insects, and smaller animals in the ground! It is a veritable fleece, beneath which the shivering earth ("the frozen hills ached with pain," says one of our young poets) is restored to warmth. When the temperature of the air is at zero, the thermometer, placed at the surface of the ground beneath a foot and a half of snow, would probably indicate but a few degrees below freezing; the snow is rendered such a perfect nonconductor of heat mainly by reason of the quantity of air that is caught and retained between the crystals. Then how, like a fleece of wool, it rounds and fills out the landscape and makes the leanest and most angular field look smooth!

The day dawned and continued as innocent and fair as the day which had preceded — two mountain peaks of sky and sun, with their valley of cloud and snow between. Walk to the nearest spring run on such a morning and you can see the Colorado valley and the great cañons of the West in miniature, carved in alabaster. In the midst of the plain of snow lie these chasms; the vertical walls, the bold headlands, the turrets and spires and obelisks, the rounded and towering capes, the carved and buttressed precipices, the branch valleys and cañons, and the winding and tortuous course of the main channel are all here — all that the Yosemite or Yellowstone have to show, except the terraces and the cascades.

But there is a more beautiful and fundamental geology than this in the snowstorm: we are admitted into nature's oldest laboratory and see the working of the law by which the foundations of the material universe were laid — the law or mystery of crystallization. The earth is built upon crystals; the granite rock is only a denser and more compact snow, or a kind of ice that was vapor once and may be vapor again. "Every stone is nothing else but a congealed lump of frozen earth," says Plutarch. By cold and pressure, air can be liquefied, perhaps solidified. A little more time, a little more heat, and the hills are but April snowbanks. Nature has but two forms, the cell and the crystal — the crystal first, the cell last. All organic nature is built up of the cell; all inorganic, of the crystal. Cell upon cell rises the vegetable, rises the animal; crystal wedded to and compacted with crystal stretches the earth beneath them. See in the falling snow the old cooling and precipitation and the shooting, radiating forms that are the architects of planet and globe.

We love the sight of the brown and ruddy earth; it is the color of life, while a snow-covered plain is the face of death; yet snow is but the mask of the life-giving rain; it, too, is the friend of man — the tender, sculpturesque, immaculate, warming, fertilizing snow.[4]

Such a winter as was that of 1880–1881 — deep snows and zero weather for nearly three months — proves especially trying to the wild creatures that attempt to face it. The supply of fat (or fuel) with which their bodies become stored in the fall is rapidly exhausted by the severe and uninterrupted cold, and the sources from which fresh supplies are usually obtained are all but wiped out. Even the fox was very hard pressed and reduced to the unusual straits of eating frozen apples; the pressure of hunger must be great, indeed, to compel Reynard to take up with such a diet.

A bevy of quail in my vicinity got through the winter by feeding upon the little black beans contained in the pods of the common locust. For many weeks their diet must have been almost entirely leguminous. The surface snow in the locust grove which they frequented was crossed in every direction with their fine tracks, like a chain stitch upon muslins, showing where they went from pod to pod and extracted the contents. Where quite a large branch, filled with pods, lay upon the snow, it looked as if the whole flock had dined or breakfasted off it. The wind seemed to shake down the pods about as fast as they were needed. When a fresh fall of snow had blotted out everything, it was not many hours before the wind had placed upon the cloth another course; but it was always the same old course — beans, beans.

What would the birds and the fowls do during such winters, if the trees and the shrubs and plants all dropped their fruit and their seeds in the fall, as they do their leaves? They would nearly all perish. The apples that cling to the trees, the pods that hang to the lowest branches, and the seeds that the various weeds and grasses hold above the deepest snows, alone make it possible for many birds to pass the winter among us. The red squirrel, too, what would he do? I have seen the ground under a wild apple tree that stood near the woods completely covered with the "chonkings" of the frozen apples, the work of the squirrels in getting at the seeds; not an apple had been left, and apparently not a seed had been lost. But the squirrels

in this particular locality evidently got pretty hard up before
spring, for they developed a new source of food supply. A
young bushy-topped sugar maple, about forty feet high, standing beside a stone fence near the woods, was attacked and more
than half denuded of its bark. The object of the squirrels
seemed to be to get at the soft, white, mucilaginous substance
(cambium layer) between the bark and the wood. The ground
was covered with fragments of the bark, and the white, naked
stems and branches had been scraped by fine teeth. When the
sap starts in the early spring, the squirrels add this to their
scanty supplies. They perforate the bark of the branches of
the maples with their chisel-like teeth and suck the sweet liquid
as it slowly oozes out. It is not much as food, but evidently it
helps.

I have said the red squirrel does not lay by a store of food
for winter use, like the chipmunk and the wood mice; yet in
the fall he sometimes hoards in a tentative, temporary kind of
way. I have seen his savings — butternuts and black walnuts —
stuck here and there in saplings and trees near his nest; sometimes carefully inserted in the upright fork of a limb or twig.
One day, late in November, I counted a dozen or more black
walnuts put away in this manner in a little grove of locusts,
chestnuts, and maples by the roadside, and could but smile at
the wise forethought of the rascally squirrel. His supplies were
probably safer that way than if more elaborately hidden. They
were well distributed; his eggs were not all in one basket, and
he could go away from home without any fear that his storehouse would be broken into in his absence. The next week,
when I passed that way, the nuts were all gone but two. I saw
the squirrel that doubtless laid claim to them, on each occasion.

There is one thing the red squirrel knows unerringly that
I do not (there are probably several other things); that is, on

which side of the butternut the meat lies. He always gnaws through the shell so as to strike the kernel broadside and thus easily extract it; while to my eyes there is no external mark or indication, in the form or appearance of the nut, as there is in the hickory nut, by which I can tell whether the edge or the side of the meat is toward me. But examine any number of nuts that the squirrels have rifled and, as a rule, you will find they always drill through the shell at the one spot where the meat will be most exposed. It stands them in hand to know, and they do know.

A hard winter affects the chipmunks very little; they are snug and warm in their burrows in the ground and under the rocks, with a bountiful store of nuts or grain. I have heard of nearly a half bushel of chestnuts being taken from a single den. They usually hole in November and do not come out again till March or April, unless the winter is very open and mild.

The woodpeckers and chickadees doubtless find food as plentiful during severe winters as during more open ones, because they confine their search almost entirely to the trunks and branches of trees, where the latter pick up the eggs of insects and various microscopic tidbits, and where the former find their accustomed fare of eggs and larvæ also. An enamel of ice upon the trees alone puts an embargo upon their supplies. At such seasons the ruffed grouse "buds" or goes hungry; while the snowbirds, snow buntings, Canada sparrows, gold-finches, shore larks, and redpolls are dependent upon the weeds and grasses that rise above the snow and upon the litter of the haystack and barnyard. Neither do the deep snows and the severe cold materially affect the supplies of the rabbit. The deeper the snow, the nearer he is brought to the tops of the tender bushes and shoots. I see in my walks where he has cropped the tops of the small, bushy, soft maples, cutting them slantingly as you would do with a knife, and quite as smoothly. Indeed, the mark was so like that of a knife that, notwithstanding the tracks, it was only after the closest scrutiny that I was convinced it was the sharp, chisellike teeth of the rabbit. He leaves no chips and apparently makes clean work of every twig he cuts off.

The wild or native mice usually lay up stores in the fall, in the shape of various nuts, grain, and seeds, yet the provident instinct, as in the red squirrel and in the jay, seems only partly developed in them; instead of carrying these supplies home, they hide them in the nearest convenient place. I have known them to carry a pint or more of hickory nuts and deposit them in a pair of boots standing in the chamber of an outhouse. Near the chestnut trees they will fill little pocketlike depressions in the ground with chestnuts; in a grain field they carry the grain under stones; under some cover beneath cherry trees they collect great numbers of cherry pits. Hence, when cold weather comes, instead of staying at home like the chipmunk, they gad about hither and thither looking up their supplies. One may see their tracks on the snow everywhere in the woods and fields and by the roadside. The advantage of this way of living is that it leads to activity and probably to sociability.

Our woods are full of these little creatures, and they appear to have a happy, social time of it, even in the severest winters. Their little tunnels under the snow and their hurried strides upon its surface may be noted everywhere. They link tree and stump, or rock and tree, by their pretty trails. They evidently travel for adventure and to hear the news, as well as for food. They know that foxes and owls are about, and they keep pretty close to cover. When they cross an exposed place, they do it hurriedly.

Birds not of a feather flock together in winter. Hard times or a common misfortune makes all the world akin. A Noah's ark with antagonistic species living in harmony is not an improbable circumstance in a forty-day and a forty-night rain. In severe weather, when the snow lies deep on the ground, I frequently see a loose, heterogeneous troop of birds pass my door, engaged in the common search for food: snowbirds, Canada sparrows, and goldfinches on the ground, and kinglets and nuthatches in the tree above — all drifting slowly in the same direction — the snowbirds and sparrows closely associated but the goldfinches rather clannish and exclusive, while the kinglets and nuthatches keep still more aloof. These birds were probably not drawn, even thus loosely, together by any social instincts, but by a common want; all were hungry, and the activity of one species attracted and drew after it another and another. "I will look that way, too," the kinglet and creeper probably said, when they saw the other birds busy and heard their merry voices.[5]

But with March our interest in these phases of animal life, which winter has so emphasized and brought out, begins to decline. Vague rumors are afloat in the air of a great and coming change. We are eager for Winter to be gone, since he, too, is fugitive and cannot keep his place. Invisible hands deface his icy statuary; his chisel has lost its cunning. The drifts, so pure and exquisite, are now earth stained and weatherworn — the flutes and scallops and fine, firm lines all gone; and what was a grace and an ornament to the hills is now a disfiguration. Like worn and unwashed linen appear the remains of that spotless robe with which he clothed the world as his bride.

But he will not abdicate without a struggle. Day after day he rallies his scattered forces, and night after night pitches his white tents on the hills and would fain regain his lost ground; but the young prince in every encounter prevails. Slowly and reluctantly the gray old hero retreats up the mountain, till finally the south rain comes in earnest, and in a night he is dead.[6]

9. Maple Sugar Days

ONE OF the features of farm life peculiar to this country, and one of the most picturesque of them all, is sugar making in the maple woods in spring. This is the first work of the season, and to the boys is more play than work. In the Old World, and in more simple and imaginative times, how such an occupation as this would have got into literature, and how many legends and associations would have clustered around it! It is woodsy and savors of the trees; it is an encampment among the maples. Before the bud swells, before the grass springs, before the plow is started, comes the sugar harvest. It is the sequel of the bitter frost; a sap run is the sweet goodbye of winter. It denotes a certain equipoise of the season; the heat of the day fully balances the frost of the night. In New York and New England the time of the sap hovers about the vernal equinox, beginning a week or ten days before and continuing a week or ten days after. As the days and nights get equal, the heat and cold get equal, and the sap mounts. A day that brings the bees out of the hive will bring the sap out of the maple tree. It is the fruit of the equal marriage of the sun and frost. When the frost is all out of the ground, and all the snow gone from its surface, the flow stops. The thermometer must not rise above 38° or 40° by day or sink below 24° or 25° at night, with wind in the northwest; a relaxing south wind, and the run is over for the present.

Sugar weather is crisp weather. How the tin buckets glisten in the gray woods; how the robins laugh; how the nuthatches call; how lightly the thin blue smoke rises among the trees! The squirrels are out of their dens; the migrating waterfowls are streaming northward; the sheep and cattle look wistfully toward the bare fields; the tide of the season, in fact, is just beginning to rise.

Sap letting does not seem to be an exhaustive process to the trees, as the trees of a sugar bush appear to be as thrifty and as long-lived as other trees. They come to have a maternal, large-waisted look, from the wounds of the axe or the auger, and that is about all.

In my sugar-making days the sap was carried to the boiling place in pails by the aid of a neck yoke and stored in hogsheads, and boiled or evaporated in immense kettles or caldrons set in huge stone arches; now, the hogshead goes to the trees hauled upon a sled by a team, and the sap is evaporated in broad, shallow, sheet-iron pans — a great saving of fuel and of labor.

Maple sugar in its perfection is rarely seen, perhaps never seen, in the market. When made in large quantities and indifferently, it is dark and coarse; but when made in small quantities — that is, quickly from the first run of sap and properly treated — it has a wild delicacy of flavor that no other sweet can match. What you smell in freshly cut maple wood or taste in the blossom of the tree, is in it. It is then, indeed, the distilled essence of the tree. Made into syrup, it is white and clear as clover honey; and crystallized into sugar, it is pure as the wax. The way to attain this result is to evaporate the sap under cover in an enameled kettle; when reduced about twelve times, allow it to settle half a day or more; then clarify with milk or the white of an egg.* The product is virgin syrup, or sugar worthy the table of the gods.[1]

---

* John Burroughs made his first money by this method. [Ed.]

In New York and northern New England the beginning of this season varies from the first to the middle of March, sometimes even holding off till April. The moment the contest between the sun and frost fairly begins, sugar weather begins; and the more even the contest, the more the sweet. I do not know what the philosophy of it is, but it seems a kind of seesaw, as if the sun drew the sap up and the frost drew it down; and an excess of either stops the flow. Before the sun has got power to unlock the frost, there is no sap; and after the frost has lost its power to lock up again the work of the sun, there is no sap. But when it freezes soundly at night, with a bright, warm sun next day, wind in the west, and no signs of a storm, the veins of the maples fairly thrill. Pierce the bark anywhere, and out gushes the clear, sweet liquid. But let the wind change to the south and blow moist and warm, destroying that crispness of the air, and the flow slackens at once, unless there be a deep snow in the woods to counteract or neutralize the warmth, in which case the run may continue till the rain sets in. The rough-coated old trees — one would not think they could scent a change so quickly through that wrapper of dead, dry bark an inch or more thick. I have to wait till I put my head out of doors and feel the air on my bare cheek and sniff it with my nose; but their nerves of taste and smell are no doubt underground, imbedded in the moisture, and if there is anything that responds quickly to atmospheric changes it is water.

A sap run seldom lasts more than two or three days. By that time there is a change in the weather, perhaps a rainstorm, which takes the frost nearly all out of the ground. Then, before there can be another run, the trees must be wound up again, the storm must have a white tail and "come off" cold. Presently the sun rises clear again and cuts the snow or softens the hard-frozen ground with his beams, and the trees take a fresh start.

The boys go through the wood, emptying out the buckets or the pans and reclaiming those that have blown away, and the delightful work is resumed. But the first run, like first love, is always the best, always the fullest, always the sweetest; while there is a purity and delicacy of flavor about the sugar that far surpasses any subsequent yield.

Trees differ much in the quantity as well as in the quality of sap produced in a given season. Indeed, in a bush or orchard of fifty or one hundred trees, as wide a difference may be observed in this respect as among that number of cows in regard to the milk they yield. I have in my mind now a sugar bush nestled in the lap of a spur of the Catskills, every tree of which is known to me and assumes a distinct individuality in my thought. I know the look and quality of the whole two hundred; and when on my annual visit to the old homestead I find one has perished or fallen before the axe, I feel a personal loss. They are all veterans and have yielded up their life's blood for the profit of two or three generations. They stand in little groups or couples. One stands at the head of a spring run and lifts a large dry branch high above the woods, where hawks and crows love to alight. Half a dozen are climbing a little hill; while others stand far out in the field, as if they had come out to get the sun. A file of five or six worthies sentry the woods on the northwest and confront a steep sidehill where sheep and cattle graze. An equal number crowd up to the line on the east; and their gray, stately trunks are seen across meadows or fields of grain. Then there is a pair of Siamese twins, with heavy, bushy tops; while in the forks of a wood road stand the two brothers, with their arms around each other's neck and their bodies in gentle contact for a distance of thirty feet.

One immense maple, known as the "old-cream-pan-tree," stands, or did stand, quite alone among a thick growth of birches and beeches. But it kept its end up and did the work of two or three ordinary trees, as its name denotes. Next to it the best milcher in the lot was a shaggy-barked tree in the edge of the field that must have been badly crushed or broken when it was little, for it had an ugly crook near the ground and seemed to struggle all the way up to get in an upright attitude, but never quite succeeded; yet it could outrun all its neighbors nevertheless. The poorest tree in the lot was a short-bodied, heavy-topped tree that stood in the edge of a spring run. It seldom produced half a gallon of sap during the whole season; but this half gallon was very sweet — three or four times as sweet as the ordinary article. In the production of sap, top seems far less important than body. It is not length of limb that wins in this race but length of trunk. A heavy, bushy-topped tree in the open field, for instance, will not, according to my observation, compare with a tall, long-trunked tree in the woods that has but a small top. Young, thrifty, thin-skinned trees start up with great spirit, indeed, fairly on a run; but they do not hold out, and their blood is very diluted.

Cattle are very fond of sap; so are sheep, and will drink enough to kill them. The honeybees get here their first sweet, and the earliest bug takes up his permanent abode on the "spile."

Maple sugar is peculiarly an American product, the discovery of it dating back into the early history of New England. The first settlers usually caught the sap in rude troughs and boiled it down in kettles slung to a pole by a chain, the fire being built around them. The first step in the way of improvement was to use tin pans instead of troughs, and a large stone arch in which the kettles or caldrons were set with the fire beneath them. But of late years, as the question of fuel has become a more important one, greater improvements have been made.

The arch has given place to an immense stove designed for that special purpose; and the kettles to broad, shallow, sheet-iron pans, the object being to economize all the heat and to obtain the greatest possible extent of evaporating surface.[2]

10. Flowering Plants

NEARLY EVERY season I make the acquaintance of one or more new flowers. It takes years to exhaust the botanical treasures of any one considerable neighborhood, unless one makes a dead set at it, like an herbalist. One likes to have his floral acquaintances come to him easily and naturally, like his other friends. Some pleasant occasion should bring you together.

Several of our harmless little wild flowers have been absurdly named out of the old mythologies: thus, Indian cucumber root, one of Thoreau's favorite flowers, is named after the sorceress Medea and is called "medeola," because it was at one time thought to possess rare medicinal properties; and medicine and sorcery have always been more or less confounded in the opinion of mankind. It is a pretty and decorative sort of plant with, when perfect, two stages or platforms of leaves, one above the other. You see a whorl of five or six leaves, a foot or more from the ground, which seems to bear a standard with another whorl of three leaves at the top of it. The small, yellowish, recurved flowers shoot out from above this top whorl. The whole expression of the plant is singularly slender and graceful. Sometimes, probably the first year, it only attains to the first circle of leaves. This is the platform from which it will rear its flower column the next year. Its white, tuberous root is crisp and tender and leaves in the mouth distinctly the taste of cu-

cumber. Whether or not the Indians used it as a relish as we
do the cucumber, I do not know.

Still another pretty flower that perpetuates the name of a
Grecian nymph, a flower that was a new find to me a few summers ago, is the arethusa. Arethusa was one of the nymphs who
attended Diana and was by that goddess turned into a fountain,
that she might escape the god of the river, Alpheus, who became desperately in love with her on seeing her at her bath.
Our arethusa is one of the prettiest of the orchids and has been
pursued through many a marsh and quaking bog by her lovers.
She is a bright pink-purple flower an inch or more long, with
the odor of sweet violets. The sepals and petals rise up and
arch over the column, which we may call the heart of the flower,
as if shielding it. In Plymouth County, Massachusetts, where the
arethusa seems common, I have heard it called Indian pink.*

My second new acquaintance the same season was the showy
lady's-slipper. Most of the floral ladies leave their slippers in
swampy places in the woods; only the stemless one (*Cypri-
pedium acaule*) leaves hers on dry ground before she reaches
the swamp, commonly under evergreen trees, where the carpet
of pine needles will not hurt her feet. But one may penetrate
many wet, mucky places in the woods before he finds the prettiest of them all, the showy lady's-slipper — the prettiest slipper,
but the stoutest and coarsest plant; the flower large and very
showy, white, tinged with purple in front; the stem two feet
high, very leafy, and coarser than bearweed. Report had come
to me, through my botanizing neighbor, that in a certain quaking sphagnum bog in the woods the showy lady's-slipper could
be found. The locality proved to be the marrowy grave of an
extinct lake or black tarn. On the borders of it the white
azalea was in bloom, fast fading. In the midst of it were spruces
and black ash and giant ferns and, low in the spongy, mossy

* Arethusa is a very rare orchid today. [Ed.]

bottom, the pitcher plant. The lady's-slipper grew in little groups and companies all about. Never have I beheld a prettier sight — so gay, so festive, so holiday looking. Were they so many gay bonnets rising above the foliage? or were they flocks of white doves with purple-stained breasts just lifting up their wings to take flight? or were they little fleets of fairy boats, with sail set, tossing on a mimic sea of wild, weedy growths? Such images throng the mind on recalling the scene and only faintly hint its beauty and animation. The long, erect, white sepals do much to give the alert, tossing look which the flower wears. The dim light, too, of its secluded haunts, and its snowy purity and freshness, contribute to the impression it makes. The purple tinge is like a stain of wine which has slightly overflowed the brim of the inflated lip or sac and run part way down its snowy sides.

This lady's-slipper is one of the rarest and choicest of our wild flowers, and its haunts and its beauty are known only to the few.

A few summers ago I struck a new and beautiful plant in the shape of a weed that had only recently appeared in that part of the country. I was walking through an August meadow when I saw, on a little knoll, a bit of most vivid orange, verging on a crimson. I knew of no flower of such a complexion frequenting such a place as that. On investigation, it proved to be a stranger. It had a rough, hairy, leafless stem about a foot high, surmounted by a corymbose cluster of flowers or flower heads of dark vivid orange color. The leaves were deeply notched and toothed, very bristly, and were pressed flat to the ground. The whole plant was a veritable Esau for hairs, and it seemed to lay hold upon the ground as if it was not going to let go easily. And what a fiery plume it had!

The next day, in another field a mile away, I chanced upon

more of the flowers. On making inquiry, I found that a small patch or colony of the plants had appeared that season or had first been noticed then, in a meadow well known to me from boyhood. They had been cut down with the grass in early July, and the first week in August had shot up and bloomed again. I found the spot aflame with them. Their leaves covered every inch of the surface where they stood, and not a spear of grass grew there. They were taking slow but complete possession; they were devouring the meadow by inches. The plant seemed to be a species of hieracium, or hawkweed, or some closely allied species of the composite family, but I could not find it mentioned in our botanies.

A few days later, on the edge of an adjoining county ten miles distant, I found, probably, its headquarters. It had appeared there a few years before and was thought to have escaped from some farmer's dooryard. Patches of it were appearing here and there in the fields, and the farmers were thoroughly alive to the danger and were fighting it like fire. Its seeds are winged like those of the dandelion, and it sows itself far and near. It would be a beautiful acquisition to our midsummer fields, supplying a tint as brilliant as that given by the scarlet poppies to English grain fields. But it would be an expensive one, as it usurps the land completely.*

Our seacoast flowers are probably more brilliant in color than the same flowers in the interior. I thought the wild rose on the Massachusetts coast deeper tinted and more fragrant than those I was used to. The steeplebush, or hardhack, had more color, as had the rose gerardia and several other plants. But when vivid color is wanted, what can surpass or equal

* This observation was made ten years ago. I have since learned that the plant is *Hieracium aurantiacum*, from Europe, a kind of hawkweed. It is fast becoming a common weed in New York and New England.

our cardinal flower? There is a glow about this flower as if color emanated from it as from a live coal. The eye is baffled and does not seem to reach the surface of the petal; it does not see the texture or material part as it does in other flowers, but rests in a steady, still radiance. It is not so much something colored as it is color itself. And then the moist, cool, shady places it affects, usually where it has no floral rivals and where the large, dark shadows need just such a dab of fire! Often, too, we see it double, its reflected image in some dark pool heightening its effect. I never have found it with its only rival in color, the monarda or bee balm, a species of mint. Farther north, the cardinal flower seems to fail, and the monarda takes its place, growing in similar localities. One may see it about a mountain spring or along a meadow brook or glowing in the shade around the head of a wild mountain lake. It stands up two feet high or more, and the flowers show like a broad scarlet cap.

The only thing I have seen in this country that calls to mind the green grain fields of Britain splashed with scarlet poppies may be witnessed in August in the marshes of the lower Hudson, when the broad sedgy and flaggy spaces are sprinkled with the great marsh mallow. It is a most pleasing spectacle — level stretches of dark green flag or waving marsh grass kindled on every square yard by these bright pink blossoms, like great burning coals fanned in the breeze. The mallow is not so deeply colored as the poppy, but it is much larger and has the tint of youth and happiness. It is an immigrant from Europe, but it is making itself at home in our great river meadows.

The same day your eye is attracted by the mallows, as your train skirts or cuts through the broad marshes, it will revel with delight in the masses of fresh bright color afforded by the purple loosestrife, which grows in similar localities and shows here and there like purple bonfires. It is a tall plant, grows in dense masses, and affords a most striking border to the broad spaces dotted with the mallow. It, too, came to us from overseas and first appeared along the Wallkill many years ago.

One sometimes seems to discover a familiar wild flower anew by coming upon it in some peculiar and striking situation. Our columbine is at all times and in all places one of the most exquisitely beautiful of flowers; yet one spring day, when I saw it growing out of a small seam on the face of a great lichen-covered wall of rock, where no soil or mold was visible — a jet of foliage and color shooting out of a black line on the face of a perpendicular mountain wall and rising up like a tiny fountain, its drops turning to flame-colored jewels that hung and danced in the air against the gray rocky surface — its beauty became something magical and audacious. On little narrow shelves in the rocky wall the corydalis was blooming, and among the loose boulders at its base the bloodroot shone conspicuous, suggesting snow rather than anything more sanguine.

ARBUTUS

Sequestered flower of April days,
Thy covert bloom in forest ways
A spell about me weaves;
Thy frosted petals' faint pink glow,
Crystals pure like urns of snow
That all with incense overflow,
Half hid beneath the leaves.

Certain flowers one makes special expeditions for every season. They are limited in their ranges and must generally be sought for in particular haunts. How many excursions to the woods does the delicious trailing arbutus give rise to! There are arbutus days in one's calendar, days when the trailing flower fairly calls him to the woods. With me, they come the latter part of April. The grass is greening here and there on the moist slopes and by the spring runs; the first furrow has been struck by the farmer; the liverleaf is in the height of its beauty, and the bright constellations of the bloodroot shine out here and there.

The arriving swallows twitter above the woods; the first chewink rustles the dry leaves; the northward-bound thrushes, the hermit and the gray-cheeked, flit here and there before you. The robin, the sparrow, and the bluebird are building their first nests, and the first shad are making their way slowly up the Hudson. Indeed, the season is fairly under way when the trailing arbutus comes. Now look out for troops of boys and girls going to the woods to gather it! and let them look out that in their greed they do not exterminate it. Within reach of our large towns, the choicer spring wild flowers are hunted mercilessly. Every fresh party from town raids them as if bent upon their destruction. One day, about ten miles from one of our Hudson River cities, there got into the train six young women loaded down with vast sheaves and bundles of trailing arbutus. Each one of them had enough for forty. They had apparently made a clean sweep of the woods. It was a pretty sight — the pink and white of the girls and the pink and white of the flowers! and the car, too, was suddenly filled with perfume — the breath of spring loaded the air; but I thought it a pity to ravish the woods in that way. The next party was probably equally greedy and, because a handful was desirable, thought an armful proportionately so; till, by and by, the flower will be driven from those woods.*

Another flower that one makes special excursions for is the pond lily. The pond lily is a star and easily takes the first place

---

* Arbutus has been exterminated in many regions. [Ed.]

among lilies; and the expeditions to her haunts and the gathering her where she rocks upon the dark secluded waters of some pool or lakelet are the crown and summit of the floral expeditions of summer. It is the expedition about which more things gather than almost any other: you want your boat, you want your lunch, you want your friend or friends with you. You are going to put in the greater part of the day; you are going to picnic in the woods and indulge in a "green thought in a green shade." When my friend and I go for pond lilies, we have to traverse a distance of three miles with our boat in a wagon. The road is what is called a "back road," and leads through woods most of the way. Black Pond,* where the lilies grow, lies about one hundred feet higher than the Hudson, from which it is separated by a range of rather bold wooded heights, one of which might well be called Mount Hymettus, for I have found a great deal of wild honey in the forest that covers it.

Our road leads us along this stream, across its rude bridges, through dark hemlock and pine woods under gray, rocky walls, now past a black pool, then within sight or hearing of a foaming rapid or fall, till we strike the outlet of the long level that leads to the lake. In this we launch our boat and paddle slowly upward over its dark surface, now pushing our way through half-submerged treetops, then ducking under the trunk of an overturned tree which bridges the stream and makes a convenient way for the squirrels and wood mice, or else forcing the boat over it when it is sunk a few inches below the surface.

As we come in sight of the lilies, where they cover the water at the outlet of the lake, a brisk gust of wind, as if it had been waiting to surprise us, sweeps down and causes every leaf to leap from the water and show its pink underside. Was it a

* Near West Park, N. Y. [Ed.]

fluttering of hundreds of wings, or the clapping of a multitude
of hands? But there rocked the lilies with their golden hearts
open to the sun and their tender white petals as fresh as crystals
of snow. What a queenly flower, indeed, the type of unsullied
purity and sweetness! Its root, like a black, corrugated, ugly
reptile, clinging to the slime, but its flower in purity and white-
ness like a star. There is something very pretty in the closed
bud making its way up through the water to meet the sun; and
there is something touching in the flower closing itself up again
after its brief career and slowly burying itself beneath the dark
wave. One almost fancies a sad, regretful look in it as the stem
draws it downward to mature its seed on the sunless bottom.
The pond lily is a flower of the morning; it closes a little after
noon.

In our walks we note the most showy and beautiful flowers
but not always the most interesting. Who, for instance, pauses
to consider that early species of everlasting, commonly called
mouse-ear,* that grows nearly everywhere by the roadside or
about poor fields? It begins to be noticeable in May, its whitish
downy appearance, its groups of slender stalks crowned with
a corymb of paperlike buds, contrasting it with the fresh green
of surrounding grass or weeds. It is a member of a very large
family, the *Compositæ,* and does not attract one by its beauty;
but it is interesting because of its many curious traits and habits. For instance, it is diœcious, that is, the two sexes are
represented by separate plants; and, what is more curious,
these plants are usually found separated from each other in
well-defined groups, like the men and women in an old-fashioned country church — always in groups; here a group of
females, there, a few yards away, a group of males. The females
may be known by their more slender and graceful appearance

* and pussy-toes. [Ed.]

and, as the season advances, by their outstripping the males in growth. Indeed, they become real amazons in comparison with their brothers. The staminate or male plants grow but a few inches high; the heads are round and have a more dusky or freckled appearance than do the pistillate; and as soon as they have shed their pollen their work is done, they are of no further use, and by the middle of May or before, their heads droop, their stalks wither, and their general collapse sets in. Then the other sex, or pistillate plants, seem to have taken a new lease of life; they wax strong, they shoot up with the growing grass and keep their heads above it; they are alert and active; they bend in the breeze; their long, tapering flower heads take on a tinge of color, and life seems full of purpose and enjoyment with them. I have discovered, too, that they are real sun worshipers; that they turn their faces to the east in the morning and follow the sun in his course across the sky till they all bend to the west at his going down. On the other hand, their brothers have stood stiff and stupid and unresponsive to any influence of sky and air, so far as I could see, till they drooped and died.

Another curious thing is that the females seem vastly more numerous — I should say almost ten times as abundant. You have to hunt for the males; the others you see far off. One season I used every day to pass several groups or circles of females in the grass by the roadside. I noted how they grew and turned their faces sunward. I observed how alert and vigorous they were, and what a purplish tinge came over their mammæ-shaped flower heads as June approached. I looked for the males; to the east, south, west, none could be found for hundreds of yards. On the north, about two hundred feet away, I found a small colony of meek and lowly males. I wondered by what agency fertilization would take place — by insects, or by the wind? I suspected it would not take place. No insects seemed to visit the flowers, and the wind surely could not be relied upon to hit the mark so far off and from such an unlikely corner, too. But by some means the vitalizing dust seemed to have been conveyed. Early in June, the plants began to shed their down, or seed-bearing pappus, still carrying their heads at the top of the grass, so that the breezes could have free access to them and sow the seeds far and wide.

As the seeds are sown broadcast by the wind, I was at first puzzled to know how the two sexes were kept separate and always in little communities, till I perceived, what I might have read in the botany, that the plant is perennial and spreads by offsets and runners, like the strawberry. This would of course keep the two kinds in groups by themselves.

Another plant which has interesting ways and is beautiful besides is the adder's-tongue, or yellow erythronium, the earliest of the lilies and one of the most pleasing. The April sunshine is fairly reflected in its revolute flowers. The lilies have bulbs that sit on or near the top of the ground. The onion is a fair type of the lily in this respect. But here is a lily with the bulb deep in the ground. How it gets there is well worth investigating. The botany says the bulb is deep in the ground, but offers no explanation. Now, it is only the bulbs of the older or flowering plants that are deep in the ground. The bulbs of the young plants are near the top of the ground. The young plants have but one leaf, the older or flowering ones have two. If you happen to be in the woods at the right time in early April, you may see these leaves compactly rolled together, piercing the matted coating of sere leaves that covers the ground like some sharp-pointed instrument. They do not burst their covering or lift it up but pierce through it like an awl.

But how does the old bulb get so deep into the ground? In digging some of them up one spring in an old meadow bottom, I had to cleave the tough fibrous sod to a depth of eight inches. The smaller ones were barely two inches below the surface. Of course they all started from the seed at the surface of the soil. The young botanist or nature lover will find here a field for original research. If, in late May or early June, after the leaves of the plant have disappeared, he finds the ground where they stood showing curious, looping, twisting growths or roots of a greenish white color, let him examine them. They are as smooth and as large as an angleworm, and very brittle. Both ends will be found in the ground, one attached to the old bulb, the other boring or drilling downward and enlarged till it suggests the new bulb. I do not know that this mother root in all cases comes to the surface. Why it should come at all is a mystery, unless it be in some way to get more power for the downward thrust. My own observations upon the subject are not complete, but I think in the foregoing I have given the clew as to how the bulb each year sinks deeper and deeper into the ground.

It is a pity that this graceful and abundant flower has no good and appropriate common name. It is the earliest of the true lilies, and it has all the grace and charm that belong to this order of flowers. *Erythronium*, its botanical name, is not good, as it is derived from a Greek word that means red, while one species of our flower is yellow and the other is white. How it came to be called "adder's-tongue" I do not know; probably from the spotted character of the leaf, which might suggest a snake, though it in no wise resembles a snake's tongue. A fawn is spotted, too, and "fawn lily" would be better than "adder's-tongue." Still better is the name "trout lily," which has recently been proposed for this plant. It blooms along the trout streams, and its leaf is as mottled as a trout's back. The name "dog's-tooth" may have been suggested by the shape and color of the bud, but how the "violet" came to be added is a puzzle, as it has not one feature of the violet. It is only another illustration of the haphazard way in which our wild flowers, as well as our birds, have been named.

In my spring rambles I have sometimes come upon a solitary specimen of this yellow lily growing beside a mossy stone where the sunshine fell full upon it, and have thought it one of the most beautiful of our wild flowers. Its two leaves stand up like a fawn's ears, and this feature, with its recurved petals, gives it an alert, wide-awake look.

Another of our common wild flowers, which I always look at with an interrogation point in my mind, is the wild ginger. Why should this plant always hide its flower? Its two fuzzy, heart-shaped green leaves stand up very conspicuously amid the rocks or mossy stones; but its one curious, brown, bell-shaped flower is always hidden beneath the moss or dry leaves, as if too modest to face the light of the open woods. As a rule, the one thing which a plant is anxious to show and to make much of, and to flaunt before all the world, is its flower. But the wild ginger reverses the rule and blooms in secret. Instead of turning upward toward the light and air, it turns downward toward the darkness and the silence. It has no corolla, but what the botanists call a lurid or brown-purple calyx, which is conspicuous like a corolla. Its root leaves in the mouth a taste precisely like that of ginger.

This plant and the closed gentian are apparent exceptions, in their manner of blooming, to the general habit of the rest of our flowers. The closed gentian does not hide its flower, but the corolla never opens; it always remains a closed bud. I used to think that this gentian could never experience the benefits

of insect visits, which Darwin showed us were of such importance in the vegetable world. I once plucked one of the flowers
into which a bumblebee had forced his way, but he had never
come out; the flower was his tomb. I am assured, however, by
recent observers, that the bumblebee does successfully enter the
closed corolla, and thus distribute its pollen.

There is yet another curious exception which I will mention, namely, the witch hazel. All our trees and plants bloom
in the spring except this one species; this blooms in the fall.
Just as its leaves are fading and falling, its flowers appear, giving out an odor along the bushy lanes and margins of the woods
that is to the nose like cool water to the hand. Why it should
bloom in the fall instead of in the spring is a mystery. And it
is probably because of this very curious trait that its branches
are used as divining rods by certain credulous persons to point
out where springs of water and precious metals are hidden.[1]

To me, nothing else about a tree is so remarkable as the
extreme delicacy of the mechanisms by which it grows and
lives, the fine hairlike rootlets at the bottom and the microscopi-
cal cells of the leaves at the top. The rootlets absorb the water
charged with mineral salts from the soil, and the leaves absorb
the sunbeams from the air. So it looks as if the tree was almost
made of matter and spirit, like man; the ether with its vibrations, on the one hand, and the earth with its inorganic com-
pounds, on the other — earth salts and sunlight. The sturdy
oak, the gigantic sequoia, are each equally finely organized in
these parts that take hold of nature. We call certain plants
gross feeders, and in a sense they are; but all are delicate feeders
in their mechanism of absorption from the earth and air.

The tree touches the inorganic world at the two finest points
of its structure — the rootlets and the leaves. These attack

the great crude world of inorganic matter with weapons so fine that only the microscope can fully reveal them to us. The animal world seizes its food in masses little and big and often gorges itself with it, but the vegetable, through the agency of the solvent power of water, absorbs its nourishment molecule by molecule.

A tree does not live by its big roots — these are mainly for strength and to hold it to the ground. How they grip the rocks, fitting themselves to them, as Lowell says, like molten metal! The tree's life is in the fine hairlike rootlets that spring from the roots. Darwin says those rootlets behave as if they had minute brains in their extremities. They feel their way into the soil; they know the elements the plant wants; some select more lime, others more potash, others more magnesia. The wheat rootlets select more silica to make the stalk; the pea rootlets select more lime: the pea does not need the silica. The individuality of plants and trees in this respect is most remarkable. The cells of each seem to know what particular elements they want from the soil, as of course they do.

The vital activity of the tree goes on at three points — in the leaves, in the rootlets, and in the cambium layer. The activity of the leaf and rootlet furnishes the starchy deposit which forms this generative layer — the milky, mucilaginous girdle of matter between the inner bark and the wood through which the tree grows and increases in size. Generation and regeneration take place through this layer. I have called it the girdle of perpetual youth. It never grows old. It is annually renewed. The heart of the old apple tree may decay and disappear, indeed the tree may be reduced to a mere shell and many of its branches may die and fall, but the few apples which it still bears attest the fact that its cambium layer, at least over a part of its surface, is still youthful and doing its work. It is this layer that the yellow-bellied woodpecker, known as the sapsucker, drills into and devours, thus drawing directly upon the vitality of the tree. But his ravages are rarely serious. Only in two instances have I seen dead branches on an apple tree that appeared to be the result of his drilling.

What we call the heart of a tree is in no sense the heart; it has no vital function but only the mechanical one of strength and support. It adds to the tree's inertia and power to resist storms. The trunk of a tree is like a community where only one generation at a time is engaged in active business, the great mass of the population being retired and adding solidity and permanence to the social organism. The rootlets of a plant or a tree are like the laborers in the field that produce for us the raw material of our food, while the leaves are like our many devices for rendering it edible and nourishing. The rootlets continue their activity in the fall, after the leaves have fallen, and thus gorge the tree with fluid against the needs of the spring. In the growing tree or vine the sap, charged with nourishment, flows down from the top to the roots. In the spring it evidently flows upward, seeking the air through the leaves. Or rather, we may say that the crude sap always flows upward, while the nutritive sap flows downward, thus giving the tree a kind of double circulation.

A tree may be no more beautiful and wonderful when we have come to a knowledge of all its hidden processes, but it certainly is no less so. We do not think of the function of the leaves or of the bark or of the roots and rootlets when we gaze upon a noble oak or an elm; we admire it for its form, its sturdiness, or its grace; it is akin to ourselves; it is the work of a vast community of cells like those that build up our own bodies; it is a fountain of living matter rising up out of the earth and splitting up and spreading out at its top in a spray of leaves and flowers; and if we could see its hidden processes we should realize how truly like a fountain it is. While in full leaf a current of water is constantly flowing through it, and flowing upward against gravity. This stream of water is truly its life current; it enters at the rootlets under the ground and escapes at the top through the leaves by a process called transpiration. All the mineral salts with which the tree builds up its woody tissues — its osseous system, so to speak — the instruments with which it imprisons and consolidates the carbon which it obtains from the air, are borne in solution in this stream of water. Its function is analogous to that of the rivers which bring the produce and other material to the great cities situated upon their banks. A cloud of invisible vapor rises from the top of every tree, and a thousand invisible rills enter it through its myriad hairlike rootlets. The trees are thus conduits in the circuit of the waters from the earth to the clouds. Our own bodies and the bodies of all living things perform a similar function. Life cannot go on without water, but water is not a food; it makes the processes of metabolism possible; assimilation and elimination go on through its agency. Water and air are the two ties between the organic and the inorganic. The function of the one is mainly mechanical, that of the other is mainly chemical.

As the water is drawn in at the roots, it flows out at the top, to which point it rises by capillary attraction and a process called osmosis. Neither of them is a strictly vital process, since both are found in the inorganic world; but they are in the service of what we call a vital principle.[2]

April, too, is the time to go budding. A swelling bud is food for the fancy and often food for the eye. Some buds begin to glow as they begin to swell. The bud scales change color and become a delicate rose pink. I note this especially in the European maple. The bud scales flush as if the effort to "keep in" brought the blood into their faces. The scales of the willow do not flush but shine like ebony, and each one presses like a hand upon the catkin that will escape from beneath it.

When spring pushes pretty hard, many buds begin to sweat as well as to glow; they exude a brown, fragrant, gummy substance that affords the honeybee her first cement and hive varnish. The hickory, the horse chestnut, the plane tree, the poplars, are all coated with this April myrrh. That of certain poplars, like the Balm of Gilead, is the most noticeable and fragrant. No spring incense is more agreeable. Its perfume is often upon the April breeze. I pick up the bud scales of the poplars along the road, long brown scales like the beaks of birds, and they leave a rich gummy odor in my hand that lasts for hours. I frequently detect the same odor about my hives when the bees are making all snug against the rains, or against the millers. When used by the bees, we call it propolis. The bees often have serious work to detach it from their leg baskets and make it stick only where they want it to.

The bud scales begin to drop in April, and by May Day the scales have fallen from the eyes of every branch in the forest. In most cases the bud has an inner wrapping that does not fall so soon. In the hickory this inner wrapping is like a great livid membrane, an inch or more in length, thick, fleshy, and shining. It clasps the tender leaves about as if both protecting and nursing them. As the leaves develop, these membranous wrappings curl back and finally wither and fall. In the plane tree, or sycamore, this inner wrapping of the bud is a little pelisse of soft yellow or tawny fur. When it is cast off, it is the size of one's thumbnail and suggests the delicate skin of some golden-haired mole. The young sycamore balls lay aside their fur

wrappings early in May. The flower tassels of the European maple, too, come packed in a slightly furry covering. The long and fleshy inner scales that enfold the flowers and leaves are of a clear olive green, thinly covered with silken hairs like the young of some animals. Our sugar maple is less striking in the bud, but the flowers are more graceful and fringelike.

Some trees have no bud scales. The sumac presents in early spring a mere fuzzy knot, from which, by and by, there emerges a soft, furry, tawny-colored kitten's paw. I know of nothing in vegetable nature that seems so really to be *born* as the ferns. They emerge from the ground rolled up, with a rudimentary and "touch-me-not" look, and appear to need a maternal tongue to lick them into shape. The sun plays the wet nurse to them, and very soon they are out of that uncanny covering in which they come swathed, and take their places with other green things.

The bud scales strew the ground in spring as the leaves do in the fall, though they are so small that we hardly notice them. All growth, all development, is a casting off, a leaving of something behind. First the bud scales drop, then the flower drops, then the fruit drops, then the leaf drops. The first two are preparatory and stand for spring; the last two are the crown and stand for autumn. Nearly the same thing happens with the seed in the ground. First the shell, or outer husk, is dropped or cast off; then the cotyledons, those nurse leaves of the young plant; then the fruit falls, and at last the stalk and leaf. A bud is a kind of seed planted in the branch instead of in the soil. It bursts and grows like a germ. In the absence of seeds and fruit, many birds and animals feed upon buds. The pine grosbeaks from the north are the most destructive budders that come among us. The snow beneath the maples they frequent is often covered with bud scales. The ruffed grouse

sometimes buds in an orchard near the woods and thus takes
the farmer's apple crop a year in advance. Grafting is but a
planting of buds. The seed is a complete, independent bud;
it has the nutriment of the young plant within itself, as the egg
holds several good lunches for the young chick. When the
spider or the wasp or the carpenter bee or the sand hornet lays
an egg in a cell and deposits food or germ, she stores food for
the young plant. Upon this it feeds till the root takes hold of
the soil and draws sustenance from thence. The bud is rooted
in the branch and draws its sustenance from the milk of the
pulpy cambium layer beneath the bark.[3]

How different the expression of the pine, in fact of all the co-
niferæ, from that of the deciduous trees! Not different merely
by reason of color and foliage, but by reason of form. The
deciduous trees have greater diversity of shapes; they tend to
branch endlessly; they divide and subdivide until the original
trunk is lost in a maze of limbs. Not so the pine and its con-
geners. Here the main thing is the central shaft; there is one
dominant shoot which leads all the rest and which points the
tree upward; the original type is never departed from: the
branches shoot out at nearly right angles to the trunk and
occur in regular whorls; the main stem is never divided unless
some accident nips the leading shoot, when two secondary
branches will often rise up and lead the tree forward. The pine
has no power to develop new buds, new shoots, like the deciduous trees; no power of spontaneous variation to meet new
exigencies, new requirements. It is, as it were, cast in a mold.
Its buds, its branches occur in regular series and after a regular
pattern. Interrupt this series, try to vary this pattern, and the
tree is powerless to adapt itself to any other. Victor Hugo, in
his old age, compared himself to a tree that had been many

times cut down but which always sprouted again. But the pines do not sprout again. The spontaneous development of a new bud or a new shoot rarely or never occurs. The hemlock seems to be under the same law. I have cut away all the branches and rubbed away all the buds of a young sapling of this species and found the tree, a year and a half later, full of life but with no leaf or bud upon it. It could not break the spell. One bud would have released it and set its currents going again, but it was powerless to develop it. Remove the bud or the new growth from the end of the central shaft of the branch of a pine, and in a year or two the branch will die back to the next joint; remove the whorl of branches here and it will die back to the next whorl, and so on.

When you cut the top of a pine or a spruce, removing the central and leading shaft, the tree does not develop and send forth a new one to take the place of the old, but a branch from the next in rank, that is, from the next whorl of limbs, is promoted to take the lead. It is curious to witness this limb rise up and get into position. One season I cut off the tops of some young hemlocks that were about ten feet high, that I had balled in the winter and had moved into position for a hedge. The next series of branches consisted of three that shot out nearly horizontally. As time passed, one of these branches, apparently the most vigorous, began to lift itself up very slowly toward the place occupied by the lost leader. The third year it stood at an angle of about forty-five degrees; the fourth year it had gained about half the remaining distance, when the clipping shears again cut it down. In five years it would probably have assumed an upright position. A white pine of about the same height lost its central shaft by a grub that developed from the egg of an insect, and I cut it away. It rose from a whorl of four branches, and it now devolved upon one of these to take the lead. Two of them, on opposite sides, were more vigorous than the other two, and the struggle now is as to which of these two shall gain the mastery. Both are rising up and turning toward the vacant chieftainship, and unless something interferes, the tree will probably become forked and led upward by two equal branches. I shall probably humble the pride of one of the rivals by nipping its central shoot. One of my neighbors has cut off a yellow pine about six inches in diameter, so as to leave only one circle of limbs seven or eight feet from the ground. It is now the third year of the tree's decapitation, and one of this circle of horizontal limbs has risen up several feet, like a sleeper rising from his couch, and seems to be looking around inquiringly, as much as to say: "Come, brothers, wake up! Someone must take the lead here; shall it be I?"

In one of my Norway spruces I have witnessed the humbling or reducing to the ranks of a would-be leading central shoot. For a couple of years the vigorous young tree was led upward by two rival branches; they appeared almost evenly matched; but on the third year one of them clearly took the lead and at the end of the season was a foot or more in advance of the other. The next year the distance between them became still greater, and the defeated leader appeared to give up the contest, so that a season or two afterward it began to lose its upright attitude and to fall more and more toward a horizontal position; it was willing to go back into the ranks of the lateral branches. Its humiliation was so great that it even for a time dropped below them; but toward midsummer it lifted up its head a little and was soon fairly in the position of a side branch, simulating defeat and willing subordination as completely as if it had been a conscious, sentient being.

The evergreens can keep a secret the year round, someone has said. How well they keep the secret of the shedding of their leaves! so well that in the case of the spruces we hardly know when it does occur. In fact, the spruces do not properly shed their leaves at all but simply outgrow them, after carrying them an indefinite time. Some of the species carry their leaves five or six years. The hemlock drops its leaves very irregularly: the winds and the storms whip them off; in winter the snow beneath them is often covered with them.

But the pine sheds its leaves periodically, though always as it were stealthily and under cover of the newer foliage. The white pine usually sheds its leaves in midsummer, though I have known all the pines to delay till October. It is on with the new love before it is off with the old. From May till near autumn it carries two crops of leaves, last year's and the present year's. Emerson's inquiry,

> *How the sacred pine tree adds*
> *To her old leaves new myriads,*

is framed in strict accordance with the facts. It is to her *old* leaves that she adds the new. Only the new growth, the outermost leaves, are carried over till the next season, thus keeping the tree always clothed and green. As its moulting season approaches, these old leaves, all the rear ranks on the limbs, begin to turn yellow, and a careless observer might think the tree was struck with death, but it is not. The decay stops just where the growth of the previous spring began, and presently the tree stands green and vigorous, with a newly laid carpet of fallen leaves beneath it.

The pine is the tree of silence. Who was the Goddess of Silence? Look for her altars amid the pines — silence above, silence below. Pass from deciduous woods into pine woods of a windy day, and you think the day has suddenly become calm.

Then how silent to the foot! One walks over a carpet of pine
needles almost as noiselessly as over the carpets of our dwellings. Do these halls lead to the chambers of the great, that all
noise should be banished from them? Let the designers come
here and get the true pattern for a carpet — a soft yellowish
brown with only a red leaf or a bit of gray moss or a dusky lichen
scattered here and there; a background that does not weary or
bewilder the eye or insult the ground-loving foot.

How friendly the pine tree is to man — so docile and available as timber and so warm and protective as shelter! Its balsam is salve to his wounds, its fragrance is long life to his nostrils; an abiding, perennial tree, tempering the climate, cool as
murmuring waters in summer and like a wrapping of fur in
winter.

The deciduous trees are inconstant friends that fail us when
adverse winds do blow; but the pine and all its tribe look winter
cheerily in the face, tossing the snow, masquerading in his
arctic livery, in fact holding high carnival from fall to spring.
The Norseman of the woods, lofty and aspiring, tree without
bluster or noise, that sifts the howling storm into a fine spray of
sound; symmetrical tree, tapering, columnar, shaped as in a
lathe, the preordained mast of ships, the mother of colossal timbers; centralized, towering, patriarchal, coming down from the
foreworld, counting centuries in thy rings and outlasting em-
pires in thy decay.

In the absence of the pine, the hemlock is a graceful and
noble tree. In primitive woods it shoots up in the same manner, drawing the ladder up after it, and attains an altitude of
nearly or quite a hundred feet. It is the poor man's pine and
destined to humbler uses than its lordlier brother. It follows
the pine like a servitor, keeping on higher and more rocky
ground and going up the minor branch valleys when the pine

follows only the main or mother stream. As an ornamental tree it is very pleasing and deserves to be cultivated more than it is. It is a great favorite with the sylvan folk, too. The ruffed grouse prefer it to the pine; it is better shelter in winter, and its buds are edible. The red squirrel has found out the seeds in its cones, and they are an important part of his winter stores.

Both the pine and the hemlock make friends with the birch, the maple, and the oak, and one of the most pleasing and striking features of our autumnal scenery is a mountainside sown broadcast with these intermingled trees, forming a combination of colors like the richest tapestry, the dark green giving body and permanence, the orange and yellow giving light and brilliancy.[4]

11. Insect and Amphibian Ways

THE HONEYBEE goes forth from the hive in spring like the dove from Noah's ark, and it is not till after many days that she brings back the olive leaf, which in this case is a pellet of golden pollen upon each hip, usually obtained from the alder or swamp willow. In a country where maple sugar is made, the bees get their first taste of sweet from the sap as it flows from the spiles, or as it dries and is condensed upon the sides of the buckets. They will sometimes, in their eagerness, come about the boiling place and be overwhelmed by the steam and the smoke. But bees appear to be more eager for bread in the spring than for honey: their supply of this article, perhaps, does not keep as well as their stores of the latter; hence fresh bread, in the shape of new pollen, is diligently sought for. My bees get their first supplies from the catkins of the willows. How quickly they find them out! If but one catkin opens anywhere within range, a bee is on hand that very hour to rifle it, and it is a most pleasing experience to stand near the hive some mild April day and see them come pouring in with their little baskets packed with this first fruitage of the spring. They will have new bread now; they have been to mill in good earnest; see their dusty coats and the golden grist they bring home with them.

The first honey is perhaps obtained from the flowers of the

red maple and the golden willow. The latter sends forth a wild, delicious perfume. The sugar maple blooms a little later, and from its silken tassels a rich nectar is gathered. My bees will not label these different varieties for me, as I really wish they would. Honey from the maple, a tree so clean and wholesome and full of such virtues every way, would be something to put one's tongue to. Or that from the blossoms of the apple, the peach, the cherry, the quince, the currant — one would like a card of each of these varieties to note their peculiar qualities. The apple blossom is very important to the bees. A single swarm has been known to gain twenty pounds in weight during its continuance. Bees love the ripened fruit, too, and in August and September will suck themselves tipsy upon varieties like the sops-of-wine.

The interval between the blooming of the fruit trees and that of the clover and raspberry is bridged over in many localities by the honey locust. What a delightful summer murmur these trees send forth at this season! I know nothing about the quality of the honey, but it ought to keep well. But when the red raspberry blooms, the fountains of plenty are unsealed indeed; what a commotion about the hives then, especially in localities where it is extensively cultivated, as in places along the Hudson! The delicate white clover, which begins to bloom about the same time, is neglected; even honey itself is passed by for this modest, colorless, all but odorless flower. A field of these berries in June sends forth a continuous murmur like that of an enormous hive. The honey is not so white as that obtained from clover, but it is easier gathered; it is in shallow cups, while that of the clover is in deep tubes. The bees are up and at it before sunrise, and it takes a brisk shower to drive them in. But the clover blooms later and blooms everywhere and is the staple source of supply of the finest quality of honey. The red clover yields up its stores only to the longer proboscis of the bumblebee, else the bee pasturage of our agricultural districts would be unequaled.

Among your stores of honey gathered before midsummer you may chance upon a card, or mayhap only a square inch or two of comb, in which the liquid is as transparent as water, of a delicious quality, with a slight flavor of mint. This is the product of the linden or basswood, of all the trees in our forest the one most beloved by the bees. Melissa, the goddess of honey, has placed her seal upon this tree. The wild swarms in the woods frequently reap a choice harvest from it.

It is the making of the wax that costs with the bee. As with the poet, the form, the receptacle, gives him more trouble than the sweet that fills it, though, to be sure, there is always more or less empty comb in both cases. The honey he can have for the gathering, but the wax he must make himself — must evolve from his own inner consciousness. When wax is to be made, the wax makers fill themselves with honey and retire into their chamber for private meditation; it is like some solemn religious rite: they take hold of hands or hook themselves together in long lines that hang in festoons from the top of the hive, and wait for the miracle to transpire. After about twenty-four hours their patience is rewarded, the honey is turned into wax, minute scales of which are secreted from between the rings of the abdomen of each bee; this is taken off and from it the comb is built up. It is calculated that about twenty-five pounds of honey are used in elaborating one pound of comb, to say nothing of the time that is lost. Hence the importance, in an economical point of view, of a recent device by which the honey is extracted and the comb returned intact to the bees. But honey without the comb is the perfume without the rose — it is sweet merely and soon degenerates into candy. Half the delectableness is in breaking down these frail and exquisite walls yourself and tasting the nectar before it has lost its freshness by contact with the air. Then the comb is a sort of shield or foil that prevents the tongue from being over-whelmed by the first shock of the sweet.

Honey was a much more important article of food with the ancients than it is with us. As they appear to have been un-acquainted with sugar, honey no doubt stood them instead. It is too rank and pungent for the modern taste; it soon cloys upon the palate. It demands the appetite of youth and the strong, robust digestion of people who live much in the open air. It is a more wholesome food than sugar, and modern confectionery is poison beside it. Beside grape sugar, honey contains manna, mucilage, pollen, acid, and other vegetable odoriferous sub-stances and juices. It is a sugar with a kind of wild natural bread added. The manna of itself is both food and medicine, and the pungent vegetable extracts have rare virtues. Honey promotes the excretions and dissolves the glutinous and starchy impedimenta of the system.

Hence it is not without reason that with the ancients a land flowing with milk and honey should mean a land abounding in all good things; and the queen in the nursery rhyme who lingered in the kitchen to eat "bread and honey" while the "king was in the parlor counting out his money," was doing a very sensible thing. Epaminondas is said to have rarely eaten anything but bread and honey. The Emperor Augustus one day inquired of a centenarian how he had kept his vigor of mind and body so long; to which the veteran replied that it was by "oil without and honey within." Cicero, in his "Old Age," classes honey with meat and milk and cheese as among the staple articles with which a well-kept farmhouse will be supplied.[1]

I turned another (to me) new page in natural history when, during the past season, I made the acquaintance of the sand wasp or hornet. From boyhood I had known the black hornet with his large paper nest, and the spiteful yellow jacket with his lesser domicile, and had cherished proper contempt for the various indolent wasps. But the sand hornet was a new bird — in fact, the harpy eagle among insects — and he made an impression. While walking along the road about midsummer, I noticed working in the towpath, where the ground was rather inclined to be dry and sandy, a large yellow hornetlike insect. It made a hole the size of one's little finger in the hard, gravelly path beside the roadbed. When disturbed, it alighted on the dirt and sand in the middle of the road. I had noticed in my walks some small bulletlike holes in the field that had piqued my curiosity, and I determined to keep an eye on these insects of the roadside. I explored their holes and found them quite shallow, and no mystery at the bottom of them. One morning in the latter part of July, walking that way, I was quickly attracted by the sight of a row of little mounds of fine, freshly dug earth resting upon the grass beside the road, a foot or more beneath the path. "What is this?" I said. "Mice or squirrels or snakes," said my neighbor. But I connected it at once with the strange insect I had seen. Neither mice nor squirrels work like that, and snakes do not dig. Above each mound of earth was a hole the size of one's largest finger leading into the bank. While speculating about the phenomenon, I saw one of the large yellow hornets I had observed, quickly enter one of the holes. That settled the query. While spade and hoe were being brought to dig him out, another hornet appeared, heavy-laden with some prey, and flew humming up and down and around the place where I was standing. I withdrew a little, when he quickly alighted upon one of the mounds of earth, and

I saw him carrying into his den no less an insect than the cicada or harvest fly.   Then another came, and after coursing up and down a few times, disturbed by my presence, alighted upon a tree with his quarry to rest.   The black hornet will capture a fly or a small butterfly and, after breaking and dismembering it, will take it to his nest; but here was this hornet carrying an insect much larger than himself and flying with ease and swiftness.   It was as if a hawk should carry a hen, or an eagle a turkey. I at once proceeded to dig for one of the hornets and, after following his hole about three feet under the footpath and to the edge of the roadbed, succeeded in capturing him and recovering the cicada.   The hornet weighed fifteen grains, and the cicada nineteen; but in bulk the cicada exceeded the hornet by more than half.   In color, the wings and thorax, or waist, of the hornet were a rich bronze; the abdomen was black, with three irregular yellow bands; the legs were large and powerful, especially the third or hindmost pair, which were much larger than the others and armed with many spurs and hooks.   In digging its hole the hornet has been seen at work very early in the morning.   It backed out with the loosened material, like any other animal under the same circumstances, holding and scraping back the dirt with its legs.   These were dug by the larger hornets or females.   There was but one inhabitant in each hole, and the holes were two to three feet apart.   One that we examined had nine chambers or galleries at the end of it, in each of which were two locusts, or eighteen in all.   The locusts of the locality had suffered great slaughter.   Some of them in the hole or den had been eaten to a mere shell by the larvæ of the hornet.   Under the wing of each insect an egg is attached; the egg soon hatches, and the grub at once proceeds to devour the food its thoughtful parent has provided.   It is said that the hornet does not sting the insect in a vital part — for in that case it would not keep fresh for its young — but introduces its poison into certain nervous ganglia, the injury to which has the effect of paralyzing the victim and making it incapable of motion, though life remains for some time.

Besides the cicada, the sand hornet captures grasshoppers and other large insects. I have never met with it before the present summer (1879), but this year I have heard of its appearance at several points along the Hudson.

If you "leave no stone unturned" in your walks through the fields, you may perchance discover the abode of one of our solitary bees. Indeed, I have often thought what a chapter of natural history might be written on "Life under a Stone," so many of our smaller creatures take refuge there — ants, crickets, spiders, wasps, bumblebees, the solitary bee, mice, toads, snakes, newts, etc. What do these things do in a country where there are no stones? A stone makes a good roof, a good shield; it is waterproof and fireproof and, until the season becomes too rigorous, frostproof, too. The field mouse wants no better place to nest than beneath a large, flat stone, and the bumblebee is entirely satisfied if she can get posssession of his old or abandoned quarters. I have even heard of a swarm of hive bees going under a stone that was elevated a little from the ground. After that, I did not marvel at Samson's bees going into the carcass or skeleton of the lion.

But to return to the solitary bee. When you go a-hunting of the honeybee and are in quest of a specimen among the asters or goldenrod in some remote field to start a line with, you shall see how much this little native bee resembles her cousin of the social hive. There appear to be several varieties, but the one I have in mind is just the size of the honeybee and of the same general form and color, and its manner among the flowers is nearly the same. On close inspection, its color proves to be lighter, while the underside of its abdomen is of a rich bronze. The body is also flatter and less tapering, and the curve inclines upward rather than downward.

I discovered its nest one day in this wise: I was lying upon the ground in a field, watching a line of honeybees to the woods, when my attention was arrested by one of these native bees flying about me in a curious, inquiring way. When it returned the third time, I said, "That bee wants something of me," which proved to be the case, for I was lying upon the entrance to its nest. On my getting up, it alighted and crawled quickly home. I turned over the stone, which was less than a foot across, when the nest was partially exposed. It consisted of four cells built in succession in a little tunnel that had been excavated in the ground. The cells, which were about three quarters of an inch long and half as far through, were made of sections cut from the leaf of the maple — cut with the mandibles of the bee, which work precisely like shears. I have seen the bee at work cutting out these pieces. She moves through the leaf like the hand of the tailor through a piece of cloth. When the pattern is detached she rolls it up and, embracing it with her legs, flies home with it, often appearing to have a bundle disproportionately large. Each cell is made up of a dozen or more pieces: the larger ones, those that form its walls, like the walls of a paper bag, are oblong and are turned down at one end, so as to form the bottom; not one thickness of leaf merely, but three or four thicknesses, each fragment of leaf lapping over another. When the cell is completed, it is filled about two thirds full of beebread — the color of that in the comb in the hive, but not so dry, and having a sourish smell. Upon this the egg is laid, and upon this the young feed when hatched. Is the paper bag now tied up? No, it is headed up; circular bits of leaves are nicely fitted into it to the number of six or seven. They are cut without pattern or compass, and yet they are all alike, and all exactly fit. Indeed, the construction of this cell or receptacle shows great ingenuity and skill. The bee was, of course, unable to manage a single section of a leaf large enough, when rolled up to form it, and so was obliged to construct it of smaller pieces, such as she could carry, lapping them one over another.

I was highly edified the past summer by observing the ways and doings of a colony of black hornets that established themselves under one of the projecting gables of my house. This hornet has the reputation of being a very ugly customer, but I found it no trouble to live on the most friendly terms with them. They were as little disposed to quarrel as I was. It is indeed the eagle among hornets and very noble and dignified in its bearing. They used to come freely into the house and prey upon the flies. You would hear that deep, mellow hum and see the black falcon poising on wing or striking here and there at the flies, that scattered on his approach like chickens before a hawk. When he had caught one, he would alight upon some object and proceed to dress and draw his game. The wings were sheared off, the legs cut away, the bristles trimmed, then the body thoroughly bruised and broken. When the work was completed, the fly was rolled up into a small pellet, and with it under his arm the hornet flew to his nest, where no doubt in due time it was properly served up on the royal board. Every dinner inside these paper walls is a state dinner, for the queen bee is always present.

I used to mount the ladder to within two or three feet of the nest and observe the proceedings. I at first thought the workshop must be inside — a place where the pulp was mixed and perhaps treated with chemicals; for each bee, when he came with his burden of materials, passed into the nest and then, after a few moments, emerged again and crawled to the place of building. But I one day stopped up the entrance with some cotton when no one happened to be on guard, and then observed that, when the loaded bee could not get inside, he, after some deliberation, proceeded to the unfinished part and went forward with his work. Hence I inferred that maybe the bee went inside to report and to receive orders, or possibly to surrender its material into fresh hands. Its career when away from the nest is beset with dangers; the colony is never large, and the safe return of every bee is no doubt a matter of solicitude to the royal mother.

The hornet was the first paper maker and holds the original patent. The paper it makes is about like that of the newspaper; nearly as firm and made of essentially the same material — woody fibres scraped from old rails and boards. And there is news on it, too, if one could make out the characters.[2]

Once, while walking in the woods, I saw quite a large nest in the top of a pine tree. On climbing up to it, I found that it had originally been a crow's nest. Then a red squirrel had appropriated it; he had filled up the cavity with the fine inner bark of the red cedar and made himself a dome-shaped nest upon the crow's foundation of coarse twigs. It is probable that the flying squirrel or the white-footed mouse had been the next tenants, for the finish of the interior suggested their dainty taste. But when I found it, its sole occupant was a bumblebee — the mother or queen bee, just planting her colony. She buzzed very loud and complainingly and stuck up her legs in protest against my rude inquisitiveness but refused to vacate the premises. She had only one sack or cell constructed, in which she had deposited her first egg, and beside that a large loaf of bread, probably to feed the young brood with, as they should be hatched.   It looked like Boston brown bread, but I examined it and found it to be a mass of dark brown pollen, quite soft and pasty.   In fact it was unleavened bread and had not been got at the baker's.   A few weeks later, if no accident befell her, she had a good working colony of a dozen or more bees.

This was not an unusual incident.   Our bumblebee, so far as I have observed, invariably appropriates a mouse nest for the site of its colony, never excavating a place in the ground nor conveying materials for a nest, to be lined with wax, like the European species.   Many other of our wild creatures take up with the leavings of their betters or strongers.   Neither the skunk nor the rabbit digs his own hole but takes up with that of a woodchuck or else hunts out a natural den among the rocks.   In England the rabbit burrows in the ground to such an extent that in places the earth is honeycombed by them, and the walker steps through the surface into their galleries.   Our white-footed mouse has been known to take up his abode in a hornet's nest, furnishing the interior to suit his taste.   A few of our birds also avail themselves of the work of others, as the titmouse, the brown creeper, the bluebird, and the house wren. But in every case they refurnish the tenement: the wren carries feathers into the cavity excavated by the woodpeckers, the blue-bird carries in fine straws, and the chickadee lays down a fine wool mat upon the floors.   When the high-hole occupies the same cavity another year, he deepens and enlarges it: the phœbe bird, in taking up her old nest, puts in a new lining; so does the robin; but cases of reoccupancy of an old nest by the last-named birds are rare.

The latter part of April, when the little peeping frogs are in full chorus, one comes upon places in his drives or walks late in the day where the air fairly palpitates with sound; from every little marshy hollow and spring run there rises an impenetrable maze or cloud of shrill musical voices. After the peepers, the next frog to appear is the clucking frog, a rather small, dark-brown frog with a harsh, clucking note, which later in the season becomes the well-known brown wood frog. Their chorus is heard for a few days only, while their spawn is being deposited. In less than a week it ceases, and I never hear them again till the next April. As the weather gets warmer, the toads take to the water and set up that long-drawn musical *tr-r-r-r-r-r-ing* note. The voice of the bullfrog, who calls, according to the boys, *jug o' rum, jug o' rum, pull the plug, pull the plug,* is not heard much before June. The peepers, the clucking frog, and the bullfrog are the only ones that call in chorus. The most interesting and the most shy and withdrawn of all our frogs and toads is the tree toad — the creature that, from the old apple or cherry tree or red cedar, announces the approach of rain and baffles your every effort to see or discover him. It has not (as some people imagine) exactly the power of the chameleon to render itself invisible by assuming the color of the object it perches upon, but it sits very close and still, and its mottled back of different shades of ashen gray blends it perfectly with the bark of nearly every tree. The only change in its color I have ever noticed is that it is lighter on a light-colored tree, like the beech or soft maple, and darker on the apple or cedar or pine. Then it is usually hidden in some cavity or hollow of the tree, when its voice appears to come from the outside.

The home of the tree toad, I am convinced, is usually a hollow limb or other cavity in the tree; here he makes his headquarters and passes most of the day. For two years a pair of them frequented an old apple tree near my house, occasionally sitting at the mouth of a cavity that led into a large branch, but usually their voices were heard from within the cavity itself.

During the present season, I obtained additional proof of the fact that the tree toad hibernates on dry land. The 12th of November was a warm, springlike day; wind southwest, with slight rain in the afternoon — just the day to bring things out of their winter retreats. As I was about to enter my door at dusk, my eye fell upon what proved to be the large tree toad in question, sitting on some low stonework at the foot of a terrace a few feet from the house. I paused to observe his movements. Presently he started on his travels across the yard toward the lawn in front. He leaped about three feet at a time, with long pauses between each leap. For fear of losing him as it grew darker, I captured him and kept him under the coal sieve till morning. He was very active at night trying to escape.

After a while I let my prisoner escape into the open air. The weather had grown much colder, and there was a hint of coming frost. The toad took the hint at once and, after hopping a few yards from the door to the edge of a grassy bank, began to prepare for winter. It was a curious proceeding. He went into the ground backward, elbowing himself through the turf with the sharp joints of his hind legs and going down in a spiral manner. His progress was very slow: at night I could still see him by lifting the grass; and as the weather changed again to warm, with southerly winds before morning, he stopped digging entirely. The next day I took him out and put him into a bottomless tub sunk into the ground and filled with soft earth, leaves, and leafmold, where he passed the winter safely and came out fresh and bright in the spring.

The little peeping frogs lead a sort of arboreal life, too, a part of the season, but they are quite different from the true tree toads above described. They appear to leave the marshes in May and to take to the woods or bushes. I have never seen

them on trees, but upon low shrubs. They do not seem to be climbers, but perchers. I caught one in May, in some low bushes a few rods from the swamp. It perched upon the small twigs like a bird and would leap about among them, sure of its hold every time. I was first attracted by its piping. I brought it home, and it piped for one twilight in a bush in my yard and then was gone. I do not think they pipe much after leaving the water. I have found them early in April upon the ground in the woods, and again late in the fall.[3]

One season, the last day of December was very warm. The bees were out of the hive, and there was no frost in the air or in the ground. I was walking in the woods when, as I paused in the shade of a hemlock tree, I heard a sound proceed from beneath the wet leaves on the ground but a few feet from me that suggested a frog. Following it cautiously up, I at last determined upon the exact spot from whence the sound issued; lifting up the thick layer of leaves, there sat a frog — the wood frog, one of the first to appear in the marshes in spring, and which I have elsewhere called the "clucking frog" — in a little excavation in the surface of the leafmold. As it sat there the top of its back was level with the surface of the ground. This, then, was its hibernaculum; here it was prepared to pass the winter, with only a coverlid of wet matted leaves between it and zero weather. Forthwith I set up as a prophet of warm weather and among other things predicted a failure of the ice crop on the river; which, indeed, others who had not heard frogs croak on the 31st of December had also begun to predict. Surely, I thought, this frog knows what it is about; here is the wisdom of nature; it would have gone deeper into the ground than that if a severe winter was approaching; so I was not anxious about my coalbin nor disturbed by longings for Florida. But what a winter followed, the winter of 1885, when the Hudson became coated with ice nearly two feet thick and when March was as cold as January! I thought of my frog under the hemlock and wondered how it was faring. So one day the latter part of March, when the snow was gone and there was a feeling of spring in the air, I turned aside in my walk to investigate it. The matted leaves were still frozen hard, but I succeeded in lifting them up and exposing the frog. There it sat as fresh and unscathed as in the fall. The ground beneath and all about it was still frozen like a rock, but apparently it had some means of its own of resisting the frost. It winked and bowed its head when I touched it but did not seem inclined to leave its retreat. Some days later, after the frost was nearly all out of the ground, I passed that way and found my frog had come out of its seclusion and was resting amid the dry leaves. There was not much jump in it yet, but its color was growing lighter. A few more warm days, and its fellows and doubtless itself too were croaking and gamboling in the marshes.

This incident convinced me of two things, namely, that frogs know no more about the coming weather than we do and that they do not retreat as deep into the ground to pass the winter as has been supposed. I used to think the muskrats could foretell an early and a severe winter, and have so written. But I am now convinced they cannot; they know as little about it as I do. Sometimes on an early and severe frost they seem to get alarmed and go to building their houses, but usually they seem to build early or late, high or low, just as the whim takes them.[4]

12. Bird Study

Years ago, when quite a youth, I was rambling in the woods one Sunday with my brothers gathering black birch, wintergreens, etc., when, as we reclined upon the ground, gazing vaguely up into the trees, I caught sight of a bird that paused a moment on a branch above me, the like of which I had never before seen or heard of. I saw it a moment as the flickering leaves parted, noted the white spot on its wing, and it was gone.* How the thought of it clung to me afterward! It was a revelation. It was the first intimation I had had that the woods we knew so well held birds that we knew not at all. Were our eyes and ears so dull, then? There was the robin, the blue jay, the bluebird, the yellowbird, the cherry bird,† the catbird, the chipping bird, the woodpecker, the highhole, an occasional redbird, and a few others, in the woods or along their borders, but who ever dreamed that there were still others that not even the hunters saw and whose names no one had ever heard?

When, one summer day later in life, I took my gun and went to the woods again in a different though perhaps a less simple spirit, I found my youthful vision more than realized. There were, indeed, other birds, plenty of them, singing, nesting,

---

* Black-throated Blue Warbler. [Ed.]
† Cedar Waxwing. [Ed.]

breeding, among the familiar trees, which I had before passed by unheard and unseen.

It is a surprise that awaits every student of ornithology, and the thrill of delight that accompanies it, and the feeling of fresh, eager inquiry that follows can hardly be awakened by any other pursuit. Take the first step in ornithology, procure one new specimen, and you are ticketed for the whole voyage. There is a fascination about it quite overpowering. It fits so well with other things — with fishing, hunting, farming, walking, camping out — with all that takes one to the fields and woods. One may go a-blackberrying and make some rare discovery; or, while driving his cow to pasture, hear a new song or make a new observation. Secrets lurk on all sides. There is news in every bush. Expectation is ever on tiptoe. What no man ever saw before may the next moment be revealed to you. What a new interest the woods have! How you long to explore every nook and corner of them! You would even find consolation in being lost in them. You could then hear the night birds and the owls and, in your wanderings, might stumble upon some unknown specimen.

In all excursions to the woods or to the shore, the student of ornithology has an advantage over his companions. He has one more resource, one more avenue of delight. He, indeed, kills two birds with one stone and sometimes three. If others wander, he can never go out of his way. His game is everywhere. The cawing of a crow makes him feel at home, while a new note or a new song drowns all care. Audubon, on the desolate coast of Labrador, is happier than any king ever was; and on shipboard is nearly cured of his seasickness when a new gull appears in sight.

One must taste it to understand or appreciate its fascination. The looker-on sees nothing to inspire such enthusiasm. Only a little feathers and a half-musical note or two; why all this ado? "Who would give a hundred and twenty dollars to know about the birds?" said an Eastern governor half contemptuously to Wilson, as the latter solicited a subscription to his great work. Sure enough. Bought knowledge is dear at any price. The most precious things have no commercial value. It is not, your Excellency, mere technical knowledge of the birds that you are asked to purchase but a new interest in the fields and woods, a new moral and intellectual tonic, a new key to the treasure house of nature. Think of the many other things your Excellency would get — the air, the sunshine, the healing fragrance and coolness and the many respites from the knavery and turmoil of political life.[1]

August is the month of the high-sailing hawks. The hen hawk* is the most noticeable. He likes the haze and calm of these long, warm days. He is a bird of leisure and seems always at his ease. How beautiful and majestic are his movements! So self-poised and easy, such an entire absence of haste, such a magnificent amplitude of circles and spirals, such a haughty, imperial grace and, occasionally, such daring aerial evolutions!

With slow, leisurely movement, rarely vibrating his pinions, he mounts and mounts in an ascending spiral till he appears a mere speck against the summer sky; then, if the mood seizes him, with wings half closed like a bent bow he will cleave the air almost perpendicularly, as if intent on dashing himself to pieces against the earth; but on nearing the ground he suddenly mounts again on broad, expanded wing, as if rebounding upon the air, and sails leisurely away. It is the sublimest feat of the season. One holds his breath till he sees him rise again.

The calmness and dignity of this hawk, when attacked by

* One of the Buteo hawks. [Ed.]

crows or the kingbird, are well worthy of him.   He seldom deigns to notice his noisy and furious antagonists but deliberately wheels about in that aerial spiral and mounts and mounts till his pursuers grow dizzy and return to earth again.   It is quite original, this mode of getting rid of an unworthy opponent, rising to heights where the braggart is dazed and bewildered and loses his reckoning!   I am not sure but it is worthy of imitation.[2]

Whir! whir! whir! and a brood of half-grown partridges start up like an explosion a few paces from me and, scattering, disappear in the bushes on all sides. Let me sit down here behind the screen of ferns and briers and hear this wild hen of the woods call together her brood. At what an early age the partridge flies! Nature seems to concentrate her energies on the wing, making the safety of the bird a point to be looked after first; and while the body is covered with down and no signs of feathers are visible, the wing quills sprout and unfold, and in an incredibly short time the young make fair headway in flying.

Hark! there arises over there in the brush a soft, persuasive cooing, a sound so subtle and wild and unobtrusive that it requires the most alert and watchful ear to hear it. How gentle and solicitous and full of yearning love! It is the voice of the mother hen. Presently a faint timid *Yeap!* which almost eludes the ear is heard in various directions — the young responding. As no danger seems near, the cooing of the parent bird is soon a very audible clucking call, and the young move cautiously in the direction. Let me step never so carefully from my hiding place, and all sounds instantly cease and I search in vain for either parent or young.

The partridge is one of our most native and characteristic birds. The woods seem good to be in where I find him. He gives a habitable air to the forest, and one feels as if the right-ful occupant was really at home. The woods where I do not find him seem to want something, as if suffering from some neglect of nature. And then he is such a splendid success, so hardy and vigorous. I think he enjoys the cold and the snow. His wings seem to rustle with more fervency in midwinter. If the snow falls very fast and promises a heavy storm, he will complacently sit down and allow himself to be snowed under. Approaching him at such times, he suddenly bursts out of the snow at your feet, scattering the flakes in all directions, and goes humming away through the woods like a bombshell — a picture of native spirit and success.

His drum is one of the most welcome and beautiful sounds of spring. Scarcely have the trees expanded their buds when, in the still April mornings or toward nightfall, you here the hum of his devoted wings. He selects not, as you would pre-dict, a dry and resinous log but a decayed and crumbling one, seeming to give the preference to old oak logs that are partly blended with the soil. Who has seen the partridge drum? It is the next thing to catching a weasel asleep, though by much caution and tact it may be done. He does not hug the log but stands very erect, expands his ruff, gives two introductory blows, pauses half a second, and then resumes, striking faster and faster till the sound becomes a continuous, unbroken whir, the whole lasting less than half a minute. The tips of his wings barely brush the log,* so that the sound is produced rather by the force of the blows upon the air and upon his own body as in flying. One log will be used for many years, though not by the same drummer. It seems to be a sort of temple and held in great respect. The bird always approaches on foot and leaves it in the same quiet manner, unless rudely disturbed.

At one point in the grayest, most shaggy part of the woods,

* Speed cameras have proved that the grouse does not strike the log. [Ed.]

I came suddenly upon a brood of screech owls, full grown, sitting together upon a dry, moss-draped limb but a few feet from the ground. I pause within four or five yards of them and am looking about me, when my eye alights upon these gray, motionless figures. They sit perfectly upright, some with their backs and some with their breasts toward me, but every head turned squarely in my direction. Their eyes are closed to a mere line; through this crack they are watching me, evidently thinking themselves unobserved. The spectacle is weird and grotesque and suggests something impish and uncanny. It is a new effect, the night side of the woods by daylight. After observing them a moment I take a single step toward them when, quick as thought, their eyes fly wide open, their attitude is changed, they bend, some this way, some that, and, instinct with life and motion, stare wildly around them. Another step, and they take flight but one, which stoops low on the branch and with the look of a frightened cat regards me for a few seconds over its shoulder. They fly swiftly and softly and disperse through the trees. I shot one, which is of a tawny red tint, like that figured by Wilson. It is a singular fact that the plumage of these owls presents two totally distinct phases which "have no relation to sex, age, or season," one being an ashen gray, the other a bright rufus.[3]

The crow may not have the sweet voice which the fox in his flattery attributed to him, but he has a good, strong, native speech nevertheless. How much character there is in it! How much thrift and independence! Of course his plumage is firm, his color decided, his wit quick. He understands you at once and tells you so; so does the hawk by his scornful, defiant *whir-r-r-r.* Hardy, happy outlaw, the crow, how I love him! Alert, social, republican, always able to look out for himself, not

afraid of the cold and the snow, fishing when flesh is scarce and stealing when other resources fail, the crow is a character I would not willingly miss from the landscape. I love to see his track in the snow or the mud and his graceful pedestrianism about the brown fields.

He is no interloper but has the air and manner of being thoroughly at home and in rightful possession of the land. He is no sentimentalist like some of the plaining, disconsolate song-birds but apparently is always in good health and good spirits. No matter who is sick or dejected or unsatisfied, or what the weather is or what the price of corn, the crow is well and finds life sweet. He is the dusky embodiment of worldly wisdom and prudence. Then he is one of nature's self-appointed constables and greatly magnifies his office. He would fain arrest every hawk or owl or grimalkin that ventures abroad. I have known a posse of them to beset the fox and cry "Thief!" till Reynard hid himself for shame. Do I say the fox flattered the crow when he told him he had a sweet voice? Yet one of the most musical sounds in nature proceeds from the crow. All the crow tribe, from the blue jay up, are capable of certain low ventriloquial notes that have peculiar cadence and charm. I often hear the crow indulging in his in winter and am reminded of the sound of the dulcimer. The bird stretches up and exerts himself like a cock in the act of crowing and gives forth a peculiarly clear, vitreous sound that is sure to arrest and reward your attention. This is no doubt the song the fox begged to be favored with, as in delivering it the crow must inevitably let drop the piece of meat.[4]

Among the birds that tarry briefly with us in the spring on their way to Canada and beyond, there is none I behold with so much pleasure as the white-crowned sparrow. I have an eye

out for him all through April and the first week in May. He
is the rarest and most beautiful of the sparrow kind. He is
crowned, as some hero or victor in the games. He is usually
in company with his congener, the white-throated sparrow, but
seldom more than in the proportion of one to twenty of the
latter. Contrasted with this bird, he looks like its more for-
tunate brother, upon whom some special distinction has been
conferred and who is, from the egg, of finer make and quality.
His sparrow color of ashen gray and brown is very clear and
bright, and his form graceful. His whole expression, however,
culminates in a singular manner in his crown. The various
tints of the bird are brought to a focus here and intensified, the
lighter ones becoming white and the deeper ones nearly black.
There is the suggestion of a crest, also, from a habit the bird
has of slightly elevating this part of its plumage, as if to make
more conspicuous its pretty markings. They are great scratch-
ers and will often remain several minutes scratching in one
place, like a hen. Yet, unlike the hen and like all hoppers,
they scratch with both feet at once, which is by no means the
best way to scratch.

The whitethroats often sing during their sojourning in both
fall and spring; but only on one occasion have I ever heard
any part of the song of the white-crowned, and that proceeded
from what I took to be a young male, one October morning
just as the sun was rising. It was pitched very low, like a half-
forgotten air, but it was very sweet. It was the song of the
vesper sparrow and the whitethroat in one. In his breeding
haunts he must be a superior songster, but he is very chary of
his music while on his travels.[5]

The bird that seems to consider he has the best right to
the bone both upon the tree and upon the sill is the downy
woodpecker, my favorite neighbor among the winter birds. His

retreat is but a few paces from my own, in the decayed limb of an apple tree which he excavated several autumns ago. I say "he" because the red plume on the top of his head proclaims the sex. It seems not to be generally known to our writers upon ornithology that certain of our woodpeckers — probably all the winter residents — each fall excavate a limb or the trunk of a tree in which to pass the winter, and that the cavity is abandoned in the spring, probably for a new one in which nidification takes place. So far as I have observed, these cavities are drilled out only by the males. Where the females take up their quarters I am not so well informed, though I suspect that they use the abandoned holes of the males of the previous year.

The particular woodpecker to which I refer drilled his first hole in my apple tree one fall four or five years ago. This he occupied till the following spring, when he abandoned it. The next fall he began a hole in an adjoining limb, later than before, and when it was about half completed a female took possession of his old quarters. I am sorry to say that this seemed to enrage the male very much, and he persecuted the poor bird whenever she appeared upon the scene. He would fly at her spitefully and drive her off.

My bird is a genuine little savage, doubtless, but I value him as a neighbor. It is a satisfaction during the cold or stormy winter nights to know he is warm and cozy there in his retreat. When the day is bad and unfit to be abroad in, he is there too. When I wish to know if he is at home, I go and rap upon his tree, and if he is not too lazy or indifferent, after some delay he shows his head in his round doorway about ten feet above and looks down inquiringly upon me — sometimes latterly I think half resentfully, as much as to say, "I would thank you not to disturb me so often." After sundown, he will not put his head out any more when I call, but as I step away I can get a glimpse of him inside looking cold and reserved. He is a late riser, especially if it is a cold or disagreeable morning, in this respect being like the barn fowls; it is sometimes near nine o'clock before I see him leave his tree. On the other hand, he comes home early, being in, if the day is unpleasant, by four P.M. He lives all alone; in this respect I do not commend his example. Where his mate is, I should like to know.

Did you think that loud, sonorous hammering which proceeded from the orchard or from the near woods on that still March or April morning was only some bird getting its breakfast? It is downy, but he is not rapping at the door of a grub; he is rapping at the door of spring, and the dry limb thrills beneath the ardor of his blows. Or, later in the season, in the dense forest or by some remote mountain lake, does that measured rhythmic beat that breaks upon the silence, first three strokes following each other rapidly, succeeded by two louder ones with longer intervals between them, and that has an effect upon the alert ear as if the solitude itself had at last found a voice — does that suggest anything less than a deliberate musical performance? In fact, our woodpeckers are just as characteristically drummers as is the ruffed grouse, and they have their particular limbs and stubs to which they resort for that purpose. Their need of expression is apparently just as great as that of the songbirds, and it is not surprising that they should have found out that there is music in a dry, seasoned limb which can be evoked beneath their beaks.

A few seasons ago a downy woodpecker, probably the individual one who is now my winter neighbor, began to drum early in March in a partly decayed apple tree that stands in the edge of a narrow strip of woodland near me. When the morning was still and mild I would often hear him through my window before I was up, or by half-past six o'clock, and he would keep it up pretty briskly till nine or ten o'clock, in this respect resembling the grouse, which do most of their drumming in the forenoon. His drum was the stub of a dry limb about the size of one's wrist. The heart was decayed and gone, but the outer shell was hard and resonant. The bird would keep his position there for an hour at a time. Between his drummings he would preen his plumage and listen as if for the response of the female or for the drum of some rival. How swift his head would go when he was delivering his blows upon the limb! His beak wore the surface perceptibly. When he wished to change the key, which was quite often, he would shift his position an inch or two to a knot which gave out a higher, shriller note. When I climbed up to examine his drum he was much disturbed. I did not know he was in the vicinity, but it seems he saw me from a near tree and came in haste to the neighboring branches and with spread plumage and a sharp note demanded plainly enough what my business was with his drum. I was invading his privacy, desecrating his shrine, and the bird was much put out.[6]

Beside my path in the woods a downy woodpecker late one fall drilled a hole in the top of a small dead black birch for his winter quarters. My attention was first called to his doings by the white chips upon the ground. Every day as I passed I would rap upon his tree, and if he was in he would appear at his door and ask plainly enough what I wanted now. One day when I rapped, something else appeared at the door — I could not make out what. I continued my rapping, when out came two flying squirrels. On the tree being given a vigorous shake, it broke off at the hole, and the squirrels went sliding down the air to the foot of a hemlock, up which they disappeared. They had dispossessed Downy of his house, had carried in some grass and leaves for a nest, and were as snug as a bug in a rug. Downy drilled another cell in a dead oak farther up the hill and, I hope, passed the winter there unmolested. Such incidents, comic or tragic, as they chance to strike us, are happening all about us, if we have eyes to see them.

The next season, near sundown of a late November day, I saw Downy trying to get possession of a hole not his own. I chanced to be passing under a maple, when white chips upon the ground again caused me to scrutinize the branches overhead. Just then I saw Downy come to the tree and, hopping around on the under side of a large dry limb, begin to make passes at something with his beak. Presently I made out a round hole there, with something in it returning Downy's thrusts. The sparring continued some moments. Downy would hop away a few feet then return to the attack, each time to be met by the occupant of the hole. I suspected an English sparrow had taken possession of Downy's cell in his absence during the day, but I was wrong. Downy flew to another branch, and I tossed up a stone against the one that contained the hole when, with a sharp, steely note, out came a hairy woodpecker and alighted on a nearby branch. Downy, then, had the "cheek" to try to turn his large rival out of doors — and it was Hairy's cell, too; one could see that by the size of the entrance. Thus loosely does the rule of *meum* and *tuum* obtain in the woods. There is no moral code in nature. Might reads right. Man in communities has evolved ethical standards of conduct, but nations, in their dealings with one another, are still largely in a state of savage nature and seek to establish the right, as dogs do, by the appeal to battle.[7]

Nature is not always consistent; she does not always choose the best means to a given end. For instance, all the wrens ex-

cept our house wren seem to use about the best material at
hand for their nests. What can be more unsuitable, untrac-
table, for a nest in a hole or cavity than the twigs the house wren
uses? Dry grasses or bits of soft bark would bend and adapt
themselves easily to the exigencies of the case; but stiff, un-
yielding twigs! What a contrast to the suitableness of the
material the hummingbird uses — the down of some plant,
which seems to have a poetic fitness!

Probably we have no other familiar bird keyed up to the
same degree of intensity as the house wren. He seems to be
the one bird whose cup of life is always overflowing. The wren
is habitually in an ecstasy either of delight or of rage. He probably gets on the nerves of more persons than any other of our
birds. He is so shrilly and overflowingly joyous, or else so
sharply and harshly angry and pugnacious — a lyrical burst
one minute and a volley of chiding, staccato notes the next.
More restless than the wind, he is a tiny dynamo of bird energy.
From his appearance in May till his last brood is out in midsummer, he repeats his shrill, hurried little strain about ten
times a minute for about ten hours a day and cackles and chatters between times. He expends enough energy in giving expression to his happiness or vent to his anger, in the course of
each day, to carry him halfway to the Gulf. He sputters, he
chatters, he carols; he excites the wrath of bluebirds, phœbes,
orioles, robins; he darts into holes; he bobs up in unexpected
places; he nests in old hats, in dinner pails, in pumps, in old
shoes. Give him a twig and a feather and a hole in almost anything, and his cup is full. How absurdly happy he is over a
few dry twigs there in that box, and his little freckled mate
sitting upon her eggs! His throat swells and throbs as if he
had all the winds of Æolus imprisoned in it, and the little
tempest of joy in there rages all the time. His song goes off

as suddenly as if someone had touched a spring or switched on a current. If feathers can have a feathered edge, the wren has it.

It repeats its song at least six thousand times a day for two or three months, at the same time that it brings many scores of insects to feed its young. But this activity does not use up all the energy of the wren. He gets rid of some of the surplus in building cock, or sham, nests in every unoccupied bird box near him. He fills the cavities up with twigs, and I have even seen him carry food into these sham nests, playing that he had young there. (I saw him do it yesterday, July 7th; he held in his beak what seemed to be a small green worm.) Not even these activities use up all his energy; it overflows in his shaking and vibrating wings while in song.

The song of the house wren is rather harsh and shrill, far inferior as a musical performance to that of the winter wren. The songs of the two differ as their nests differ, or as soft green moss and feathers differ from dry twigs and a little dry grass. A truly sylvan strain is that of the winter wren, suggesting deep wildwood solitudes, while that of the house wren is more in keeping with the noise and clatter of the farm and dooryard. He begins singing by or before four o'clock in the morning and for the first hour hardly stops to take breath, and all the forenoon the pauses between his volleys of notes are of but a few seconds.

This season there are four wrens' nests about my place, in hollow limbs and boxes which we have put up, and three blue-birds' nests. The wrens and the bluebirds often come into collision; mainly, I think, because they are rivals for the same nesting sites. The bluebird, with all his soft, plaintive notes, has a marked vein of pugnacity in him and is at times a lively "scrapper"; and the wren is no "peace-at-any-price" bird and will stand up for his rights very bravely against his big blue-coated rival.[8]

It would be interesting to know how long our chimney swifts saw the open chimney stacks of the early settlers beneath them before they abandoned the hollow trees in the woods and entered the chimneys for nesting and roosting purposes. Was the act an act of judgment or simply an unreasoning impulse, like so much else in the lives of the wild creatures?

In the choice of nesting material the swift shows no change of habit. She still snips off the small dry twigs from the tree tops and glues them together, and to the side of the chimney, with her own glue. The soot is a new obstacle in her way that she does not yet seem to have learned to overcome, as the rains often loosen it and cause her nest to fall to the bottom.

She has a pretty way of trying to frighten you off when your head suddenly darkens the opening above her. At such times she leaves the nest and clings to the side of the chimney near it. Then, slowly raising her wings, she suddenly springs out from the wall and back again, making as loud a drumming with them in the passage as she is capable of. If this does not frighten you away, she repeats it three or four times. If your face still hovers above her, she remains quiet and watches you.

What a creature of the air this bird is, never touching the ground, so far as I know, and never tasting earthly food! The swallow does perch now and then and descend to the ground for nesting material; but the swift, I have reason to believe, even outrides the summer storms, facing them on steady wing, high in air. The twigs for her nest she gathers on the wing, sweeping along like children on a merry-go-round who try to seize a ring or to do some other feat as they pass a given point. If the swift misses the twig, or it fails to yield to her the first time, she tries again and again, each time making a wider circuit, as if to tame and train her steed a little and bring him up more squarely to the mark next time.

The swift is a stiff flyer: there appear to be no joints in her

wings; she suggests something made of wires or of steel. Yet
the air of frolic and of superabundance of wing power is more
marked with her than with any other of our birds. Her feeding
and twig gathering seem like asides in a life of endless play.
Several times both in spring and fall I have seen swifts gather
in immense numbers toward nightfall, to take refuge in large,
unused chimney stacks. On such occasions they seem to be
coming together for some aerial festival or grand celebration;
and, as if bent upon a final effort to work off a part of their
superabundant wing power before settling down for the night,
they circle and circle high above the chimney top, a great cloud
of them, drifting this way and that, all in high spirits and chippering as they fly. Their numbers constantly increase as other
members of the clan come dashing in from all points of the
compass. Swifts seem to materialize out of empty air on all
sides of the chippering, whirling ring, as an hour or more this
assembling of the clan and this flight festival go on. The birds
must gather in from whole counties, or from half a State. They
have been on the wing all day, and yet now they seem as tireless
as the wind and as if unable to curb their powers.

One fall they gathered in this way and took refuge for the
night in a large chimney stack in a city near me, for more than
a month and a half. Several times I went to town to witness
the spectacle, and a spectacle it was: ten thousand of them, I
should think, filling the air above a whole square like a whirling swarm of huge black bees but saluting the ear with a
multitudinous chippering, instead of a humming. People
gathered upon the sidewalks to see them. It was a rare circus
performance, free to all. After a great many feints and playful
approaches the whirling ring of birds would suddenly grow
denser above the chimney; then a stream of them, as if drawn
down by some power of suction, would pour into the opening.

For only a few seconds would this downward rush continue; then, as if the spirit of frolic had again got the upper hand of them, the ring would rise, and the chippering and circling go on. In a minute or two the same manœuvre would be repeated, the chimney, as it were, taking its swallows at intervals to prevent choking. It usually took a half hour or more for the birds all to disappear down its capacious throat. There was always an air of timidity and irresolution about their approach to the chimney, just as there always is about their approach to the dead treetop from which they procure their twigs for nest building. Often did I see birds hesitate above the opening and then pass on, apparently as though they had not struck it at just the right angle. On one occasion a solitary bird was left flying, and it took three or four trials either to make up its mind or to catch the trick of the descent. On dark or threatening or stormy days the birds would begin to assemble by midafternoon, and by four or five o'clock were all in their lodgings.

The chimney is a capacious one, forty or fifty feet high and nearly three feet square, yet it did not seem adequate to afford breathing space for so many birds. I was curious to know how they disposed themselves inside. At the bottom was a small opening. Holding my ear to it, I could hear a continuous chippering and humming, as if the birds were still all in motion, like an agitated beehive. At nine o'clock this multitudinous sound of wings and voices was still going on and doubtless it was kept up all night. What was the meaning of it? Was the press of birds so great that they needed to keep their wings moving to ventilate the shaft, as do certain of the bees in a crowded hive? Or were these restless spirits unable to fold their wings even in sleep? I was very curious to get a peep inside that chimney when the swifts were in it. So one afternoon this opportunity was afforded me by the removal of the large smoke pipe of

the old steam boiler. This left an opening into which I could
thrust my head and shoulders. The sound of wings and voices
filled the hollow shaft. On looking up, I saw the sides of the
chimney for about half its length paved with the restless birds;
they sat so close together that their bodies touched. Moreover,
a large number of them were constantly on the wing, showing
against the sky light as if they were leaving the chimney. But
they did not leave it. They rose up a few feet and then resumed their positions upon the sides, and it was this movement
that caused the humming sound. All the while the droppings
of the birds came down like a summer shower. At the bottom
of the shaft was a mine of guano three or four feet deep, with a
dead swift here and there upon it. Probably one or more birds
out of such a multitude died every night. I had fancied there
would be many more. It was a long time before it dawned
upon me what this uninterrupted flight within the chimney
meant. Finally I saw that it was a sanitary measure: only thus
could the birds keep from soiling each other with their droppings. Birds digest very rapidly, and had they all continued to
cling to the sides of the wall, they would have been in a sad predicament before morning. Like other acts of cleanliness on
the part of birds, this was doubtless the prompting of instinct
and not of judgment. It was nature looking out for her own.[9]

One of the new pleasures of country life when one has made
the acquaintance of the birds is to witness the northward bird
procession as it passes or tarries with us in the spring — a procession which lasts from April till June and has some new
feature daily.

The migrating wild creatures, whether birds or beasts,
always arrest the attention. They seem to link up animal life
with the great currents of the globe. It is moving day on a

continental scale. It is the call of the primal instinct to increase and multiply, suddenly setting in motion whole tribes and races. The first phœbe bird, the first song sparrow, the first robin or bluebird in March or early April, is like the first ripple of the rising tide on the shore.

In my boyhood the vast armies of the passenger pigeons were one of the most notable spring tokens. Often late in March or early in April the naked beechwoods would suddenly become blue with them and vocal with their soft, childlike calls; or all day the sky would be streaked with the long lines or dense masses of the moving armies. The last great flight of them that I ever beheld was on the 10th of April, 1875, when, for the greater part of the day, one could not at any movement look skyward above the Hudson River Valley without seeing several flocks, great and small, of the migrating birds. But that spectacle was never repeated as it had been for generations before. The pigeons never came back. Death and destruction, in the shape of the greed and cupidity of man, were on their trail. The hosts were pursued from State to State by professional pothunters and netters, and the numbers so reduced and their flocking instinct so disorganized that their vast migrating bands disappeared, and they were seen only in loosely scattered and diminishing flocks in different parts of the West during the remainder of the century. A friend of mine shot a few in Indiana in the early eighties, and scattered bands of them have occasionally been reported, here and there, up to within a few years. The last time that my eyes beheld a passenger pigeon was in the fall of 1876 when I was out for grouse. I saw a solitary cock sitting in a tree. I killed it, little dreaming that, so far as I was concerned, I was killing the last pigeon.

What man now in his old age who witnessed in youth that spring or fall festival and migration of the passenger pigeons would not hail it as one of the gladdest hours of his life if he could be permitted to witness it once more? It was such a spectacle of bounty, of joyous, copious animal life, of fertility in the air and in the wilderness, as to make the heart glad. I have seen the fields and woods fairly inundated for a day or two with these fluttering, piping, blue-and-white hosts. The very air at times seemed suddenly to turn to pigeons.[10]

13. Bird Song—a Challenge

J UNE, OF all the months, the student of ornithology can least afford to lose. Most birds are nesting then, and in full song and plumage. And what is a bird without its song? Do we not wait for the stranger to speak? It seems to me that I do not know a bird till I have heard its voice; then I come nearer it at once, and it possesses a human interest to me. I have met the gray-cheeked thrush in the woods and held him in my hand; still I do not know him. The silence of the cedarbird throws a mystery about him which neither his good looks nor his petty larcenies in cherry time can dispel. A bird's song contains a clew to its life and establishes a sympathy, an understanding, between itself and the listener.

I descend a steep hill and approach the hemlocks through a large sugarbush. When twenty rods distant, I hear all along the line of the forest the incessant warble of the red-eyed vireo, cheerful and happy as the merry whistle of a schoolboy. He is one of our most common and widely distributed birds. Approach any forest at any hour of the day, in any kind of weather, from May to August, in any of the Middle or Eastern districts, and the chances are that the first note you hear will be his. Rain or shine, before noon or after, in the deep forest or in the village grove — when it is too hot for the thrushes or too cold and windy for the warblers — it is never out of time or place

for this little minstrel to indulge his cheerful strain. In the
deep wilds of the Adirondacks, where few birds are seen and
fewer heard, his note was almost constantly in my ear. Always
busy, making it a point never to suspend for one moment his
occupation to indulge his musical taste, his lay is that of industry and contentment. There is nothing plaintive or
especially musical in his performance, but the sentiment expressed is eminently that of cheerfulness. Indeed, the songs of
most birds have some human significance, which, I think, is the
source of the delight we take in them.[1]

The songbirds might all have been brooded and hatched in
the human heart. They are typical of its highest aspirations,
and nearly the whole gamut of human passion and emotion is
expressed more or less fully in their varied songs. Among our
own birds there is the song of the hermit thrush for devoutness
and religious serenity; that of the wood thrush for the musing,
melodious thoughts of twilight; the song sparrow's for simple
faith and trust, the bobolink's for hilarity and glee, the mourn-
ing dove's for hopeless sorrow, the vireo's for all-day and everyday contentment, and the nocturne of the mockingbird for
love. Then there are the plaintive singers, the soaring, ecstatic
singers, the confident singers, the gushing and voluble singers,
and the half-voiced, inarticulate singers. The note of the wood
pewee is a human sigh; the chickadee has a call full of unspeak-
able tenderness and fidelity. There is pride in the song of the
tanager, and vanity in that of the catbird. There is something
distinctly human about the robin; his is the note of boyhood.[2]

Some birds passing north in the spring are provokingly
silent. Every April I see the hermit thrush hopping about the
woods and in case of a sudden snowstorm seeking shelter about

the outbuildings; but I never hear even a fragment of his wild, silvery strain.   The fox sparrow, who passes earlier (sometimes in March), is also chary of the music with which he is so richly endowed.   It is not every season that I hear him, though my ear is on the alert for his strong, finely modulated whistle.

Nearly all the warblers sing in passing.   I hear them in the orchards, in the groves, in the woods, as they pause to feed in their northward journey, their brief, lisping, shuffling, insect-like notes requiring to be searched for by the ear, as their forms by the eye.[3]

A very interesting feature of our bird songs is the wing song, or song of ecstasy.   It is not the gift of many of our birds.   Indeed, less than a dozen species are known to me as ever singing on the wing.   It seems to spring from more intense excitement and self-abandonment than the ordinary song delivered from the perch.   When its joy reaches the point of rapture, the bird is literally carried off its feet, and up it goes into the air, pouring out its song as a rocket pours out its sparks.   The skylark and the bobolink habitually do this, while a few others of our birds do it only on occasions.   One summer, up in the Catskills, I added another name to my list of ecstatic singers — that of the vesper sparrow.   Several times I heard a new song in the air and caught a glimpse of the bird as it dropped back to the earth.   My attention would be attracted by a succession of hurried chirping notes, followed by a brief burst of song then by the vanishing form of the bird.   One day I was lucky enough to see the bird as it was rising to its climax in the air and to identify it as the vesper sparrow.   The burst of song that crowned the upward flight of seventy-five or one hundred feet was brief; but it was brilliant and striking and entirely unlike the leisurely chant of the bird while upon the ground.   It suggested a lark but was less buzzing or humming. The preliminary chirping notes, uttered faster and faster as the bird mounted in the air, were like the trail of sparks which a rocket emits before its grand burst of color at the top of its flight.

Probably the perch songster among our ordinary birds that is most regularly seized with the fit of ecstasy that results in this lyric burst in the air, as I described in my first book, *Wake-Robin,* over thirty years ago, is the ovenbird,* or wood accentor — the golden-crowned thrush of the old ornithologists.[4]

Coming to a drier and less mossy place in the woods, I am amused with the golden-crowned thrush — which, however, is no thrush at all but a warbler. He walks on the ground ahead of me with such an easy gliding motion and with such an unconscious, preoccupied air, jerking his head like a hen or a partridge, now hurrying, now slackening his pace, that I pause to observe him. I sit down, he pauses to observe me and extends his pretty ramblings on all sides, apparently very much engrossed with his own affairs but never losing sight of me. But few of the birds are walkers, most being hoppers, like the robin.

Satisfied that I have no hostile intentions, the pretty pedestrian mounts a limb a few feet from the ground and gives me the benefit of one of his musical performances, a sort of accelerating chant. Commencing in a very low key, which makes him seem at a very uncertain distance, he grows louder and louder till his body quakes and his chant runs into a shriek, ringing in my ear with a peculiar sharpness. This lay may be represented thus: "Teacher, *teacher,* TEACHER, TEACHER, *TEACHER!*" — the accent on the first syllable and each word uttered with increased force and shrillness. No writer with whom I am

* Whose song is described in *Wake-Robin.* [Ed.]

acquainted gives him credit for more musical ability than is displayed in this strain. Yet in this the half is not told. He has a far rarer song, which he reserves for some nymph whom he meets in the air. Mounting by easy flights to the top of the tallest tree, he launches into the air with a sort of suspended, hovering flight, like certain of the finches, and bursts into a perfect ecstasy of song — clear, ringing, copious, rivaling the goldfinch's in vivacity and the linnet's in melody. This strain is one of the rarest bits of bird melody to be heard and is oftenest indulged in late in the afternoon or after sundown. Over the woods, hid from view, the ecstatic singer warbles his finest strain.

Passing down through the maple arches, barely pausing to observe the antics of a trio of squirrels — two gray ones and a black one — I cross an ancient brush fence and am fairly within the old hemlocks and in one of the most primitive, undisturbed nooks. In the deep moss I tread as with muffled feet, and the pupils of my eyes dilate in the dim, almost religious light. The irreverent red squirrels, however, run and snicker at my approach or mock the solitude with their ridiculous chattering and frisking.

This nook is the chosen haunt of the winter wren. This is the only place and these the only woods in which I find him in this vicinity. His voice fills these dim aisles, as if aided by some marvelous sounding board. Indeed, his song is very strong for so small a bird and unites in a remarkable degree brilliancy and plaintiveness. I think of a tremulous vibrating tongue of silver. You may know it is the song of a wren, from its gushing lyrical character; but you must needs look sharp to see the little minstrel, especially while in the act of singing. He is nearly the color of the ground and the leaves; he never ascends the tall trees but keeps low, flitting from stump to stump and from root to root, dodging in and out of his hiding places and watching all intruders with a suspicious eye. He has a very pert, almost comical look. His tail stands more than perpendicular: it points straight toward his head. He is the least ostentatious singer I know of. He does not strike an attitude and lift up his head in preparation and, as it were, clear his throat; but sits there on a log and pours out his music, looking straight before him or even down at the ground. As a songster, he has but few superiors. I do not hear him after the first week in July.

Ever since I entered the woods, even while listening to the lesser songsters or contemplating the silent forms about me, a strain has reached my ears from out the depths of the forest that to me is the finest sound in nature — the song of the hermit thrush. I often hear him thus a long way off, sometimes over a quarter of a mile away, when only the stronger and more perfect parts of his music reach me; and through the general chorus of wrens and warblers I detect this sound rising pure and serene, as if a spirit from some remote height were slowly chanting a divine accompaniment. This song appeals to the sentiment of the beautiful in me and suggests a serene religious beatitude as no other sound in nature does. It is perhaps more of an evening than a morning hymn, though I hear it at all hours of the day. It is very simple, and I can hardly tell the secret of its charm. *O spheral, spheral!* he seems to say; *O holy, holy! O clear away, clear away! O clear up, clear up!* interspersed with the finest trills and the most delicate preludes. It is not a proud, gorgeous strain, like the tanager's or the grosbeak's; suggests no passion or emotion — nothing personal — but seems to be the voice of that calm, sweet solemnity one attains to in his best moments. It realizes a peace and a deep, solemn joy that only the finest souls may know. A few

nights ago I ascended a mountain to see the world by moonlight, and when near the summit the hermit commenced his
evening hymn a few rods from me. Listening to this strain on
the lone mountain, with the full moon just rounded from the
horizon, the pomp of your cities and the pride of your civilization seemed trivial and cheap.[5]

THE HERMIT THRUSH

In the primal forest's hush,
Listen! . . . the hermit thrush!
Silver cords of purest sound
Pealing through the depths profound,
Tranquil rapture, unafraid
In the fragrant shade.

A dapper bird that sulks and hides,
Now courtsying on a mossy stone,
Then ducking 'neath a tree-trunk prone;
Pert his mien, his wonderous throat
Quivers and throbs with rapid note —
A lyric burst with power imbued
To thrill and shake the solitude.

If we take the quality of melody as the test, the wood thrush,
hermit thrush, and the veery thrush stand at the head of our
list of songsters. The emotions excited by the songs of these
thrushes belong to a higher order, springing as they do from
our deepest sense of the beauty and harmony of the world.

The wood thrush is worthy of all, and more than all, the
praises he has received; and considering the number of his
appreciative listeners, it is not a little surprising that his rela-
tive and equal, the hermit thrush, should have received so
little notice. Both the great ornithologists, Wilson and Audubon, are lavish in their praises of the former but have little or

nothing to say of the song of the latter. Audubon says it is
sometimes agreeable but evidently has never heard it. Nuttall,
I am glad to find, is more discriminating and does the bird
fuller justice.

The cast of its song is very much like that of the wood thrush,
and a good observer might easily confound the two. But hear
them together and the difference is quite marked: the song of
the hermit is in a higher key and is more wild and ethereal.
His instrument is a silver horn which he winds in the most
solitary places. The song of the wood thrush is more golden
and leisurely. Its tone comes near to that of some rare stringed
instrument. One feels that perhaps the wood thrush has more
compass and power, if he would only let himself out, but on
the whole he comes a little short of the pure, serene, hymnlike
strain of the hermit.

Yet those who have heard only the wood thrush may well
place him first on the list. He is truly a royal minstrel and,
considering his liberal distribution throughout our Atlantic
seaboard, perhaps contributes more than any other bird to
our sylvan melody. One may object that he spends a little too
much time in tuning his instrument, yet his careless and uncertain touches reveal its rare compass and power.[6]

We have no well-known pastoral bird in the Eastern States
that answers to the skylark. The American pipit or titlark and
the shore lark, both birds of the far north, and seen in the States
only in fall and winter, are said to sing on the wing in a similar
strain.

Throughout the northern and eastern parts of the Union
the lark would find a dangerous rival in the bobolink, a bird
that has no European prototype and no near relatives anywhere, standing quite alone, unique and, in the qualities of

hilarity and musical tintinnabulation, with a song unequaled. He has already a secure place in general literature, having been laureated by a no less poet than Bryant and invested with a lasting human charm in the sunny pages of Irving, and is the only one of our songsters, I believe, the mockingbird cannot parody or imitate. He affords the most marked example of exuberant pride and a glad, rollicking, holiday spirit that can be seen among our birds. Every note expresses complacency and glee. He is a beau of the first pattern and, unlike any other bird of my acquaintance, pushes his gallantry to the point of wheeling gayly into the train of every female that comes along, even after the season of courtship is over and the matches all settled; and when she leads him on too wild a chase, he turns lightly about and breaks out with a song that is precisely analogous to a burst of gay and self-satisfied laughter, as much as to say, *Ha! ha! ha! I must have my fun, Miss Silverthimble, thimble, thimble, if I break every heart in the meadow, see, see, see!*

At the approach of the breeding season the bobolink undergoes a complete change; his form changes, his color changes, his flight changes. From mottled brown or brindle he becomes black and white, earning in some localities the shocking name of "skunk bird"; his small, compact form becomes broad and conspicuous, and his ordinary flight is laid aside for a mincing, affected gait, in which he seems to use only the very tips of his wings. It is very noticeable what a contrast he presents to his mate at this season, not only in color but in manners, she being as shy and retiring as he is forward and hilarious. Indeed, she seems disagreeably serious and indisposed to any fun or jollity, scurrying away at his approach and apparently annoyed at every endearing word and look. It is surprising that all this parade of plumage and tinkling of cymbals should be gone through with and persisted in to please a creature so coldly indifferent as she really seems to be. If Robert O'Lincoln has been stimulated into acquiring this holiday uniform and this musical gift by the approbation of Mrs. Robert, as Darwin, with his sexual selection principle, would have us believe, then there must have been a time when the females of this tribe were not quite so chary of their favors as they are now. Indeed, I never knew a female bird of any kind that did not appear utterly indifferent to the charms of voice and plumage that the male birds are so fond of displaying. But I am inclined to believe that the males think only of themselves and of out-shining each other and not at all of the approbation of their mates, as, in an analogous case in a higher species, it is well known whom the females dress for and whom they want to kill with envy!

Numerous others of our birds would seem to challenge attention by their calls and notes. There is the Maryland yellow-throat, for instance, standing in the door of his bushy tent and calling out as you approach, *which way, sir! which way, sir!* If he says this to the ear of common folk, what would he not say to the poet? One of the pewees says *stay there!* with great emphasis. The cardinal grosbeak calls out *what cheer, what cheer;* the bluebird says *purity, purity, purity;* the brown thrasher, or ferruginous thrush, according to Thoreau, calls out to the farmer planting his corn *drop it, drop it, cover it up, cover it up.* The yellow-breasted chat says *who, who,* and *tea-boy.* What the robin says, caroling that simple strain from the top of the tall maple, or the crow with his hardy *haw-haw,* or the pedestrian meadow lark sounding his piercing and long-drawn note in the spring meadows, the poets ought to be able to tell us. I only know the birds all have a language which is very expressive and which is easily translatable into the human tongue.[7]

I have observed numerous song sparrows with songs peculiarly their own. Last season, the whole summer through, one sang about my grounds like this: *swee-e-t, swee-e-t, swee-e-t, bitter.* Day after day from May to September I heard this strain, which I thought a simple but very profound summing up of life, and wondered how the little bird had learned it so quickly. The present season, I heard another with a song equally original but not so easily worded. Among a large troop of them in April, my attention was attracted to one that was a master songster — some Shelley or Tennyson among his kind. The strain was remarkably prolonged, intricate, and animated and far surpassed anything I ever before heard from that source.

But the most noticeable instance of departure from the standard song of a species I ever knew of was in the case of a wood thrush. The bird sang, as did the sparrow, the whole season through, at the foot of my lot near the river. The song began correctly and ended correctly; but interjected into it about midway was a loud, piercing, artificial note at utter variance with the rest of the strain. When my ear first caught this singular note, I started out, not a little puzzled, to make, as I supposed, a new acquaintance, but had not gone far when I discovered whence it proceeded. Brass amid gold, or pebbles amid pearls are not more out of place than was this discordant scream or cry in the melodious strain of the wood thrush. It pained and startled the ear. It seemed as if the instrument of the bird was not under control, or else that one note was sadly out of tune, and when its turn came, instead of giving forth one of those sounds that are indeed like pearls, it shocked the ear with a piercing discord. Yet the singer appeared entirely unconscious of the defect; or had he grown used to it, or had his friends persuaded him that it was a variation to be coveted? Sometimes, after the brood had hatched and the bird's pride was at its full, he would make a little triumphal tour of the locality, coming from under the hill quite up to the house and flaunting his cracked instrument in the face of whoever would listen. He did not return again the next season; or, if he did, the malformation of his song was gone.

A prominent April bird that one does not have to go to the woods or away from his own door to see and hear, is the hardy and ever-welcome meadow lark. What a twang there is about this bird, and what vigor! It smacks of the soil. It is the winged embodiment of the spirit of our spring meadows. What emphasis in its *z-d-t, z-d-t,* and what character in its long, piercing note! Its straight, tapering sharp beak is typical of its voice. Its note goes like a shaft from a crossbow; it is a little too sharp and piercing when near at hand, but heard in the proper perspective it is eminently melodious and pleasing. It is one of the major notes of the fields at this season. In fact, it easily dominates all others. *Spring o' the year! spring o' the year!* it says, with a long-drawn breath, a little plaintive but not complaining or melancholy. At times it indulges in something much more intricate and larklike while hovering on the wing in mid-air, but a song is beyond the compass of its instrument, and the attempt usually ends in a breakdown. A clear, sweet, strong, high-keyed note, uttered from some knoll or rock or stake in the fence, is its proper vocal performance.[8]

14. Birds' Nests

Birds'-nesting is by no means a failure, even though you find no birds' nests. You are sure to find other things of interest, plenty of them. A friend of mine says that in his youth he used to go hunting with his gun loaded for wild turkeys, and though he frequently saw plenty of smaller game, he generally came home empty-handed, because he was loaded only for turkeys. But the student of ornithology, who is also a lover of nature in all her shows and forms, does not go out loaded for turkeys merely, but for everything that moves or grows, and is quite sure, therefore, to bag some game, if not with his gun then with his eye or his nose or his ear. Even a crow's nest is not amiss, or a den in the rocks where the coons or the skunks live, or a log where a partridge drums, or the partridge himself starting up with spread tail and walking a few yards in advance of you before he goes humming through the woods, or a woodchuck hole, with well-beaten and worn entrance and with the saplings gnawed and soiled about it, or the strong, fetid smell of the fox, which a sharp nose detects here and there and which is a good perfume in the woods. And then it is enough to come upon a spring in the woods and stoop down and drink of the sweet, cold water and bathe your hands in it, or to walk along a trout brook which has absorbed the shadows till it has itself become but a denser shade. Then I am always drawn out of my way by a ledge of rocks and love nothing better than to explore the caverns and dens, or to sit down under the overhanging crags and let the wild scene absorb me.

There is a fascination about ledges! They are an unmistakable feature and give emphasis and character to the scene. I feel their spell and must pause awhile. Time, old as the hills and older, looks out of their scarred and weatherworn face. The woods are of today, but the ledges, in comparison, are of eternity. One pokes about them as he would about ruins, and with something of the same feeling. They are ruins of the fore world. Here the foundations of the hills were laid; here the earth giants wrought and builded. They constrain one to silence and meditation; the whispering and rustling trees seem trivial and impertinent.

And then there are birds' nests about ledges, too, exquisite mossy tenements with white, pebbly eggs, that I can never gaze upon without emotion. The little brown bird, the phœbe, looks at you from her niche till you are within a few feet of her, when she darts away. Occasionally you may find the nest of some rare wood warbler forming a little pocket in the apron of moss that hangs down over the damp rocks.

But I am making slow headway toward finding the birds' nests, for I had set out on this occasion in hopes of finding a rare nest—the nest of the black-throated blue-backed warbler,* which, it seemed, with one or two others was still wanting to make the history of our warblers complete. The woods were extensive and full of deep, dark tangles, and looking for any particular nest seemed about as hopeless a task as searching for a needle in a haystack, as the old saying is. Where to begin, and how? But the principle is the same as in looking for a hen's nest — first find your bird, then watch its movements.

* Now called black-throated blue warbler. [Ed.]

Before long, just as we were about to plunge down a hill into a dense, swampy part of the woods, we discovered a pair of the birds we were in quest of. They had food in their beaks and, as we paused, showed great signs of alarm, indicating that the nest was in the immediate vicinity. This was enough. We would pause here and find this nest, anyhow. To make a sure thing of it, we determined to watch the parent birds till we had wrung from them their secret. So we doggedly crouched down and watched them, and they watched us. It was diamond cut diamond. But as we felt constrained in our movements, desiring, if possible, to keep so quiet that the birds would after a while see in us only two harmless stumps or prostrate logs, we had much the worst of it. The mosquitoes were quite taken with our quiet and knew us from logs and stumps in a moment. Neither were the birds deceived, not even when we tried the Indian's tactics and plumed ourselves with green branches. Ah, the suspicious creatures, how they watched us with the food in their beaks, abstaining for one whole hour from ministering that precious charge which otherwise would have been visited every moment! Quite near us they would come at times, between us and the nest, eying us so sharply. Then they would move off and apparently try to forget our presence. Was it to deceive us or to persuade himself and mate that there was no serious cause for alarm, that the male would now and then strike up in full song and move off to some distance through the trees? But the mother bird did not allow herself to lose sight of us at all, and both birds, after carrying the food in their beaks a long time, would swallow it themselves. Then they would obtain another morsel and apparently approach very near the nest, when their caution or prudence would come to their aid, and they would swallow the food and hasten away. I thought the young birds would cry out, but not a

syllable from them. Yet this was, no doubt, what kept the
parent birds away from the nest. The clamor the young would
have set up on the approach of the old with food would have
exposed everything.

After a time I felt sure I knew within a few feet where the
nest was concealed. Indeed, I thought I knew the identical
bush. Then the birds approached each other again and grew
very confidential about another locality some rods below. This
puzzled us and, seeing the whole afternoon might be spent
in this manner, and the mystery unsolved, we determined to
change our tactics and institute a thorough search of the locality. This procedure soon brought things to a crisis, for, as
my companion clambered over a log by a little hemlock, a few
yards from where we had been sitting, with a cry of alarm out
sprang the young birds from their nest in the hemlock and,
scampering and fluttering over the leaves, disappeared in different directions. This brought the parent birds on the scene
in an agony of alarm. Their distress was pitiful. They threw
themselves on the ground at our very feet and fluttered and
cried and trailed themselves before us, to draw us away from
the place or distract our attention from the helpless young. I
shall not forget the male bird, how bright he looked, how sharp
the contrast as he trailed his painted plumage there on the
dry leaves. Apparently he was seriously disabled. He would
start up as if exerting every muscle to fly away, but no use;
down he would come with a helpless, fluttering motion before he had gone two yards, and apparently you had only to
go and pick him up. But before you could pick him up, he
had recovered somewhat and flown a little farther; and thus,
if you were tempted to follow him, you would soon find yourself some distance from the scene of the nest, and both old and
young well out of your reach. The female bird was not less

solicitous and practiced the same arts upon us to decoy us away, but her dull plumage rendered her less noticeable. The male was clad in holiday attire, but his mate in an everyday working garb.

The nest was built in the fork of a little hemlock, about fifteen inches from the ground, and was a thick, firm structure composed of the finer material of the woods, with a lining of very delicate roots or rootlets. There were four young birds and one addled egg.[1]

The woodpeckers all build in about the same manner, excavating the trunk or branch of a decayed tree and depositing the eggs on the fine fragments of wood at the bottom of the cavity. Though the nest is not especially an artistic work — requiring strength rather than skill — yet the eggs and the young of few other birds are so completely housed from the elements or protected from their natural enemies, the jays, crows, hawks, and owls. A tree with a natural cavity is never selected but one which has been dead just long enough to have become soft and brittle throughout. The bird goes in horizontally for a few inches, making a hole perfectly round and smooth and adapted to his size, then turns downward, gradually enlarging the hole, as he proceeds, to the depth of ten, fifteen, twenty inches, according to the softness of the tree and the urgency of the mother bird to deposit her eggs. While excavating, male and female work alternately. After one has been engaged fifteen or twenty minutes, drilling and carrying out chips, it ascends to an upper limb, utters a loud call or two, when its mate soon appears and, alighting near it on the branch, the pair chatter and caress a moment, then the fresh one enters the cavity and the other flies away.

A few days since, I climbed up to the nest of the downy woodpecker, in the decayed top of a sugar maple. For better protection against driving rains, the hole, which was rather more than an inch in diameter, was made immediately beneath a branch which stretched out almost horizontally from the main stem. It appeared merely a deeper shadow upon the dark and mottled surface of the bark with which the branches were covered, and could not be detected by the eye until one was within a few feet of it. The young chirped vociferously as I approached the nest, thinking it was the old one with food; but the clamor suddenly ceased as I put my hand on that part of the trunk in which they were concealed, the unusual jarring and rustling alarming them into silence. The cavity, which was about fifteen inches deep, was gourd shaped and was wrought out with great skill and regularity. The walls were quite smooth and clean and new.[2]

One day in May, walking in the woods, I came upon the nest of a whip-poor-will, or rather its eggs, for it builds no nest — two elliptical whitish spotted eggs lying upon the dry leaves. My foot was within a yard of the mother bird before she flew. I wondered what a sharp eye would detect curious or characteristic in the ways of the bird, so I came to the place many times and had a look. It was always a task to separate the bird from her surroundings, though I stood within a few feet of her and knew exactly where to look. One had to bear on with his eye, as it were, and refuse to be baffled. The sticks and leaves and bits of black or dark-brown bark were all exactly copied in the bird's plumage. And then she did sit so close and simulate so well a shapeless, decaying piece of wood or bark! Twice I brought a companion and, guiding his eye to the spot, noted how difficult it was for him to make out there, in full view upon the dry leaves, any semblance to a bird. When the bird returned after being disturbed, she would alight within a few inches of her eggs and then, after a moment's pause, hobble awkwardly upon them.

After the young had appeared, all the wit of the bird came into play. I was on hand the next day, I think. The mother bird sprang up when I was within a pace of her, and in doing so fanned the leaves with her wings till they sprang up, too; as the leaves started the young started, and, being of the same color, to tell which was the leaf and which the bird was a trying task to any eye. I came the next day, when the same tactics were repeated. Once a leaf fell upon one of the young birds and nearly hid it. The young are covered with a reddish down, like a young partridge, and soon follow their mother about. When disturbed, they gave but one leap then settled down, perfectly motionless and stupid, with eyes closed. The parent bird, on these occasions, made frantic efforts to decoy me away from her young. She would fly a few paces and fall upon her breast, and a spasm like that of death would run through her tremulous outstretched wings and prostrate body. She kept a sharp eye out the meanwhile to see if the ruse took, and if it did not, she was quickly cured and, moving about to some other point, tried to draw my attention as before. When followed she always alighted upon the ground, dropping down in a sudden peculiar way. The second or third day both old and young had disappeared.

The whip-poor-will walks as awkwardly as a swallow, which is as awkward as a man in a bag, and yet she manages to lead her young about the woods. The latter, I think, move by leaps and sudden spurts, their protective coloring shielding them most effectively.[3]

Birds with whom the struggle for life is the sharpest seem

to be more prolific than those whose nest and young are exposed
to fewer dangers. The robin, the sparrow, the pewee, etc., will
rear, or make the attempt to rear, two and sometimes three
broods in a season; but the bobolink, the oriole, the kingbird,
the goldfinch, the cedarbird, the birds of prey, and the woodpeckers, that build in safe retreats in the trunks of trees, have
usually but a single brood.[4]

None of our familiar birds endear themselves to us more
than does the bluebird. The first bluebird in the spring is as
welcome as the blue sky itself. The season seems softened and
tempered as soon as we hear his note and see his warm breast
and azure wing. His gentle manners, his soft, appealing voice,
not less than his pleasing hues, seem born of the bright and
genial skies. He is the spirit of the April days incarnated in a
bird. He has the quality of winsomeness, like the violet
and the speedwell among the flowers. Not strictly a songster,
yet his every note and call is from out the soul of harmony. The
bluebird is evidently an off-shoot from the thrush family, and
without the thrush's gift of song; still his voice affords us much
of the same pleasure.

How readily the bluebirds become our friends and neighbors
when we offer them suitable nesting retreats! Bring them
something from nature, something with the bark on — a section of a dry beech or maple limb in which the downy woodpecker has excavated his chamber and passed the winter or
reared his brood; fasten it in early spring upon the corner of
your porch or on the trunk of a nearby tree, and see what interesting neighbors you will soon have. One summer I brought
home from one of my walks to the woods a section, two or three
feet long, of a large yellow birch limb which contained such a
cavity as I speak of, and I wired it to one of the posts of the

rustic porch at Woodchuck Lodge. The next season a pair of bluebirds reared two broods in it.[5]

But the nest of nests, the ideal nest, after we have left the deep woods, is unquestionably that of the Baltimore oriole. It is the only perfectly pensile nest we have. The nest of the orchard oriole is indeed mainly so, but this bird generally builds lower and shallower, more after the manner of the vireos.

The Baltimore oriole loves to attach its nest to the swaying branches of the tallest elms, making no attempt at concealment but satisfied if the position be high and the branch pendent. This nest would seem to cost more time and skill than any other bird structure. A peculiar flaxlike substance seems to be always sought after and always found. The nest when completed assumes the form of a large, suspended gourd. The walls are thin but firm, and proof against the most driving rain. The mouth is hemmed or overhanded with horsehair, and the sides are usually sewed through and through with the same.[6]

The oriole nests in many kinds of trees — oaks, maples, apple trees, elms — but her favorite is the elm. She chooses the end of one of the long drooping branches where a group of small swaying twigs affords her suitable support. It is the most unlikely place imaginable for any but a pendent nest, woven to half a dozen or more slender, vertical twigs and swaying freely in the wind. Few nests are so secure, so hidden, and so completely sheltered from the rains by the drooping leaves above and around it. It is rarely discoverable except from directly beneath it. I think a well-built oriole's nest would sustain a weight of eight or ten pounds before it would be torn from its moorings. They are also very partial to the ends of branches that swing low over the highway. One May I saw two female orioles building their nests twenty or twenty-five feet above our State Road, where automobiles and other vehicles passed nearly every minute all the day. An oriole's nest in a remote field far from highways and dwellings is a rare occurrence.

Birds of different species differ as widely in skill in nest-building as they do in song. From the rude platform of dry twigs and other coarse material of the cuckoo, to the pendent, closely woven pouch of the oriole, the difference in the degree of skill displayed is analogous to the difference between the simple lisp of the cedarbird or the little tin whistle of the "chippie," and the golden notes of the wood thrush or the hilarious song of the bobolink.

Real castles in the air are the nests of the orioles; no other nests are better hidden or apparently more safe from the depredations of crows and squirrels. To start the oriole's nest successfully is quite an engineering feat. The birds inspect the branches many times before they make a decision. When they have decided on the site, the mother bird brings her first string or vegetable fiber and attaches it to a twig by winding it around and around many times, leaving one or both ends hanging free. I have nests where these foundation strings are wound around a twig a dozen times. In her blind windings and tuckings and loopings the bird occasionally ties a substantial knot, but it is never the result of a deliberate purpose as some observers contend, but purely a matter of chance. When she uses only wild vegetable fibers, she fastens it to the twig by a hopeless kind of tangle. It is about the craziest kind of knitting imaginable. After the builder has fastened many lines to opposite twigs, their ends hanging free, she proceeds to span the little gulf by weaving them together. She stands with her claws clasped one to each side and uses her beak industriously, looping up and fastening the loose ends. I have stood in the road under the nest looking straight up till my head swam, trying to make out just how she did it, but all I could see was the bird standing astride the chasm she was trying to bridge and busy with the hanging strings. Slowly the maze of loose threads takes a sacklike form, the bottom of the nest thickens, till some morning you see the movement of the bird inside it; her beak comes through the sides from within, like a needle or an awl, seizes a loose hair or thread, and jerks it back through the wall and tightens it. It is a regular stitching or quilting process. The course of any particular thread of fiber is as irregular and haphazard as if it were the work of the wind or the waves. There is plan, but no conscious method of procedure. In fact, a birds' nest is a growth. It is not something builded as we build, in which judgment, design, forethought enter; it is the result of the blind groping of instinct which rarely errs but which does not see the end from the beginning, as reason does. The oriole sometimes overhands the rim of her nest with strings and fibers to make it firm and to afford a foundation for her to perch upon, but it is like the pathetic work which an un-taught blind child might do under similar conditions.[7]

Most country boys, I fancy, know the marsh hawk. It is he you see flying low over the fields, beating about bushes and marshes and dipping over the fences, with his attention direct-ed to the ground beneath him. He is a cat on wings. He keeps so low that the birds and mice do not see him till he is fairly upon them. When I was a boy, I used to call him the long-tailed hawk. The male is a bluish slate color; the female a red-dish brown, like the hen-hawk, with a white rump.

Unlike the other hawks, they nest on the ground in low, thick marshy places. For several seasons a pair have nested in a bushy marsh a few miles back of me, near the house of a farmer friend of mine who has a keen eye for the wild life about him. Two years ago he found the nest, but when I got over to see it the next week it had been robbed, probably by some boys in the neighborhood. The past season, in April or May, by watching the mother bird, he found the nest again. It was in a marshy place, several acres in extent, in the bottom of a valley and thickly grown with hardhack, prickly ash, smilax, and other low thorny bushes. My friend brought me to the brink of a low hill, and pointed out to me in the marsh below us, as nearly as he could, just where the nest was located. Then we crossed the pasture, entered upon the marsh, and made our way cautiously toward it. The wild thorny growths, waist high, had to be carefully dealt with. As we neared the spot, I used my eyes the best I could, but I did not see the hawk till she sprang into the air not ten yards away from us. She went screaming upward and was soon sailing in a circle far above us. There, on a coarse matting of twigs and weeds, lay five snow-white eggs, a little more than half as large as hens' eggs. My companion said the male hawk would probably soon appear and join the female, but he did not. She kept drifting away to the east and was soon gone from our sight.

We soon withdrew and secreted ourselves behind the stone wall, in hopes of seeing the mother hawk return. She appeared in the distance, but seemed to know she was being watched, and kept away.

In about a week I paid another visit to the hawk's nest. The eggs were all hatched, and the mother bird was hovering near. I shall never forget the curious expression of those young hawks sitting there on the ground. The expression was not one of youth but of extreme age. Such an ancient, infirm look as they had — the sharp, dark, and shrunken look about the face and eyes, and their feeble, tottering motions! They sat upon their elbows and the hind part of their bodies, and their pale, withered legs and feet extended before them in the most helpless fashion. Their angular bodies were covered with a pale yellowish down, like that of a chicken; their heads had a plucked, seedy appearance; and their long, strong, naked wings hung down by their sides till they touched the ground: power and ferocity in the first rude draught, shorn of everything but its sinister ugliness. Another curious thing was the gradation of the young in size; they tapered down regularly from the first to the fifth, as if there had been, as probably there was, an interval of a day or two between the hatchings.

The two older ones showed some signs of fear on our approach, and one of them threw himself upon his back and put up his impotent legs and glared at us with open beak. The two smaller ones regarded us not at all. Neither of the parent birds appeared during our stay.

When I visited the nest again, eight or ten days later, the birds were much grown, but of as marked a difference in size as before and with the same look of extreme old age — old age in men of the aquiline type, nose and chin coming together, and eyes large and sunken. They now glared upon us with a wild, savage look and opened their beaks threateningly.

The next week, when my friend visited the nest, the larger of the hawks fought him savagely. But one of the brood, probably the last to hatch, had made but little growth. It appeared to be on the point of starvation. The mother hawk (for the male seemed to have disappeared) had perhaps found her family too large for her and was deliberately allowing one of the number to perish; or did the larger and stronger young devour all the food before the weaker member could obtain any? Probably this was the case.

Arthur brought the feeble nestling away, and the same day my little boy got it and brought it home, wrapped in a woolen rag. It was clearly a starved bantling. It cried feebly but would not lift up its head.

We first poured some warm milk down its throat, which soon revived it, so that it would swallow small bits of flesh. In a day or two we had it eating ravenously, and its growth became noticeable. Its voice had the sharp whistling character of that of its parents and was stilled only when the bird was asleep. We made a pen for it about a yard square in one end of the study, covering the floor with several thicknesses of newspapers; and here, upon a bit of brown woolen blanket for a nest, the hawk waxed strong day by day. An uglier looking pet, tested by all the rules we usually apply to such things, would have been hard to find. There he would sit upon his elbows, his helpless feet out in front of him, his great featherless wings touching the floor, and shrilly cry for more food. For a time we gave him water daily from a stylograph-pen filler, but the water he evidently did not need or relish. Fresh meat, and plenty of it, was his demand. And we soon discovered that he liked game, such as mice, squirrels, birds, much better than butcher's meat.

His plumage very soon began to show itself, crowding off tufts of the down. The quills on his great wings sprouted and grew apace. What a ragged, uncanny appearance he presented! but his look of extreme age gradually became modified. What a lover of the sunlight he was! We would put him out upon the grass in the full blaze of the morning sun, and he would spread his wings and bask in it with the most intense enjoyment. In the nest the young must be exposed to the full power of the mid-day sun during our first heated terms in June and July, the thermometer often going up to ninety-three or ninety-five degrees, so that sunshine seemed to be a need of his nature. He liked the rain equally well, and when put out in a shower would sit down and take it as if every drop did him good.

His legs developed nearly as slowly as his wings. He could not stand steadily upon them till about ten days before he was ready to fly. The talons were limp and feeble. When we came with food, he would hobble along toward us like the worst kind of a cripple, drooping and moving his wings and treading upon his legs from the foot back to the elbow, the foot remaining closed and useless. Like a baby learning to stand, he made many trials before he succeeded. He would rise up on his trembling legs only to fall back again.

One day, in the summerhouse, I saw him for the first time stand for a moment squarely upon his legs with the feet fully spread beneath them. He looked about him as if the world suddenly wore a new aspect.

His plumage now grew quite rapidly. One red squirrel a day, chopped fine with an axe, was his ration. He began to hold his game with his foot while he tore it. The study was full of his shed down. His dark-brown mottled plumage began to grow beautiful. The wings drooped a little, but gradually he got control of them and held them in place.

It was now the 20th of July, and the hawk was about five weeks old. In a day or two he was walking or jumping about the ground. He chose a position under the edge of a Norway spruce, where he would sit for hours dozing or looking out upon the landscape. When we brought him game, he would advance to meet us with wings slightly lifted, and uttering a shrill cry. Toss him a mouse or sparrow, and he would seize it with one foot and hop off to his cover, where he would bend above it, spread his plumage, look this way and that, uttering all the time the most exultant and satisfied chuckle.

About this time he began to practice striking with his talons, as an Indian boy might begin practicing with his bow and arrow. He would strike at a dry leaf in the grass, or at a fallen apple, or at some imaginary object. He was learning the use of his weapons. His wings also — he seemed to feel them sprouting from his shoulders. He would lift them straight up and hold them expanded, and they would seem to quiver with excitement. Every hour in the day he would do this. The pressure was beginning to centre there. Then he would strike playfully at a leaf or a bit of wood and keep his wings lifted.

The next step was to spring into the air and beat his wings. He seemed now to be thinking entirely of his wings. They itched to be put to use.

A day or two later he would leap and fly several feet. A pile of brush ten or twelve feet below the bank was easily reached. Here he would perch in true hawk fashion, to the bewilderment and scandal of all the robins and catbirds in the vicinity. Here he would dart his eye in all directions, turning his head over and glancing up into the sky.

The last week in July he began to fly quite freely, and it was necessary to clip one of his wings. As the clipping embraced only the ends of his primaries, he soon overcame the difficulty, and by carrying his broad, long tail more on that side flew with considerable ease. He made longer and longer excursions into the surrounding fields and vineyards and did not always return. On such occasions we would go find him and fetch him back.

Late one rainy afternoon he flew away into the vineyard, and when, an hour later, I went after him, he could not be found, and we never saw him again. We hoped hunger would soon drive him back, but we have had no clew to him from that day to this.[8]

If I were a bird, in building my nest I should follow the example of the bobolink, placing it in the midst of a broad meadow, where there was no spear of grass, or flower, or growth unlike another to mark its site. She selects the most monotonous and uniform place she can find amid the daisies or the timothy and clover, and places her simple structure upon the ground in the midst of it. There is no concealment, except as the great conceals the little, as the desert conceals the pebble, as the myriad conceals the unit. You may find the nest once, if your course chances to lead you across it, and your eye is quick enough to note the silent brown bird as she darts swiftly away; but step three paces in the wrong direction, and your search will probably be fruitless. My friend and I found a nest by accident one day, and then lost it again one minute afterward. I moved away a few yards to be sure of the mother bird, charging my friend not to stir from his tracks. When I returned, he had moved two paces, he said (he had really moved four), and we spent a half hour stooping over the daisies and the buttercups, looking for the lost clew. We grew desperate and fairly felt the ground over with our hands, but without avail. I marked the spot with a bush and came the next day and, with the bush as a centre, moved about it in slowly increasing circles, covering, I thought, nearly every inch of ground with my feet, and laying hold of it with all the visual power I could command, till my patience was exhausted and I gave up, baffled. I began to doubt the ability of the parent birds themselves to find it, and so secreted myself and watched. After much delay, the male bird appeared with food in his beak and, satisfying himself that the coast was clear, dropped into the grass which I had trodden down in my search. Fastening my eye upon a particular meadow lily, I walked straight to the spot, bent down, and gazed long and intently into the grass. Finally my eye separated the nest and its young from its surroundings. My foot had barely missed them in my search, but how much they had escaped my eye I could not tell. Probably not by distance at all, but simply by unrecognition. They were virtually invisible. The dark gray and yellowish brown grass and stubble of the meadow bottom were exactly copied in the color of the half-fledged young. More than that, they hugged the nest so closely and formed such a compact mass that though there were five of them, they preserved the unit of expression — no single head or form was defined; they were one, and that one was without shape or color and not separable except by closest scrutiny from the one of the meadow bottom. The nest prospered, as bobolinks' nests doubtless generally do; for, notwithstanding the enormous slaughter of the birds during their fall migrations by Southern sportsmen, the bobolink appears to hold its own, and its music does not diminish in our Northern meadows.[9]

The first wild egg in New York and New England is probably that of an owl, the great horned owl, it is said, laying as early as March. They probably shelter their eggs from the frost and the snow before incubation begins. The little screech owl waits till April and seeks the deep, snug cavity of an old tree; the heart of a decayed apple tree suits him well. Begin your search by the middle of April, and before the month is past you will find the four white, round eggs resting upon a little dry grass or a few dry leaves in the bottom of a long cavity. Owls' eggs are inclined to be spherical. You would expect to see a big, round-headed, round-eyed creature come out of such an egg.

There is a last egg of summer as well as a first egg of spring, but one cannot name either with much confidence. Both the robin and the chippie sometimes rear a third brood in August; but the birds that delay their nesting till midsummer are the goldfinch and the cedarbird, the former waiting for the thistle to ripen its seeds and the latter probably for the appearance of certain insects which it takes on the wing.[10]

15. The Way of the Mammal

T HERE IS no prettier bit of natural history upon four legs than the red fox, especially when you surprise him in your morning walk or he surprises you in his. He, too, is a night prowler, but often he does not get home till after sun-up. Early one October morning, as I stood in the road looking out over the landscape, a belated fox jumped over the wall a few yards from me and loped unconcernedly along parallel with the road, then turned and scaled the fence and crossed the road and went bounding up the hill toward the woods with a grace and ease impossible to describe.[1]

The red fox is the only species that abounds in my locality; the little gray fox seems to prefer a more rocky and precipitous country and less rigorous climate; the cross fox is occasionally seen, and there are traditions of the silver gray among the oldest hunters. But the red fox is the sportsman's prize and the only fur bearer worthy of note in these mountains. I go out in the morning, after a fresh fall of snow, and see at all points where he has crossed the road. Here he has leisurely passed within rifle range of the house, evidently reconnoitring the premises with an eye to the hen roost. That clear, sharp track — there is no mistaking it for the clumsy footprint of a little dog. All his wildness and agility are photographed in it. Here he has

taken fright or suddenly recollected an engagement, and in long, graceful leaps, barely touching the fence, has gone careering up the hill as fleet as the wind.

The wild, buoyant creature, how beautiful he is! I had often seen his dead carcass and at a distance had witnessed the hounds drive him across the upper fields; but the thrill and excitement of meeting him in his wild freedom in the woods were unknown to me till, one cold winter day, drawn thither by the baying of a hound, I stood near the summit of the mountain, waiting a renewal of the sound, that I might determine the course of the dog and choose my position — stimulated by the ambition of all young Nimrods to bag some notable game. Long I waited and patiently till, chilled and benumbed, I was about to turn back, when, hearing a slight noise, I looked up and beheld a most superb fox, loping along with inimitable grace and ease, evidently disturbed but not pursued by the hound and so absorbed in his private meditations that he failed to see me, though I stood transfixed with amazement and admiration not ten yards distant. I took his measure at a glance — a large male with dark legs and massive tail tipped with white — a most magnificent creature; but so astonished and fascinated was I by this sudden appearance and matchless beauty that not till I had caught the last glimpse of him as he disappeared over a knoll, did I awake to my duty as a sportsman and realize what an opportunity to distinguish myself I had unconsciously let slip. I clutched my gun, half angrily, as if it was to blame, and went home out of humor with myself and all foxkind. But I have since thought better of the experience and concluded that I bagged the game after all, the best part of it, and fleeced Reynard of something more valuable than his fur, without his knowledge.

One of the most notable features of the fox is his large and massive tail. When he is seen running on the snow at a distance, his tail is quite as conspicuous as his body; and, so far from appearing a burden, seems to contribute to his lightness and buoyancy. It softens the outline of his movements and repeats or continues to the eye the ease and poise of his carriage.[2]

In the Middle and Eastern States our woodchuck takes the place, in some respects, of the English rabbit, burrowing in every hillside and under every stone wall and jutting ledge and large boulder, from whence it makes raids upon the grass and clover and sometimes upon the garden vegetables. It is quite solitary in its habits, seldom more than one inhabiting the same den, unless it be a mother and her young. It is not now so much a *wood*chuck as a *field*chuck. Occasionally, however, one seems to prefer the woods and is not seduced by the sunny slopes and the succulent grass, but feeds, as did his fathers before him, upon roots and twigs, the bark of young trees, and upon various wood plants.

One summer day, as I was swimming across a broad, deep pool in the creek in a secluded place in the woods, I saw one of these sylvan chucks amid the rocks but a few feet from the edge of the water where I proposed to touch. He saw my approach, but doubtless took me for some waterfowl or for some cousin of his of the muskrat tribe; for he went on with his feeding and regarded me not till I paused within ten feet of him and lifted myself up. Then he did not know me, having, perhaps, never seen Adam in his simplicity, but he twisted his nose around to catch my scent; and the moment he had done so he sprang like a jumping jack and rushed into his den with the utmost precipitation.

The woodchuck is the true serf among our animals; he belongs to the soil and savors of it. He is of the earth, earthy.

There is generally a decided odor about his dens and lurking places, but it is not at all disagreeable in the clover-scented air; and his shrill whistle, as he takes to his hole or defies the farm dog from the interior of the stone wall, is a pleasant summer sound. In form and movement the woodchuck is not captivating. His body is heavy and flabby. Indeed, such a flaccid, fluid, pouchy carcass I have never before seen. It has absolutely no muscular tension or rigidity but is as baggy and shaky as a skin filled with water. The legs of the woodchuck are short and stout and made for digging rather than running. The latter operation he performs by short leaps, his belly scarcely clearing the ground. For a short distance he can make very good time, but he seldom trusts himself far from his hole, and when surprised in that predicament, makes little effort to escape but, grating his teeth, looks the danger squarely in the face.

The woodchuck always burrows on a sidehill. This enables him to guard against being drowned out, by making the termination of the hole higher than the entrance. He digs in slantingly for about two or three feet, then makes a sharp upward turn and keeps nearly parallel with the surface of the ground for a distance of eight or ten feet farther, according to the grade. Here he makes his nest and passes the winter, holing up in October or November and coming out again in April. This is a long sleep and is rendered possible only by the amount of fat with which the system has become stored during the summer. The fire of life still burns, but very faintly and slowly, as with the draughts all closed and the ashes heaped up. Respiration is continued, but at longer intervals, and all the vital processes are nearly at a standstill. Dig one out during hibernation (Audubon did so), and you find it a mere inanimate ball that suffers itself to be moved and rolled about without showing signs of awakening. But bring it in by the fire, and it presently unrolls and opens its eyes and crawls feebly about and if left to itself will seek some dark hole or corner, roll itself up again, and resume its former condition.[3]

My most interesting note of the season of 1893 relates to a weasel. One day in early November, my boy and I were sitting on a rock at the edge of a tamarack swamp in the woods, hoping to get a glimpse of some grouse which we knew were in the habit of feeding in the swamp. We had not sat there very long before we heard a slight rustling in the leaves below us, which we at once fancied was made by the cautious tread of a grouse. (We had no gun.) Presently, through the thick brushy growth, we caught sight of a small animal running along that we at first took for a red squirrel. A moment more, and it came into full view but a few yards from us, and we saw that it was a weasel. A second glance showed that it carried something in its mouth which, as it drew near, we saw was a mouse or a mole of some sort. The weasel ran nimbly along, now the length of a decayed log, then over stones and branches, pausing a moment every three or four yards, and passed within twenty feet of us and disappeared behind some rocks on the bank at the edge of the swamp. "He is carrying food into his den," I said, "let us watch him." In four or five minutes he reappeared, coming back over the course along which he had just passed, running over and under the same stones and down the same decayed log, and was soon out of sight in the swamp. We had not moved, and evidently he had not noticed us. After about six minutes we heard the same rustle as at first, and in a moment saw the weasel coming back with another mouse in his mouth. He kept to his former route as if chained to it, making the same pauses and gestures and repeating exactly his former movements. He disappeared on our left as before, and after a few moments' delay re-emerged and took his course down into the swamp again. We waited about the same length of time as before, when back he came with another mouse. He evidently had a big crop of mice down there amid the bogs and bushes, and he was gathering his harvest in very industriously. We became curious to see exactly where his den was, and so walked around where he had seemed to disappear each time, and waited. He was as punctual as usual and was back with his game exactly on time. It happened that we had stopped within two paces of his hole, so that, as he approached it, he evidently discovered us. He paused, looked steadily at us, and then without any sign of fear entered his den. The entrance was not under the rocks as we had expected, but was in the bank a few feet beyond them. We remained motionless for some time, but he did not reappear. Our presence had made him suspicious and he was going to wait awhile. Then I removed some dry leaves and exposed his doorway, a small, round hole, hardly as large as the chipmunk makes, going straight down into the ground. We had a lively curiosity to get a peep into his larder. If he had been carrying in mice at this rate very long, his cellars must be packed with them. With a sharp stick I began digging into the red clayey soil but soon encountered so many roots from near trees that I gave it up, deciding to return next day with a mattock. So I repaired the damages I had done as well as I could, replaced the leaves, and we moved off.

The next day, which was mild and still as usual, I came back armed, as I thought, to unearth the weasel and his treasures. I sat down where we had sat the day before and awaited developments. I was curious to know if the weasel was still carrying in his harvest. I had sat but a few minutes when I heard again the rustle in the dry leaves and saw the weasel coming home with another mouse. I observed him till he had made three trips; about every six or seven minutes, I calculated, he brought in a mouse. Then I went and stood near his hole. This time he had a fat meadow mouse. He laid it down near the entrance, went in and turned around, and reached out and drew the mouse in after him. That store of mice I am bound to see, I thought, and then fell to with the heavy mattock. I followed the hole down about two feet, when it turned to the north. I kept the clew by thrusting into the passage slender twigs; these it was easy to follow. Two or three feet more and the hole branched, one part going west, the other northeast. I followed the west one a few feet till it branched. Then I turned to the easterly tunnel and pursued it till it branched. I followed one of these ways till it divided. I began to be embarrassed and hindered by the accumulations of loose soil. Evidently this weasel had foreseen just such an assault upon his castle as I was making and had planned it accordingly. He was not to be caught napping. I found several enlargements in the various tunnels, breathing spaces, or spaces to turn around in, or to meet and chat with a companion, but nothing that looked like a terminus, a permanent living room. I tried removing the soil a couple of paces away with the mattock, but found it slow work. I was getting warm and tired, and my task was apparently only just begun. The farther I dug, the more numerous and intricate became the passages. I concluded to stop and come again the next day, armed with a shovel in addition to the mattock.

Accordingly, I came back on the morrow and fell to work vigorously. I soon had quite a large excavation; I found the bank a labyrinth of passages, with here and there a large chamber. One of the latter I struck only six inches under the surface, by making a fresh breach a few feet away.

This swamp, maybe, had been his hunting ground for many

years, and he had added another hall to his dwelling each year. After further digging I struck at least one of his banqueting halls, a cavity about the size of one's hat, arched over by a network of fine tree roots. The occupant evidently lodged or rested here also. There was a warm, dry nest, made of leaves and the fur of mice and moles. I took out two or three handfuls. In finding this chamber I had followed one of the tunnels around till it brought me within a foot of the original entrance. A few inches to one side of this cavity there was what I took to be a back alley where the weasel threw his waste; there were large masses of wet, decaying fur here, and fur pellets such as are regurgitated by hawks and owls. In the nest there was the tail of a flying squirrel, showing that the weasel sometimes had a flying squirrel for supper or dinner.

I continued my digging with renewed energy; I should yet find the grand depot where all these passages centred; but the farther I exacavated, the more complex and baffling the problem became; the ground was honeycombed with passages. What enemy has this weasel, I said to myself, that he should provide so many ways of escape, that he should have a back door at every turn? To corner him would be impossible; to be lost in his fortress were like being lost in Mammoth Cave. How he could bewilder his pursuer by appearing now at this door, now at that; now mocking him from the attic, now defying him from the cellar! So far, I had discovered but one entrance; but some of the chambers were so near the surface that it looked as if the planner had calculated upon an emergency when he might want to reach daylight quickly in a new place.

Finally I paused, rested upon my shovel awhile, eased my aching back upon the ground, and then gave it up, feeling as I never had before the force of the old saying, that you cannot catch a weasel asleep. I had made an ugly hole in the bank, had handled over two or three times a ton or more of earth, and was apparently no nearer the weasel and his store of mice than when I began.

Then I regretted that I had broken into his castle at all; that I had not contented myself with coming day after day and counting his mice as he carried them in, and continued my observation upon him each succeeding year. Now the rent in his fortress could not be repaired, and he would doubtless move away, as he most certainly did, for his doors, which I had closed with soil, remained unopened after winter had set in.

But little seems known about the intimate private lives of any of our lesser wild creatures. It was news to me that any of the weasels lived in dens in this way and that they stored up provisions against a day of need. This species was probably the little ermine, eight or nine inches long, with tail about five inches. It was still in its summer dress of dark chestnut brown above and whitish below.

It was a mystery where the creature had put the earth which it must have removed in digging its den; not a grain was to be seen anywhere, and yet a bushel or more must have been taken out. Externally, there was not the slightest sign of that curious habitation there under the ground. The entrance was hidden beneath dry leaves and was surrounded by little passages and flourishes between the leaves and the ground. If any of my readers find a weasel's den, I hope they will be wiser than I was and observe his goings and comings without disturbing his habitation.[4]

The first chipmunk in March is as sure a token of the spring as the first bluebird or the first robin; and it is quite as welcome. Some genial influence has found him out there in his burrow, deep under the ground, and waked him up and enticed him forth into the light of day. The red squirrel has been more or less active all winter; his track has dotted the surface of every new-fallen snow throughout the season. But the chipmunk retired from view early in December and has passed the rigorous months in his nest, beside his hoard of nuts, some feet underground, and hence, when he emerges in March and is seen upon his little journeys along the fences or perched upon a log or rock near his hole in the woods, it is another sign that spring is at hand.

Apparently the first thing he does on coming forth, as soon as he is sure of himself, is to go courting. So far as I have observed, the love-making of the chipmunk occurs in March. A single female will attract all the males in the vicinity. One early March day I was at work for several hours near a stone fence, where a female had apparently taken up her quarters. What a train of suitors she had that day! How they hurried up and down, often giving each other a spiteful slap or bite as they passed. The young are born in May, four or five at a birth.

The chipmunk is quite a solitary creature; I have never known more than one to occupy the same den. Apparently no two can agree to live together. What a clean, pert, dapper, nervous little fellow he is! How fast his heart beats, as he stands up on the wall by the roadside and, with hands spread out upon his breast, regards you intently! A movement of your arm, and he darts into the wall with a saucy *chip-r-r,* which has the effect of slamming the door behind him.[5]

It is interesting to see how well these wild creatures are groomed — every hair in its place and shining as if it had just been polished. The tail of my chipmunk is simply perfect — not a hair missing or soiled or worn. In fact, the whole animal looks as new and fresh as a coin just minted or a flower just opened. His underground habits leave no mark or stain upon him, and his daily labors do not ruffle a hair.

The whole character of the squirrel culminates and finds expression in its tail — all its nervous restlessness and wild beauty, all its jauntiness, archness, and suspicion, and every change of emotion, seem to ripple out along this appendage.

How furtive and nervous my chipmunk is, rushing about by little jerks incessantly, not stopping for anything! His bright, unwinking eyes, his palpitating body, his sudden spasmodic movements, his eagerness, his industry, his sleekness and cleanliness — what a picture he makes!

After I had cracked some hickory nuts for my little friend this morning and he had got a taste of the sweet morsel inside, he quickly began to stuff the whole nuts into his pockets and carry them to his storehouse. It was amusing to see him struggle with the larger nuts, first moistening them with his tongue, to force them into those secret and apparently inadequate pockets. The smooth, trim cheeks would suddenly assume the appearance of enormous wens, extending well down on the sides of the neck. The pouches are not merely passive receptacles; they evidently possess some power of muscular action, like the throat muscles, which enables them to force the grain and nuts along their whole course. As the little squirrel picks the corn from the floor you can see the pouches swell, first on the one side, then on the other. He seems to pick up the kernels and swallow them. What part the tongue plays in the process, one cannot see. In forcing a whole or a half hickory nut into them, the chipmunk uses his paws. The pouches are doubtless emptied by muscular movements similar to those by which they were filled — a self-acting piece of machinery, a pocket that can fill and empty itself.

From previous experience I calculated the capacity of his chamber to be not more than four or five quarts. One day I gave him all I thought he could manage — enough, I fancied, to fill his chamber full — two quarts of hickory nuts and some corn. How he responded to the invitation! How he flew over the course from my den to his! He fairly panted. The day might prove too short for him, or some other chipmunk might discover the pile of treasures. Three, and often four, nuts at a time went into his pockets. If one of them was too large to go in readily, he would take it between his teeth. He would first bite off the sharp point from the nut to keep it from pricking or irritating his pouches. I do not think he feared a puncture. I renewed the pile of nuts from time to time and looked on with interest. The day was cloudy and wet, but he ran his express train all day.

The next day he was back again, carrying away a fresh supply of nuts as eagerly as ever. Two more quarts disappeared before night. The next day was rainy, and though other chipmunks were hurrying about, my little miser rested from his labors. A day later a fresh supply of nuts arrived — two quarts of chestnuts and one of hickory nuts, and the greed of the little squirrel rose to the occasion. He made his trips as frequently as ever.

On my return at the end of the week, the enthusiasm of the chipmunk had greatly abated. He was seldom out of his den. A nut or two placed at its entrance disappeared, but he visited me no more in my camp. Other chipmunks were active on all sides, but his solicitude about the winter had passed, or rather his hoarding instinct had been sated.

When the spring came I was seized with a curiosity to know how much of his stores my little friend had disposed of, and which of his various assortment of nuts and grain had proved his favorites. To settle these points there was only one course to pursue: we must dig him out. So one April day we proceeded to do so. We at once discovered a new hole or entrance, only a few inches from the other, and apparently more in use than it was. We found his chamber about three feet below the surface with its usual nest of dry leaves and grass, and a few shells of hickory nuts and cherry pits, but dig as we would, we could not find any recess or granary large enough to hold the peck or more of nuts that I had seen him carry in. We searched carefully for side chambers into which he might have stored the surplus of his unexpected harvest, but we found none.

The shells we found accounted for only a small fraction of those with which we had supplied him. Not a chestnut or a peach pit or a hickory nut did we find, nor any corn, nor wild seeds of any sort. I was much puzzled, and am still, as to just what had happened. The chipmunk either had been plundered by his neighbors or else had freely distributed his supplies among them. What did the new hole signify? The old one was ample and led to the same chamber. We did not find the chipmunk in his den, nor any convincing evidence that he had recently been there. Although I spent the following summer in the same bush camp, I am not certain that I ever saw my little neighbor that season. But the next following season, he or another was again my neighbor under the apple trees and disclosed to me a refreshing bit of natural history — that of a chipmunk digging his hole.

I happened to discover my chipmunk probably the second day after he had begun to dig. Some people were calling on me at my bush camp when, as they turned to go, one of them said, "See that chipmunk!" I looked and saw him sitting up amid a little fresh earth, washing his face. His face certainly needed washing; it was so soiled it looked comical. Presently I investigated the spot and found a rude hole a few inches deep, with the loosened earth in front of it. "Evidently a green-horn," I said; "a pretty dooryard he will have by the time he finishes, with a hole big enough to admit a red squirrel!"

Next morning there was more fresh earth in front of the hole; indeed, the grass was full of it a foot or more away, and a dump pile had just been begun. From the hole to this pile there was a deep, wide groove in the loose soil, which I soon saw was made by the squirrel shoving the loosened earth from the hole to the dump, using his nose as a shovel. Day after day, for nearly a week thereafter, I saw him at work, digging and pushing the soil up to the mouth of his hole and then pushing it along this groove or channel to the dump heap. His movements were so quick and energetic that, at the final stroke, the soil, a half teaspoonful or more, would shoot from his nose four or five inches. As he turned back along his roadway he would rapidly paw the earth behind him and then, before entering his hole, would take a quick look all around. He was never for a moment off guard; the sense of danger was ever present with him. As he entered his hole, a succession of quick jets of earth, forming little parabolas in the air, would shoot up behind him. Then all would be still for from three to four minutes, when he would again emerge, shoving the soil before him and continuing to butt it, quickly glancing right and left the while, till he shot it upon his dump.

This was his invariable procedure. Every motion was repeated like clockwork, the forward shoving, the retreating pawing, and the flying spray of earth as he disappeared in his hole.

I fancied him there underground loosening the soil with his paws for two or three minutes, then either kicking it up toward the exit or else shoving it in front of him. When at work he was intensely preoccupied; only one other feeling seemed to possess him — that of impending danger.

One day, when I paused before my little neighbor's mound of earth, I saw that the hole was nearly stopped up, and while I was looking, the closure was completed from within. Loose earth was being shoved up from below and pressed into the opening; the movement of the soil could be seen. It flashed upon me at once that here was the key to the secret that had so puzzled me — he would obliterate that ugly and irregular work hole and the littered dooryard, bury them beneath his mound of earth and, working from within, would make a new and neater outlet somewhere through the turf near by. He was probably carrying out that scheme at that moment and was disposing of the loose earth in the way I had observed. The next day the mound of earth had been extended over the place where the hole had been, and the chipmunk was still active beneath it, pushing up fresh earth like a ground mole. At intervals of a few moments the fresh soil would slowly heave or boil up, as it does when a hidden crayfish or mole is at work. Twice while I looked the head of the digger came through the thin screen of earth, as if by accident; he winked and blinked as the dirt slid off his head and over his eyes, then ducked beneath it and proceeded with his work. I began to look in the turf around me for the new entrance which I knew would soon be, if it were not already, made. I did not that day find it, but the next morning there it was, not more than four inches from the edge of the dumpheap — a little round shadow under the grass-blades and wild-strawberry leaves, about half the size of the work hole, with no stain of the soil about it and having such a look of neatness and privacy as could not have been given to it if it had been made from without. How furtive and secretive it looked! Still the little miner kept at work, still the fresh earth

boiled up above the old entrance. He is excavating his chamber, I thought; he requires a den or vault down there, of several quarts' capacity, in which to build his nest and store his food.

My chipmunk was engaged for nearly three weeks in his excavations. I knew when he had finished by his boldly coming into my camp one morning, a minute or two after he had seen me enter it. Looking intently up in my face for a few seconds, he proceeded to stuff his mouth with the dry leaves most to his liking that my bushy walls afforded. He did not try to pack the leaves in his cheek pouches, but crammed four or five into his mouth and then made off to his den. He was furnishing his house. Many mouthfuls of dry leaves and fine grass doubtless went to the furnishing, though I chanced to witness only this one. His bedroom is his granary; his winter stores are packed all around and under his nest.[6]

16. The Soil in Ferment

W HEN ONE first catches the smell of the sea, his lungs seem involuntarily to expand, the same as they do when he steps into the open air after long confinement indoors. On the beach he is simply emerging into a larger and more primitive out-of-doors. There before him is aboriginal space, and the breath of it thrills and dilates his body. He stands at the open door of the continent and eagerly drinks the large air. This breeze savors of the original element; it is a breath out of the morning of the world — bitter, but so fresh and tonic! He has taken salt grossly and at second hand all his days; now let him inhale it at the fountainhead, and let its impalpable crystals penetrate his spirit and prick and chafe him into new activity.

Nothing is more singular and unexpected to the landsman than the combing of the waves — a momentary perpendicular or incurving wall of water, a few yards from shore, with other water spilling or pouring over it as over a milldam, thus exhibiting for an instant a clear, perfectly formed cataract. But instantly the wall crumbles, or is crushed down, and in place of it there is a wild caldron of foaming, boiling water and sand.

There seems to be something more cosmic, or shall I say astronomic, in the sea than in the shore. Here you behold the round back of the globe: the lines are planetary. You feel that here is the true surface of the sphere, the curving, delicate sides of this huge bubble. On the land, amid the wrinkles of the hills, you have place, fixedness, locality, a nook in the chimney corner; but upon the sea you are literally adrift; place is not, boundaries are not, space is vacant. You are upon the smooth disk of the planet, like a man bestriding the moon. Under your feet runs the line of the earth's rotundity, and round about you the same curve bounds your vision.

We seem to breathe a larger air on the coast. It is the place for large types, large thoughts. 'Tis not farms or a township we see now, but God's own domain. Possession, ownership, civilization, boundary lines cease, and there within reach is a clear page of terrestrial space, as unmarred and as unmarrable as if plucked from the sidereal heavens.

How inviting and adventurous the ships look, dropping behind the rim of the horizon or gently blown along its edge, their yardarms pointing to all quarters of the globe! Mystery, adventure, the promise of unknown lands, beckon to us from the full-rigged ships. One does not see them come or depart; they dawn upon him like his own thoughts, some dim and shadowy, just hovering on the verge of consciousness, others white and full, a solace to the eye. But presently, while you ponder, they are gone or else vaguely notch the horizon line. Illusion, enchantment, hover over the sail ships. They have the charm of the ancient world of fable and romance. They are blown by Homeric winds. They are a survival from the remotest times. But yonder comes a black steamship, cutting across this enchanted circle in defiance of wind and tide; this is the modern world snubbing and dispelling our illusions and putting our poets to flight.

But the veritable oceanic brine there before one, the continental, primordial, original liquid, the hoary, eternal sea itself — what can a lover of fields and woods make of it? None of the

charms or solacements of birds and flowers here, or of rural
sights and sounds; no repose, no plaintiveness, no dumb com-
panionship; but a spirit threatening, hungering, remorseless,
decoying, fascinating, serpentine, rebelling and forever rebelling against the fiat, "Thus far shalt thou come, and no
farther." The voice of the sea is unlike any other sound in
nature; more riant and chafing than any roar of woods or
storms. One never ceases to hear the briny, rimy, weltering
quality — it is salt to the ear no less than to the smell. One
fancies he hears the friction and clashing of the invisible crystals. A shooting avalanche of snow might have this frosty,
beaded, anfractuous sound. The sands and pebbles and
broken shells have something to do with it; but without these
that threatening, serrated edge remains — the grainy, saline
voice of the sea.

The sea shifts its pillow like an uneasy sleeper. The contour
of the beach is seldom two days alike; that round, smooth
bolster of sand is at times very prominent. The waves stroke
and caress it and slide their delicate sea draperies over it, as if
they were indeed making their bed. When you walk there
again it is gone, carried down under the waves, and the beach
is low and naked.

Sometimes the waves look like revolving cylindrical knives,
carving the coast. Then they thrust up their thin, crescent-
shaped edges, like reapers, reaping only shells and sand; yet one
seems to hear the hiss of a great sickle, the crackle of stubble,
the rustle of sheaves, and the screening of grain. Then again
there is mimic thunder as the waves burst, followed by a sound
like the downpouring of torrents of rain. How it shovels the
sand and sifts and washes it forever! Every particle of silt goes
seaward; it is the earth pollen with which the sunken floors of
the sea are deeply covered. What material for future conti-

nents, new worlds, and new peoples is hoarded within its sun-less depths! How Darwin longed to read the sealed book of the earth's history that lies buried beneath the sea! He thought it probable that the first continents were there; that the areas of elevation and of subsidence had changed places in the remote past.

And yet famine and thirst, dismay and death, stalk the wave. Contradictory, multitudinous sea! the despoiler and yet the renewer; barren as a rock, yet as fruitful as a field; old as Time, and young as today; merciless as Fate, and tender as Love; the fountain of all waters, yet mocking its victims with the most horrible thirst; smiting like a hammer and caressing like a lady's palm; falling upon the shore like a wall of rock then creeping up the sands as with the rustle of an infant's drapery; cesspool of the continents, yet "creating a sweet clime by its breath"; pit of terrors, gulf of despair, caldron of hell, yet health, power, beauty, enchantment, dwell forever with the sea.[1]

About all we have in mind when we think of the earth is this thin pellicle of soil with which the granite framework of the globe is clothed — a red and brown film of pulverized and oxi-dized rock, scarcely thicker, relatively, than the paint or enamel which some women put on their cheeks, and which the rains often wash away as a tear washes off the paint and powder. But it is the main thing to us. Out of it we came and unto it we return. "Earth to earth, and dust to dust." The dust becomes warm and animated for a little while, takes on form and color, stalks about recuperating itself from its parent dust underfoot, and then fades and is resolved into the original earth elements. We are built up out of the ground quite as literally as the trees are, but not quite so immediately. The vegetable is between us and the soil, but our dependence is none the less real. "As common as dust" is one of our sayings, but the common, the universal, is always our mainstay in this world. When we see the dust turned into fruit and flowers and grain by that intangible thing called vegetable life, or into the bodies of men and women by the equally mysterious agency of animal life, we think better of it. The trembling gold of the pond lily's heart and its petals like carved snow are no more a transformation of a little black muck and ooze by the chemistry of the sunbeam than our bodies and minds, too, are a transformation of the soil underfoot.

We are rooted to the air through our lungs and to the soil through our stomachs. We are walking trees and floating plants. The soil which in one form we spurn with our feet and in another take into our mouths and into our blood — what a composite product it is! It is the grist out of which our bread of life is made, the grist which the mills of the gods, the slow patient gods of Erosion, have been so long grinding — grinding probably more millions of years than we have any idea of. The original stuff, the pulverized granite, was probably not very nourishing, but the fruitful hand of time has made it so. It is the kind of grist that improves with the keeping, and the more the meal worms have worked in it, the better the bread. Indeed, until it has been eaten and digested by our faithful servitors the vegetables, it does not make the loaf that is our staff of life. The more death has gone into it, the more life comes out of it; the more it is a cemetery, the more it becomes a nursery; the more the rocks perish, the more the fields flourish.

This story of the soil appeals to the imagination. To have a bit of earth to plant, to hoe, to delve in, is a rare privilege. If one stops to consider, one cannot turn it with his spade without emotion. We look back with the mind's eye through the vista of geologic time and we see islands and continents of barren, jagged rocks, not a grain of soil anywhere. We look again and behold a world of rounded hills and fertile valleys and plains, depth of soil where before were frowning rocks. The hand of time with its potent fingers of heat, frost, cloud, and air has passed slowly over the scene, and the miracle is done. The rocks turn to herbage, the fetid gases to the breath of flowers. The mountain melts down into a harvest field; volcanic scoria changes into garden mold; where towered a cliff now basks a green slope; where the strata yawned now bubbles a fountain; where the earth trembled, verdure now undulates. Your lawn and your meadow are built up of the ruins of the foreworld. The leanness of granite and gneiss has become the fat of the land. What transformation and promotion! — the decrepitude of the hills becoming the strength of the plains, the decay of the heights resulting in the renewal of the valleys!

Many of our hills are but the stumps of mountains which the hand of time has cut down. Hence we may say that if God made the mountains, time made the hills.

What adds to the wonder of the earth's grist is that the millstones that did the work and are still doing it are the gentle forces that career above our heads — the sunbeam, the cloud, the air, the frost. The rain's gentle fall, the air's velvet touch, the sun's noiseless rays, the frost's exquisite crystals, these combined are the agents that crush the rocks and pulverize the mountains and transform continents of sterile granite into a world of fertile soils. It is as if baby fingers did the work of giant powder and dynamite. Give the clouds and the sunbeams time enough, and the Alps and the Andes disappear before them or are transformed into plains where corn may grow and cattle graze. The snow falls as softly as down and lies almost as lightly, yet the crags crumble beneath it; compacted by gravity, out of it grew the tremendous ice sheet that ground off the mountain summits, that scooped out lakes and valleys, and modeled our northern landscapes as the sculptor his clay image.

Not only are the mills of the gods grinding here, but the great cosmic mill in the sidereal heavens is grinding also, and some of its dust reaches our planet. Cosmic dust is apparently falling on the earth at all times. It is found in the heart of hail-stones and in Alpine snows and helps make up the mud of the ocean floors.

During the unthinkable time of the revolution of the earth around the sun, the amount of cosmic matter that has fallen upon its surface from out the depths of space must be enor-mous.

The soil underfoot, or that we turn with our plow, how it thrills with life or the potencies of life! What a fresh, good odor it exhales when we turn it with our spade or plow in spring! It is good. No wonder children and horses like to eat it!

How inert and dead it looks, yet what silent, potent fer-mentations are going on there — millions and trillions of minute organisms ready to further your scheme of agriculture or horticulture. Plant your wheat or your corn in it, and behold the miracle of a birth of a plant or a tree. How it pushes up, fed and stimulated by the soil, through the agency of heat and moisture! It makes visible to the eye the life that is latent or held in suspense there in the cool, impassive ground. The acorn, the chestnut, the maple keys, have but to lie on the surface of the moist earth to feel its power and send down root-lets to meet it.

There is no better illustration of the way decay and death play into the hands of life than the soil underfoot. The earth dies daily and has done so through countless ages. But life and youth spring forever from its decay; indeed, could not spring at all till the decay began. All the soil was once rock, perhaps many times rock, as the water that flows by may have been many times ice.

The soft, slow, aerial forces, how long and patiently they have worked! Oxygen has played its part in the way of oxidation and dioxidation of minerals. Carbon or carbonic acid has played its part, hydrogen has played its. Even granite yields slowly but surely to the action of rain water. The sun is of course the great dynamo that runs the earth machinery and, through moisture and the air currents, reduces the rocks to soil. Without solar heat we should have no rain, and without rain we should have no soil. The decay of a mountain makes a hill of fertile fields. The soil, as we know it, is the product of three great processes — mechanical, chemical, and vital — which have been going on for untold ages. The mechanical we see in the friction of winds and waves and the grinding of glaciers, and in the destructive effects of heat and cold upon the rocks; the chemical in the solvent power of rain water and of water charged with various acids and gases. The soil is rarely the color of the underlying rock from which it came, by reason of the action of the various gases of the atmosphere. Iron is black, but when turned into rust by the oxygen of the air, it is red.

The vital processes that have contributed to the soil, we see going on about us in the decay of animal and vegetable matter. It is this process that gives the humus to the soil, in fact, almost humanizes it, making it tender and full of sentiment and memories, as it were, so that it responds more quickly to our needs and to our culture. The elements of the soil remember all those forms of animal and vegetable life of which they once

made a part, and they take them on again the more readily.
Hence the quick action of wood ashes upon vegetable life.
Iron and lime and phosphorus that have once been taken up by
growing plants and trees seem to have acquired new properties
and are the more readily taken up again.

We hardly realize how life itself has stored up life in the soil,
how the organic has wedded and blended with the inorganic in
the ground we walk upon.   Many if not all of the sedimentary
rocks that were laid down in the abysms of the old ocean, out of
which our soil has been produced, and that are being laid down
now, out of which future soils will be produced, were and are
largely of organic origin, the leavings of untold myriads of
minute marine animals that lived millions of years ago.   Our
limestone rocks, thousands of feet thick in places, the decom-
position of which furnishes some of our most fertile soils, are
mainly of plant and animal origin.

Our senses are too dull and coarse to apprehend the subtle
and incessant play of forces about us — the finer play and ema-
nations of matter that go on all about us and through us.   From
a lighted candle or gas jet or glowing metal, shoot corpuscles or
electrons, the basic constituents of matter, of inconceivable
smallness — a thousand times smaller than an atom of hydrogen
— and at the inconceivable speed of 10,000 to 90,000 miles a
second.   Think how we are bombarded by these bullets as we
sit around the lamp or under the gas jet at night and are all
unconscious of them!   We are immersed in a sea of forces and
potentialities of which we hardly dream.   Of the scale of
temperatures, from absolute zero to the heat of the sun, human
life knows only a minute fraction.   So of the elemental play of
forces about us and over us, terrestrial and celestial — too fine
for our apprehension on the one hand, and too large on the
other — we know but a fraction.

The quivering and the throbbing of the earth under our feet in changes of temperature, the bendings and oscillations of the crust under the tread of the great atmospheric waves, the vital fermentations and oxidations in the soil — are all beyond the reach of our dull senses. We hear the wind in the treetops, but we do not hear the humming of the sap in the trees. We feel the pull of gravity, but we do not feel the medium through which it works. During the solar storms and disturbances all our magnetic and electrical instruments are agitated, but you and I are all unconscious of the agitation.

There are no doubt vibrations from out the depths of space that might reach our ears as sound were they attuned to the ether as the eye is when it receives a ray of light. We might hear the rush of the planets along their orbits, we might hear the explosions and uprushes in the sun; we might hear the wild whirl and dance of the nebulæ, where suns and systems are being formed; we might hear the "wreck of matter and the crush of worlds" that evidently takes place now and then in the abysms of space, because all these things must send through the ether impulses and tremblings that reach our planet. But if we felt or heard or saw or were conscious of all that was going on in the universe, what a state of agitation we should be in! Our scale of apprehension is wisely limited, mainly to things that concern our well-being.[2]

How closely every crack and corner of nature is packed with life, especially in our northern temperate zone! I was impressed with this fact when during several June days I was occupied with road mending on the farm where I was born. To open up the loosely piled and decaying laminated rocks was to open up a little biological and zoological museum, so many of our smaller forms of life harbored there. From chipmunks to ants and spiders, animal life flourished. We disturbed the chipmunks in their den a foot and a half or more beneath the loosely piled rocks. There were two of them in a soft, warm nest of dry, shredded maple leaves. They did not wait to be turned out of doors but when they heard the racket overhead bolted precipitately. Two living together surprised me, as heretofore I had never known but one in a den. Near them a milk snake had stowed himself away in a crevice, and in the little earthquake which we set up got badly crushed. Two little red-bellied snakes about one foot long had also found harbor there.

The ants rushed about in great consternation when their eggs were suddenly exposed. In fact, there was live natural history under every stone about us. Some children brought me pieces of stone, which they picked up close by, which sheltered a variety of cocoon-building spiders. One small, dark-striped spider was carrying about its ball of eggs, the size of a large pea, attached to the hind part of its body. This became detached, when she seized it eagerly and bore it about held between her legs. Another fragment of stone, the size of one's hand, sheltered the chrysalis of some species of butterfly which was attached to it at its tail. It was surprising to see this en-shrouded creature, blind and deaf, wriggle and thrash about as if threatening us with its wrath for invading its sanctuary. One would about as soon expect to see an egg protest.

Thus the naturalist finds his pleasures everywhere. Every solitude to him is peopled. Every morning or evening walk yields him a harvest to eye or ear.[3]

For twenty years or more the chipmunks have been slowly disappearing from all parts of the country with which I am familiar; hardly one of late years where there used to be ten when I was a boy. But suddenly last year they began to be noticeable, and the present season they are here in something like their old-time numbers. I hear of them from different parts of the State — the result of migration, I was at first inclined to think, till John Lewis Childs told me they had become suddenly numerous on Long Island. This fact seems to exclude the idea of migration from some other part of the country. Some parasite, some plague — chipmunk smallpox or cholera — may have kept their numbers down for years, when suddenly the enemy vanishes and the race recovers.

These vicissitudes, these ebbs and flows, probably run all through the life of nature about us and we observe them not. I know an ash tree by the roadside that year after year, early in the season, lost part of its foliage by some form of leaf blight. Surely, I thought, that tree is doomed; then there came a season when the blight did not appear, and it has not appeared since.

Of late years the prairie horned lark has appeared upon my native hills in the Catskills, where, in my youth, they were never seen. Such game birds as the quail ebb and flow in New York and New England, according as the winters are mild or severe. Not many years ago a series of mild winters gave the quail a great lift in the Hudson River Valley, where I live. The call of Bob White lent a new charm to the spring fields. Then came two or three very severe winters and the cheery call of the quail is heard in our fields no more. The same severe winters cut off the race of 'possums, which had multiplied in our country till they were as common as rabbits. A few years ago there was a fearful ebb in the life of the ruffed grouse, all over the country from Maine to Minnesota. More than fifty per cent of the birds vanished in a single season. The cause of it has not yet been cleared up. Now the birds are slowly reappearing.

The natural balance of life in any field cannot long be disturbed. Though nature at times seems to permit excesses, yet she sooner or later corrects them and restores the balance. The life of the globe could never have attained its present development on any other plane. A certain peace and harmony have come out of the perpetual struggle and warfare of opposing tendencies and forces.

The weasel is the most fierce and bloodthirsty of all our smaller mammals; mice and rats, squirrels and rabbits, and birds vanish before him, yet he does not overrun our fields and woods; he is quite a rare beast; some unknown enemy or condition keeps him in check. The defenseless rabbit, upon which so many creatures prey, easily holds its own because it is so very prolific. It also has another advantage; it can and does sleep with its eyes open. The flying squirrel would seem to have a great advantage over the chipmunk, yet it is far less numerous in our woods; it pays for its wings in some way; it is probably less handy and resourceful. Few animals will molest the skunk, yet the world is not filled with skunks; where they are found side by side, the woodchuck, which has many more natural enemies, is far more abundant, not because it is more prolific, which does not seem to be the case, but because, among other things, its food supply is simpler and more universal. The limitation of the natural food supply is, of course, the great factor in the limitation of animal life everywhere. If our spring is late and cold, the robins nest later and have smaller broods than during a warm, early spring.

Man, of course, disturbs the balance of nature wherever he goes. Some forms of life disappear before him, while others thrive and increase in his footsteps. He adds greatly to the food supply of some species, while he cuts off that of others. Most of the field animals partake of his bounty, but the forest animals vanish before him. That any species has actually become extinct through his instrumentality, unless it be that of the passenger pigeon, may well be doubted, though he hastened the extinction of the great auk and maybe the Labrador duck. The buffalo would have become extinct under his ruthless slaughter, had he not stayed his hand in time. Whole tribes and races of animals, some of them fearfully and wonderfully made, became extinct in geologic time, long before man could have played any part in hastening their doom. A change in their environment, through slow crustal movements of the earth or through change of climate that affected their food supply, probably rendered them unfit to survive.[4]

I suspect that, like most countrymen, I was born with a chronic anxiety about the weather. Is it going to rain or snow, be hot or cold, wet or dry? — are inquiries upon which I would fain get the views of every man I meet, and I find that most men are fired with the same desire to get my views upon the same set of subjects. To a countryman the weather means something — to a farmer especially. The farmer has sowed and planted and reaped and vended nothing but weather all his life. The weather must lift the mortgage on his farm and pay his taxes and feed and clothe his family. Of what use is his labor unless seconded by the weather? Hence there is speculation in his eye whenever he looks at the clouds or the moon or the sunset or the stars; for even the Milky Way, in his view, may point the direction of the wind tomorrow and hence is closely related to the price of butter. He may not take the sage's advice to "hitch his wagon to a star," but he pins his hopes to the moon and plants and sows by its phases.

But I am not going to abuse the weather; rather to praise it and make some amends for the many ill-natured things I have said, within hearing of the clouds, when I have been caught in the rain or been parched and withered by the drought.

But the great fact about the rain is that it is the most beneficent of all the operations of nature; more immediately than sunlight even, it means life and growth.   Moisture is the Eve of the physical world, the soft teeming principle given to wife to Adam or heat, and the mother of all that lives.   Sunshine abounds everywhere, but only where the rain or dew follows is there life.

I suppose there is some compensation in a drought; nature doubtless profits by it in some way.   It is a good time to thin out her garden and give the law of the survival of the fittest a chance to come into play.   How the big trees and big plants do rob the little ones! there is not drink enough to go around, and the strongest will have what there is.   It is a rest to vegetation, too, a kind of torrid winter that is followed by a fresh awakening.   Every tree and plant learns a lesson from it, learns to shoot its roots down deep into the perennial supplies of moisture and life.

But when the rain does come, the warm, sun-distilled rain; the far-traveling, vapor-born rain; the impartial, undiscriminating, unstinted rain; equable, bounteous, myriad eyed, searching out every plant and every spear of grass, finding every hidden thing that needs water, falling upon the just and upon the unjust, sponging off every leaf of every tree in the forest and every growth in the fields; music to the ear, a perfume to the smell, an enchantment to the eye; healing the earth, cleansing the air, renewing the fountains; honey to the bee, manna to the herds, and life to all creatures — what spectacle so fills the heart?[5]

Weeds are nature's makeshift.   She rejoices in the grass and the grain, but when these fail to cover her nakedness she resorts to weeds. It is in her plan or a part of her economy to keep the ground constantly covered with vegetation of some sort, and she has layer upon layer of seeds in the soil for this purpose, and the wonder is that each kind lies dormant until it is wanted. If I uncover the earth in any of my fields, ragweed and pigweed spring up; if these are destroyed, harvest grass or quack grass or purslane appears. The spade or plow that turns these under is sure to turn up some other variety, as chickweed, sheep sorrel, or goosefoot. The soil is a storehouse of seeds.

The old farmers say that wood ashes will bring in the white clover, and it will; the germs are in the soil wrapped in a profound slumber, but this stimulus tickles them until they awake. Stramonium has been known to start up on the site of an old farm building when it had not been seen in that locality for thirty years.

Weeds are so full of expedients, and the one engrossing purpose with them is to multiply. The wild onion multiplies at both ends — at the top by seed and at the bottom by offshots. Toadflax travels underground and above ground. Never allow a seed to ripen and yet it will cover your field. Cut off the head of the wild carrot, and in a week or two there are five heads in room of this one; cut off these and by fall there are ten looking defiance at you from the same root. Plant corn in August, and it will go forward with its preparations as if it had the whole season before it. Not so with the weeds; they have learned better. If amaranth, or abutilon, or burdock gets a late start, it makes great haste to develop its seed; it foregoes its tall stalk and wide-flaunting growth and turns all its energies into keeping up the succession of the species. Certain fields under the plow are always infested with "blind nettles," others with wild buckwheat, black bindweed, or cockle. The seed lies dormant under the sward, the warmth and the moisture affect it not until other conditions are fulfilled.

The way in which one plant thus keeps another down is a great mystery. Germs lie there in the soil and resist the stimulating effect of the sun and the rains for years and show no sign. Presently something whispers to them, "Arise, your chance has come; the coast is clear"; and they are up and doing in a twinkling.

Weeds are great travelers; they are, indeed, the tramps of the vegetable world. They are going east, west, north, south; they walk; they fly; they swim; they steal a ride; they travel by rail, by flood, by wind; they go underground, and they go above, across lots, and by the highway. But like other tramps, they find it safest by the highway: in the fields they are intercepted and cut off; but on the public road, every boy, every passing herd of sheep or cows, gives them a lift. Hence the incursion of a new weed is generally first noticed along the highway or the railroad.

A weed which one ruthlessly demolishes when he finds it hiding from the plow amid the strawberries or under the currant bushes and grapevines is the dandelion; yet who would banish it from the meadows or the lawns, where it copies in gold upon the green expanse the stars of the midnight sky? After its first blooming comes its second and finer and more spiritual inflorescence, when its stalk, dropping its more earthly and carnal flower, shoots upward and is presently crowned by a globe of the most delicate and aerial texture. It is like the poet's dream, which succeeds his rank and golden youth. This globe is a fleet of a hundred fairy balloons, each one of which bears a seed which it is destined to drop far from the parent source.

Most weeds have their uses; they are not wholly malevolent.

Emerson says a weed is a plant whose virtues we have not yet discovered; but the wild creatures discover their virtues if we do not. The bumblebee has discovered that the hateful toadflax, which nothing will eat and which in some soils will run out the grass, has honey at its heart. Narrow-leaved plantain is readily eaten by cattle, and the honeybee gathers much pollen from it. The oxeye daisy makes a fair quality of hay if cut before it gets ripe. The cows will eat the leaves of the burdock and the stinging nettles of the woods. But what cannot a cow's tongue stand? She will crop the poison ivy with impunity, and I think would eat thistles if she found them growing in the garden. Leeks and garlics are readily eaten by cattle in the spring and are said to be medicinal to them. Weeds that yield neither pasturage for bee nor herd, yet afford seeds to the fall and winter birds. This is true of most of the obnoxious weeds of the garden and of thistles.

Yet it is pleasant to remember that, in our climate, there are no weeds so persistent and lasting and universal as grass. Grass is the natural covering of the fields. There are but four weeds that I know of — milkweed, live-forever, Canada thistle, and toadflax — that it will not run out in a good soil. We crop it and mow it year after year; and yet, if the season favors, it is sure to come again. Fields that have never known the plow and never been seeded by man are yet covered with grass. And in human nature, too, weeds are by no means in the ascendant, troublesome as they are. The good green grass of love and truthfulness and common sense is more universal and crowds the idle weeds to the wall.[6]

17. The Sound of Nature

O<small>NE SUMMER</small> day, while I was walking along the country road on the farm where I was born, a section of the stone wall opposite me and not more than three or four yards distant suddenly fell down. Amid the general stillness and immobility about me, the effect was quite startling. The question at once arose in my mind as to just what happened to that bit of stone wall at that particular moment to cause it to fall. Maybe the slight vibration imparted to the ground by my tread caused the minute shifting of forces that brought it down. But the time was ripe; a long, slow, silent process of decay and disintegration, or a shifting of the points of bearing amid the fragments of stone by the action of the weather, culminated at that instant, and the wall fell. It was the sudden summing up of half a century or more of atomic changes in the material of the wall. A grain or two of sand yielded to the pressure of long years, and gravity did the rest. It was as when the keystone of an arch crumbles or weakens to the last particle, and the arch suddenly collapses.

In the ordinary course of nature, the great beneficent changes come slowly and silently. The noisy changes, for the most part, mean violence and disruption. The roar of storms and tornados, the explosions of volcanoes, the crash of the thunder, are the result of a sudden break in the equipoise of the elements; from a condition of comparative repose and silence they become fearfully swift and audible. The still small voice is the voice of life and growth and perpetuity. In the stillness of a bright summer day what work is being accomplished! what processes are being consummated! When the tornado comes, how quickly much of it may be brought to naught! In the history of a nation it is the same.

What a noise politics makes in the world, our politics especially! But some silent thinker in his study or some inventor in his laboratory is starting currents that will make or unmake politics for generations to come. How noiseless is the light, yet what power dwells in the sunbeams — mechanical power at one end of the spectrum, in the red and infrared rays, and chemical power at the other or violet and ultraviolet end! It is the mechanical forces — the winds, the rains, the movements of ponderable bodies — that fill the world with noise; the chemical changes that disintegrate the rocks and set the currents of life going are silent. The great loom in which is woven all the living textures that clothe the world with verdure and people it with animated forms makes no sound. Think of the still small voice of radioactivity — so still and small that only molecular science is aware of it, yet physicists believe it to be the mainspring of the universe.

The vast ice engine that we call a glacier is almost as silent as the slumbering rocks and, to all but the eye of science, nearly as immobile, save where it discharges into the sea. It is noisy in its dying, but in the height of its power it is as still as the falling snow of which it is made. Yet give it time enough, and it scoops out the valleys and grinds down the mountains and turns the courses of rivers or makes new ones.

The unknown, the inaudible forces that make for good in every state and community — the gentle word, the kind act, the forgiving look, the quiet demeanor, the silent thinkers and workers, the cheerful and unwearied toilers, the scholar in his study, the scientist in his laboratory — how much more we owe to these things than to the clamorous and discordant voices of the world of politics and the newspaper! Art, literature, philosophy, all speak with the still small voice. How much more potent the voice that speaks out of a great solitude and reverence than the noisy, acrimonious, and disputatious voice! Strong conviction and firm resolution are usually chary of words. Depth of feeling and parsimony of expression go well together.

The mills of the gods upon the earth's surface grind exceeding slow, and exceeding still. They are grinding up the rocks everywhere — pulverizing the granite, the limestone, the sandstone, the basalt, between the upper and nether millstones of air and water to make the soil, but we hear no sound and mark no change; only in geologic time are the results recorded. In still waters we get the rich deposits that add to the fat of the land, and in peaceful, untroubled times is humanity enriched, and the foundations are laid upon which the permanent institutions of a nation are built.

We all know what can be said in favor of turmoil, agitation, war; we all know, as Goethe said, that a man comes to know himself not in thought but in action; and the same is true of a nation. Equally do we know the value of repose, and the slow, silent activities both in the soul of man and in the processes of nature. The most potent and beneficent forces are stillest. The strength of a sentence is not in its adjectives but in its verbs and nouns, and the strength of men and of nations is in their calm, sane, meditative moments. In a time of noise and hurry and materialism like ours, the gospel of the still small voice is always seasonable.[1]

When I was a young man (twenty-five), I wrote a little poem called "Waiting," which has had quite a history, and the burden of which is, "My own shall come to me."

All the best things of my life have come to me unsought but I hope not unearned. That would contradict the principle of equity I have been illustrating. A man does not, in the long run, get wages he has not earned. What I mean is that most of the good things of my life — friends, travel, opportunity — have been unexpected. I do not feel that fortune has driven sharp bargains with me. I am not a disappointed man. Blessed is he who expects little but works as if he expected much.

"Serene I fold my hands and wait," but if I have waited one day, I have hustled the next. If I have had faith that my own would come to me, I have tried to make sure that it was my own and not that of another. Waiting with me has been mainly a cheerful acquiescence in the order of the universe as I found it — a faith in the essential veracity of things. I have waited for the sun to rise and for the seasons to come; I have waited for a chance to put in my oar. Which way do the currents of my being set? What do I love that is worthy and of good report? I will extend myself in this direction; I will annex this territory. I will not wait to see if this or that pays, if this or that notion draws the multitude. I will wait only till I can see my way clearly. In the meantime I will be clearing my eyes and training them to know the real values of life when they see them.

Waiting for someone else to do your work, for what you have not earned to come to you, is to murder time. Waiting for something to turn up is equally poor policy, unless you have already set the currents going that will cause a particular something to turn up. The farmer waits for his harvest after he has sown the seed. The sailor waits for a breeze after he has spread his sail. Much of life is taken up in waiting — fruitful waiting.

I am bound to praise the simple life, because I have lived
it and found it good. When I depart from it, evil results follow. I love a small house, plain clothes, simple living. Many
persons know the luxury of a skin bath — a plunge in the pool
or the wave unhampered by clothing. That is the simple life
— direct and immediate contact with things, life with the false
wrappings torn away — the fine house, the fine equipage, the
expensive habits, all cut off. How free one feels, how good
the elements taste, how close one gets to them, how they fit
one's body and one's soul! To see the fire that warms you or,
better yet, to cut the wood that feeds the fire that warms you;
to see the spring where the water bubbles up that slakes your
thirst and to dip your pail into it; to see the beams that are the
stay of your four walls and the timbers that uphold the roof
that shelters you; to be in direct and personal contact with the
sources of your material life; to want no extras, no shields; to
find the universal elements enough; to find the air and the
water exhilarating; to be refreshed by a morning walk or an
evening saunter; to find a quest of wild berries more satisfying
than a gift of tropic fruit; to be thrilled by the stars at night; to
be elated over a bird's nest or a wild flower in spring — these are
some of the rewards of the simple life.[2]

BOOKS BY JOHN BURROUGHS

Notes on Walt Whitman, Poet and Person (1867)
Wake-Robin (1871)
Winter Sunshine (1875)
Birds and Poets (1877)
Locusts and Wild Honey (1879)
Pepacton (1881)
Fresh Fields (1884)
Signs and Seasons (1886)
Indoor Studies (1889)
Riverby (1894)
Whitman: A Study (1896)
The Light of Day (1900)
(The poem "Waiting" was published in this book)

Literary Values (1902)
Far and Near (1904)
Ways of Nature (1905)
Leaf and Tendril (1908)
Time and Change (1912)
The Summit of the Years (1913)
The Breath of Life (1915)
Under the Apple-Trees (1916)
Field and Study (1919)
Accepting the Universe (1920)
Under the Maples (1921)
The Last Harvest (1922)

Under the Maples and *The Last Harvest* were compiled and edited by Dr. Clara Barrus, Burroughs' biographer, author of *The Life and Letters of John Burroughs,* published in 1925 by Houghton Mifflin, and of *John Burroughs Boy and Man* published in 1926 by Doubleday and Co.

SOURCES OF QUOTATIONS
USED IN THIS BOOK

INDEX

A CATALOG OF SELECTED
DOVER BOOKS
IN ALL FIELDS OF INTEREST

A CATALOG OF SELECTED DOVER
BOOKS IN ALL FIELDS OF INTEREST

CONCERNING THE SPIRITUAL IN ART, Wassily Kandinsky. Pioneering work by father of abstract art. Thoughts on color theory, nature of art. Analysis of earlier masters. 12 illustrations. 80pp. of text. 5⅜ × 8½. 23411-8 Pa. $3.95

ANIMALS: 1,419 Copyright-Free Illustrations of Mammals, Birds, Fish, Insects, etc., Jim Harter (ed.). Clear wood engravings present, in extremely lifelike poses, over 1,000 species of animals. One of the most extensive pictorial sourcebooks of its kind. Captions. Index. 284pp. 9 × 12. 23766-4 Pa. $12.95

CELTIC ART: The Methods of Construction, George Bain. Simple geometric techniques for making Celtic interlacements, spirals, Kells-type initials, animals, humans, etc. Over 500 illustrations. 160pp. 9 × 12. (USO) 22923-8 Pa. $9.95

AN ATLAS OF ANATOMY FOR ARTISTS, Fritz Schider. Most thorough reference work on art anatomy in the world. Hundreds of illustrations, including selections from works by Vesalius, Leonardo, Goya, Ingres, Michelangelo, others. 593 illustrations. 192pp. 7⅛ × 10¼. 20241-0 Pa. $9.95

CELTIC HAND STROKE-BY-STROKE (Irish Half-Uncial from "The Book of Kells"): An Arthur Baker Calligraphy Manual, Arthur Baker. Complete guide to creating each letter of the alphabet in distinctive Celtic manner. Covers hand position, strokes, pens, inks, paper, more. Illustrated. 48pp. 8¼ × 11. 24336-2 Pa. $3.95

EASY ORIGAMI, John Montroll. Charming collection of 32 projects (hat, cup, pelican, piano, swan, many more) specially designed for the novice origami hobbyist. Clearly illustrated easy-to-follow instructions insure that even beginning papercrafters will achieve successful results. 48pp. 8¼ × 11. 27298-2 Pa. $2.95

THE COMPLETE BOOK OF BIRDHOUSE CONSTRUCTION FOR WOOD-WORKERS, Scott D. Campbell. Detailed instructions, illustrations, tables. Also data on bird habitat and instinct patterns. Bibliography. 3 tables. 63 illustrations in 15 figures. 48pp. 5¼ × 8½. 24407-5 Pa. $1.95

BLOOMINGDALE'S ILLUSTRATED 1886 CATALOG: Fashions, Dry Goods and Housewares, Bloomingdale Brothers. Famed merchants' extremely rare catalog depicting about 1,700 products: clothing, housewares, firearms, dry goods, jewelry, more. Invaluable for dating, identifying vintage items. Also, copyright-free graphics for artists, designers. Co-published with Henry Ford Museum & Greenfield Village. 160pp. 8¼ × 11. 25780-0 Pa. $9.95

HISTORIC COSTUME IN PICTURES, Braun & Schneider. Over 1,450 costumed figures in clearly detailed engravings—from dawn of civilization to end of 19th century. Captions. Many folk costumes. 256pp. 8⅜ × 11¾. 23150-X Pa. $11.95

STICKLEY CRAFTSMAN FURNITURE CATALOGS, Gustav Stickley and L. & J. G. Stickley. Beautiful, functional furniture in two authentic catalogs from 1910. 594 illustrations, including 277 photos, show settles, rockers, armchairs, reclining chairs, bookcases, desks, tables. 183pp. 6½ × 9¼.   23838-5 Pa. $9.95

AMERICAN LOCOMOTIVES IN HISTORIC PHOTOGRAPHS: 1858 to 1949, Ron Ziel (ed.). A rare collection of 126 meticulously detailed official photographs, called "builder portraits," of American locomotives that majestically chronicle the rise of steam locomotive power in America. Introduction. Detailed captions. xi + 129pp. 9 × 12.   27393-8 Pa. $12.95

AMERICA'S LIGHTHOUSES: An Illustrated History, Francis Ross Holland, Jr. Delightfully written, profusely illustrated fact-filled survey of over 200 American lighthouses since 1716. History, anecdotes, technological advances, more. 240pp. 8 × 10¾.   25576-X Pa. $11.95

TOWARDS A NEW ARCHITECTURE, Le Corbusier. Pioneering manifesto by founder of "International School." Technical and aesthetic theories, views of industry, economics, relation of form to function, "mass-production split" and much more. Profusely illustrated. 320pp. 6⅛ × 9¼. (USO)   25023-7 Pa. $9.95

HOW THE OTHER HALF LIVES, Jacob Riis. Famous journalistic record, exposing poverty and degradation of New York slums around 1900, by major social reformer. 100 striking and influential photographs. 233pp. 10 × 7⅞.

    22012-5 Pa $10.95

FRUIT KEY AND TWIG KEY TO TREES AND SHRUBS, William M. Harlow. One of the handiest and most widely used identification aids. Fruit key covers 120 deciduous and evergreen species; twig key 160 deciduous species. Easily used. Over 300 photographs. 126pp. 5⅜ × 8½.   20511-8 Pa. $3.95

COMMON BIRD SONGS, Dr. Donald J. Borror. Songs of 60 most common U.S. birds: robins, sparrows, cardinals, bluejays, finches, more—arranged in order of increasing complexity. Up to 9 variations of songs of each species.

    Cassette and manual 99911-4 $8.95

ORCHIDS AS HOUSE PLANTS, Rebecca Tyson Northen. Grow cattleyas and many other kinds of orchids—in a window, in a case, or under artificial light. 63 illustrations. 148pp. 5⅜ × 8½.   23261-1 Pa. $4.95

MONSTER MAZES, Dave Phillips. Masterful mazes at four levels of difficulty. Avoid deadly perils and evil creatures to find magical treasures. Solutions for all 32 exciting illustrated puzzles. 48pp. 8¼ × 11.   26005-4 Pa. $2.95

MOZART'S DON GIOVANNI (DOVER OPERA LIBRETTO SERIES), Wolfgang Amadeus Mozart. Introduced and translated by Ellen H. Bleiler. Standard Italian libretto, with complete English translation. Convenient and thoroughly portable—an ideal companion for reading along with a recording or the performance itself. Introduction. List of characters. Plot summary. 121pp. 5¼ × 8½.

    24944-1 Pa. $2.95

TECHNICAL MANUAL AND DICTIONARY OF CLASSICAL BALLET, Gail Grant. Defines, explains, comments on steps, movements, poses and concepts. 15-page pictorial section. Basic book for student, viewer. 127pp. 5⅜ × 8½.

    21843-0 Pa. $4.95

BRASS INSTRUMENTS: Their History and Development, Anthony Baines. Authoritative, updated survey of the evolution of trumpets, trombones, bugles, cornets, French horns, tubas and other brass wind instruments. Over 140 illustrations and 48 music examples. Corrected and updated by author. New preface. Bibliography. 320pp. 5⅜ × 8½. 27574-4 Pa. $9.95

HOLLYWOOD GLAMOR PORTRAITS, John Kobal (ed.). 145 photos from 1926–49. Harlow, Gable, Bogart, Bacall; 94 stars in all. Full background on photographers, technical aspects. 160pp. 8⅜ × 11¼. 23352-9 Pa. $11.95

MAX AND MORITZ, Wilhelm Busch. Great humor classic in both German and English. Also 10 other works: "Cat and Mouse," "Plisch and Plumm," etc. 216pp. 5⅜ × 8½. 20181-3 Pa. $5.95

THE RAVEN AND OTHER FAVORITE POEMS, Edgar Allan Poe. Over 40 of the author's most memorable poems: "The Bells," "Ulalume," "Israfel," "To Helen," "The Conqueror Worm," "Eldorado," "Annabel Lee," many more. Alphabetic lists of titles and first lines. 64pp. 5³⁄₁₆ × 8¼. 26685-0 Pa. $1.00

SEVEN SCIENCE FICTION NOVELS, H. G. Wells. The standard collection of the great novels. Complete, unabridged. First Men in the Moon, Island of Dr. Moreau, War of the Worlds, Food of the Gods, Invisible Man, Time Machine, In the Days of the Comet. Total of 1,015pp. 5⅜ × 8½. (USO) 20264-X Clothbd. $29.95

AMULETS AND SUPERSTITIONS, E. A. Wallis Budge. Comprehensive discourse on origin, powers of amulets in many ancient cultures: Arab, Persian, Babylonian, Assyrian, Egyptian, Gnostic, Hebrew, Phoenician, Syriac, etc. Covers cross, swastika, crucifix, seals, rings, stones, etc. 584pp. 5⅜ × 8½. 23573-4 Pa. $12.95

RUSSIAN STORIES/PYCCKNE PACCKA3bl: A Dual-Language Book, edited by Gleb Struve. Twelve tales by such masters as Chekhov, Tolstoy, Dostoevsky, Pushkin, others. Excellent word-for-word English translations on facing pages, plus teaching and study aids, Russian/English vocabulary, biographical/critical introductions, more. 416pp. 5⅜ × 8½. 26244-8 Pa. $8.95

PHILADELPHIA THEN AND NOW: 60 Sites Photographed in the Past and Present, Kenneth Finkel and Susan Oyama. Rare photographs of City Hall, Logan Square, Independence Hall, Betsy Ross House, other landmarks juxtaposed with contemporary views. Captures changing face of historic city. Introduction. Captions. 128pp. 8¼ × 11. 25790-8 Pa. $9.95

AIA ARCHITECTURAL GUIDE TO NASSAU AND SUFFOLK COUNTIES, LONG ISLAND, The American Institute of Architects, Long Island Chapter, and the Society for the Preservation of Long Island Antiquities. Comprehensive, well-researched and generously illustrated volume brings to life over three centuries of Long Island's great architectural heritage. More than 240 photographs with authoritative, extensively detailed captions. 176pp. 8¼ × 11. 26946-9 Pa. $14.95

NORTH AMERICAN INDIAN LIFE: Customs and Traditions of 23 Tribes, Elsie Clews Parsons (ed.). 27 fictionalized essays by noted anthropologists examine religion, customs, government, additional facets of life among the Winnebago, Crow, Zuni, Eskimo, other tribes. 480pp. 6⅛ × 9¼. 27377-6 Pa. $10.95

FRANK LLOYD WRIGHT'S HOLLYHOCK HOUSE, Donald Hoffmann. Lavishly illustrated, carefully documented study of one of Wright's most controversial residential designs. Over 120 photographs, floor plans, elevations, etc. Detailed perceptive text by noted Wright scholar. Index. 128pp. 9¼ × 10¾.
27133-1 Pa. $11.95

THE MALE AND FEMALE FIGURE IN MOTION: 60 Classic Photographic Sequences, Eadweard Muybridge. 60 true-action photographs of men and women walking, running, climbing, bending, turning, etc., reproduced from rare 19th-century masterpiece. vi + 121pp. 9 × 12.
24745-7 Pa. $10.95

1001 QUESTIONS ANSWERED ABOUT THE SEASHORE, N. J. Berrill and Jacquelyn Berrill. Queries answered about dolphins, sea snails, sponges, starfish, fishes, shore birds, many others. Covers appearance, breeding, growth, feeding, much more. 305pp. 5¼ × 8¼.
23366-9 Pa. $7.95

GUIDE TO OWL WATCHING IN NORTH AMERICA, Donald S. Heintzelman. Superb guide offers complete data and descriptions of 19 species: barn owl, screech owl, snowy owl, many more. Expert coverage of owl-watching equipment, conservation, migrations and invasions, etc. Guide to observing sites. 84 illustrations. xiii + 193pp. 5⅜ × 8½.
27344-X Pa. $8.95

MEDICINAL AND OTHER USES OF NORTH AMERICAN PLANTS: A Historical Survey with Special Reference to the Eastern Indian Tribes, Charlotte Erichsen-Brown. Chronological historical citations document 500 years of usage of plants, trees, shrubs native to eastern Canada, northeastern U.S. Also complete identifying information. 343 illustrations. 544pp. 6½ × 9¼.
25951-X Pa. $12.95

STORYBOOK MAZES, Dave Phillips. 23 stories and mazes on two-page spreads: Wizard of Oz, Treasure Island, Robin Hood, etc. Solutions. 64pp. 8¼ × 11.
23628-5 Pa. $2.95

NEGRO FOLK MUSIC, U.S.A., Harold Courlander. Noted folklorist's scholarly yet readable analysis of rich and varied musical tradition. Includes authentic versions of over 40 folk songs. Valuable bibliography and discography. xi + 324pp. 5⅜ × 8½.
27350-4 Pa. $7.95

MOVIE-STAR PORTRAITS OF THE FORTIES, John Kobal (ed.). 163 glamor, studio photos of 106 stars of the 1940s: Rita Hayworth, Ava Gardner, Marlon Brando, Clark Gable, many more. 176pp. 8⅜ × 11¼.
23546-7 Pa. $11.95

BENCHLEY LOST AND FOUND, Robert Benchley. Finest humor from early 30s, about pet peeves, child psychologists, post office and others. Mostly unavailable elsewhere. 73 illustrations by Peter Arno and others. 183pp. 5⅜ × 8½.
22410-4 Pa. $5.95

YEKL and THE IMPORTED BRIDEGROOM AND OTHER STORIES OF YIDDISH NEW YORK, Abraham Cahan. Film Hester Street based on Yekl (1896). Novel, other stories among first about Jewish immigrants on N.Y.'s East Side. 240pp. 5⅜ × 8½.
22427-9 Pa. $6.95

SELECTED POEMS, Walt Whitman. Generous sampling from Leaves of Grass. Twenty-four poems include "I Hear America Singing," "Song of the Open Road," "I Sing the Body Electric," "When Lilacs Last in the Dooryard Bloom'd," "O Captain! My Captain!"—all reprinted from an authoritative edition. Lists of titles and first lines. 128pp. 5³⁄₁₆ × 8¼.
26878-0 Pa. $1.00

THE BEST TALES OF HOFFMANN, E. T. A. Hoffmann. 10 of Hoffmann's most important stories: "Nutcracker and the King of Mice," "The Golden Flowerpot," etc. 458pp. 5⅜ × 8½. 21793-0 Pa. $8.95

FROM FETISH TO GOD IN ANCIENT EGYPT, E. A. Wallis Budge. Rich detailed survey of Egyptian conception of "God" and gods, magic, cult of animals, Osiris, more. Also, superb English translations of hymns and legends. 240 illustrations. 545pp. 5⅜ × 8½. 25803-3 Pa. $11.95

FRENCH STORIES/CONTES FRANÇAIS: A Dual-Language Book, Wallace Fowlie. Ten stories by French masters, Voltaire to Camus: "Micromegas" by Voltaire; "The Atheist's Mass" by Balzac; "Minuet" by de Maupassant; "The Guest" by Camus, six more. Excellent English translations on facing pages. Also French-English vocabulary list, exercises, more. 352pp. 5⅜ × 8½. 26443-2 Pa. $8.95

CHICAGO AT THE TURN OF THE CENTURY IN PHOTOGRAPHS: 122 Historic Views from the Collections of the Chicago Historical Society, Larry A. Viskochil. Rare large-format prints offer detailed views of City Hall, State Street, the Loop, Hull House, Union Station, many other landmarks, circa 1904–1913. Introduction. Captions. Maps. 144pp. 9⅜ × 12¼. 24656-6 Pa. $12.95

OLD BROOKLYN IN EARLY PHOTOGRAPHS, 1865–1929, William Lee Younger. Luna Park, Gravesend race track, construction of Grand Army Plaza, moving of Hotel Brighton, etc. 157 previously unpublished photographs. 165pp. 8⅞ × 11¾. 23587-4 Pa. $13.95

THE MYTHS OF THE NORTH AMERICAN INDIANS, Lewis Spence. Rich anthology of the myths and legends of the Algonquins, Iroquois, Pawnees and Sioux, prefaced by an extensive historical and ethnological commentary. 36 illustrations. 480pp. 5⅜ × 8½. 25967-6 Pa. $8.95

AN ENCYCLOPEDIA OF BATTLES: Accounts of Over 1,560 Battles from 1479 B.C. to the Present, David Eggenberger. Essential details of every major battle in recorded history from the first battle of Megiddo in 1479 B.C. to Grenada in 1984. List of Battle Maps. New Appendix covering the years 1967–1984. Index. 99 illustrations. 544pp. 6½ × 9¼. 24913-1 Pa. $14.95

SAILING ALONE AROUND THE WORLD, Captain Joshua Slocum. First man to sail around the world, alone, in small boat. One of great feats of seamanship told in delightful manner. 67 illustrations. 294pp. 5⅜ × 8½. 20326-3 Pa. $5.95

ANARCHISM AND OTHER ESSAYS, Emma Goldman. Powerful, penetrating, prophetic essays on direct action, role of minorities, prison reform, puritan hypocrisy, violence, etc. 271pp. 5⅜ × 8½. 22484-8 Pa. $5.95

MYTHS OF THE HINDUS AND BUDDHISTS, Ananda K. Coomaraswamy and Sister Nivedita. Great stories of the epics; deeds of Krishna, Shiva, taken from puranas, Vedas, folk tales; etc. 32 illustrations. 400pp. 5⅜ × 8½. 21759-0 Pa. $9.95

BEYOND PSYCHOLOGY, Otto Rank. Fear of death, desire of immortality, nature of sexuality, social organization, creativity, according to Rankian system. 291pp. 5⅜ × 8½. 20485-5 Pa. $8.95

A THEOLOGICO-POLITICAL TREATISE, Benedict Spinoza. Also contains unfinished Political Treatise. Great classic on religious liberty, theory of government on common consent. R. Elwes translation. Total of 421pp. 5⅜ × 8½. 20249-6 Pa. $8.95

MY BONDAGE AND MY FREEDOM, Frederick Douglass. Born a slave, Douglass became outspoken force in antislavery movement. The best of Douglass' autobiographies. Graphic description of slave life. 464pp. 5⅜ × 8½.　22457-0 Pa. $8.95

FOLLOWING THE EQUATOR: A Journey Around the World, Mark Twain. Fascinating humorous account of 1897 voyage to Hawaii, Australia, India, New Zealand, etc. Ironic, bemused reports on peoples, customs, climate, flora and fauna, politics, much more. 197 illustrations. 720pp. 5⅜ × 8½.　26113-1 Pa. $15.95

THE PEOPLE CALLED SHAKERS, Edward D. Andrews. Definitive study of Shakers: origins, beliefs, practices, dances, social organization, furniture and crafts, etc. 33 illustrations. 351pp. 5⅜ × 8½.　21081-2 Pa. $8.95

THE MYTHS OF GREECE AND ROME, H. A. Guerber. A classic of mythology, generously illustrated, long prized for its simple, graphic, accurate retelling of the principal myths of Greece and Rome, and for its commentary on their origins and significance. With 64 illustrations by Michelangelo, Raphael, Titian, Rubens, Canova, Bernini and others. 480pp. 5⅜ × 8½.　27584-1 Pa. $9.95

PSYCHOLOGY OF MUSIC, Carl E. Seashore. Classic work discusses music as a medium from psychological viewpoint. Clear treatment of physical acoustics, auditory apparatus, sound perception, development of musical skills, nature of musical feeling, host of other topics. 88 figures. 408pp. 5⅜ × 8½. 21851-1 Pa. $9.95

THE PHILOSOPHY OF HISTORY, Georg W. Hegel. Great classic of Western thought develops concept that history is not chance but rational process, the evolution of freedom. 457pp. 5⅜ × 8½.　20112-0 Pa. $9.95

THE BOOK OF TEA, Kakuzo Okakura. Minor classic of the Orient: entertaining, charming explanation, interpretation of traditional Japanese culture in terms of tea ceremony. 94pp. 5⅜ × 8½.　20070-1 Pa. $3.95

LIFE IN ANCIENT EGYPT, Adolf Erman. Fullest, most thorough, detailed older account with much not in more recent books, domestic life, religion, magic, medicine, commerce, much more. Many illustrations reproduce tomb paintings, carvings, hieroglyphs, etc. 597pp. 5⅜ × 8½.　22632-8 Pa. $10.95

SUNDIALS, Their Theory and Construction, Albert Waugh. Far and away the best, most thorough coverage of ideas, mathematics concerned, types, construction, adjusting anywhere. Simple, nontechnical treatment allows even children to build several of these dials. Over 100 illustrations. 230pp. 5⅜ × 8½.　22947-5 Pa. $7.95

DYNAMICS OF FLUIDS IN POROUS MEDIA, Jacob Bear. For advanced students of ground water hydrology, soil mechanics and physics, drainage and irrigation engineering, and more. 335 illustrations. Exercises, with answers. 784pp. 6⅛ × 9¼.　65675-6 Pa. $19.95

SONGS OF EXPERIENCE: Facsimile Reproduction with 26 Plates in Full Color, William Blake. 26 full-color plates from a rare 1826 edition. Includes "The Tyger," "London," "Holy Thursday," and other poems. Printed text of poems. 48pp. 5¼ × 7.　24636-1 Pa. $4.95

OLD-TIME VIGNETTES IN FULL COLOR, Carol Belanger Grafton (ed.). Over 390 charming, often sentimental illustrations, selected from archives of Victorian graphics—pretty women posing, children playing, food, flowers, kittens and puppies, smiling cherubs, birds and butterflies, much more. All copyright-free. 48pp. 9¼ × 12¼.　27269-9 Pa. $5.95

PERSPECTIVE FOR ARTISTS, Rex Vicat Cole. Depth, perspective of sky and sea, shadows, much more, not usually covered. 391 diagrams, 81 reproductions of drawings and paintings. 279pp. 5⅜ × 8½. 22487-2 Pa. $6.95

DRAWING THE LIVING FIGURE, Joseph Sheppard. Innovative approach to artistic anatomy focuses on specifics of surface anatomy, rather than muscles and bones. Over 170 drawings of live models in front, back and side views, and in widely varying poses. Accompanying diagrams. 177 illustrations. Introduction. Index. 144pp. 8⅜ × 11¼. 26723-7 Pa. $8.95

GOTHIC AND OLD ENGLISH ALPHABETS: 100 Complete Fonts, Dan X. Solo. Add power, elegance to posters, signs, other graphics with 100 stunning copyright-free alphabets: Blackstone, Dolbey, Germania, 97 more—including many lower-case, numerals, punctuation marks. 104pp. 8⅛ × 11. 24695-7 Pa. $8.95

HOW TO DO BEADWORK, Mary White. Fundamental book on craft from simple projects to five-bead chains and woven works. 106 illustrations. 142pp. 5⅜ × 8. 20697-1 Pa. $4.95

THE BOOK OF WOOD CARVING, Charles Marshall Sayers. Finest book for beginners discusses fundamentals and offers 34 designs. "Absolutely first rate . . . well thought out and well executed."—E. J. Tangerman. 118pp. 7¾ × 10⅝. 23654-4 Pa. $5.95

ILLUSTRATED CATALOG OF CIVIL WAR MILITARY GOODS: Union Army Weapons, Insignia, Uniform Accessories, and Other Equipment, Schuyler, Hartley, and Graham. Rare, profusely illustrated 1846 catalog includes Union Army uniform and dress regulations, arms and ammunition, coats, insignia, flags, swords, rifles, etc. 226 illustrations. 160pp. 9 × 12. 24939-5 Pa. $10.95

WOMEN'S FASHIONS OF THE EARLY 1900s: An Unabridged Republication of "New York Fashions, 1909," National Cloak & Suit Co. Rare catalog of mail-order fashions documents women's and children's clothing styles shortly after the turn of the century. Captions offer full descriptions, prices. Invaluable resource for fashion, costume historians. Approximately 725 illustrations. 128pp. 8⅜ × 11¼. 27276-1 Pa. $11.95

THE 1912 AND 1915 GUSTAV STICKLEY FURNITURE CATALOGS, Gustav Stickley. With over 200 detailed illustrations and descriptions, these two catalogs are essential reading and reference materials and identification guides for Stickley furniture. Captions cite materials, dimensions and prices. 112pp. 6½ × 9¼. 26676-1 Pa. $9.95

EARLY AMERICAN LOCOMOTIVES, John H. White, Jr. Finest locomotive engravings from early 19th century: historical (1804–74), main-line (after 1870), special, foreign, etc. 147 plates. 142pp. 11⅜ × 8¼. 22772-3 Pa. $10.95

THE TALL SHIPS OF TODAY IN PHOTOGRAPHS, Frank O. Braynard. Lavishly illustrated tribute to nearly 100 majestic contemporary sailing vessels: Amerigo Vespucci, Clearwater, Constitution, Eagle, Mayflower, Sea Cloud, Victory, many more. Authoritative captions provide statistics, background on each ship. 190 black-and-white photographs and illustrations. Introduction. 128pp. 8⅞ × 11¾. 27163-3 Pa. $13.95

EARLY NINETEENTH-CENTURY CRAFTS AND TRADES, Peter Stockham (ed.). Extremely rare 1807 volume describes to youngsters the crafts and trades of the day: brickmaker, weaver, dressmaker, bookbinder, ropemaker, saddler, many more. Quaint prose, charming illustrations for each craft. 20 black-and-white line illustrations. 192pp. 4⅝ × 6.   27293-1 Pa. $4.95

VICTORIAN FASHIONS AND COSTUMES FROM HARPER'S BAZAR, 1867–1898, Stella Blum (ed.). Day costumes, evening wear, sports clothes, shoes, hats, other accessories in over 1,000 detailed engravings. 320pp. 9⅜ × 12¼.

22990-4 Pa. $13.95

GUSTAV STICKLEY, THE CRAFTSMAN, Mary Ann Smith. Superb study surveys broad scope of Stickley's achievement, especially in architecture. Design philosophy, rise and fall of the Craftsman empire, descriptions and floor plans for many Craftsman houses, more. 86 black-and-white halftones. 31 line illustrations. Introduction. 208pp. 6½ × 9¼.   27210-9 Pa. $9.95

THE LONG ISLAND RAIL ROAD IN EARLY PHOTOGRAPHS, Ron Ziel. Over 220 rare photos, informative text document origin (1844) and development of rail service on Long Island. Vintage views of early trains, locomotives, stations, passengers, crews, much more. Captions. 8⅞ × 11¾.   26301-0 Pa. $13.95

THE BOOK OF OLD SHIPS: From Egyptian Galleys to Clipper Ships, Henry B. Culver. Superb, authoritative history of sailing vessels, with 80 magnificent line illustrations. Galley, bark, caravel, longship, whaler, many more. Detailed, informative text on each vessel by noted naval historian. Introduction. 256pp. 5⅜ × 8½.   27332-6 Pa. $6.95

TEN BOOKS ON ARCHITECTURE, Vitruvius. The most important book ever written on architecture. Early Roman aesthetics, technology, classical orders, site selection, all other aspects. Morgan translation. 331pp. 5⅜ × 8½. 20645-9 Pa. $8.95

THE HUMAN FIGURE IN MOTION, Eadweard Muybridge. More than 4,500 stopped-action photos, in action series, showing undraped men, women, children jumping, lying down, throwing, sitting, wrestling, carrying, etc. 390pp. 7⅞ × 10⅝.

20204-6 Clothbd. $24.95

TREES OF THE EASTERN AND CENTRAL UNITED STATES AND CANADA, William M. Harlow. Best one-volume guide to 140 trees. Full descriptions, woodlore, range, etc. Over 600 illustrations. Handy size. 288pp. 4½ × 6⅜.

20395-6 Pa. $5.95

SONGS OF WESTERN BIRDS, Dr. Donald J. Borror. Complete song and call repertoire of 60 western species, including flycatchers, juncoes, cactus wrens, many more—includes fully illustrated booklet.   Cassette and manual 99913-0 $8.95

GROWING AND USING HERBS AND SPICES, Milo Miloradovich. Versatile handbook provides all the information needed for cultivation and use of all the herbs and spices available in North America. 4 illustrations. Index. Glossary. 236pp. 5⅜ × 8½.   25058-X Pa. $6.95

BIG BOOK OF MAZES AND LABYRINTHS, Walter Shepherd. 50 mazes and labyrinths in all—classical, solid, ripple, and more—in one great volume. Perfect inexpensive puzzler for clever youngsters. Full solutions. 112pp. 8⅛ × 11.

22951-3 Pa. $4.95

PIANO TUNING, J. Cree Fischer. Clearest, best book for beginner, amateur. Simple repairs, raising dropped notes, tuning by easy method of flattened fifths. No previous skills needed. 4 illustrations. 201pp. 5⅜ × 8½. 23267-0 Pa. $5.95

A SOURCE BOOK IN THEATRICAL HISTORY, A. M. Nagler. Contemporary observers on acting, directing, make-up, costuming, stage props, machinery, scene design, from Ancient Greece to Chekhov. 611pp. 5⅜ × 8½. 20515-0 Pa. $11.95

THE COMPLETE NONSENSE OF EDWARD LEAR, Edward Lear. All nonsense limericks, zany alphabets, Owl and Pussycat, songs, nonsense botany, etc., illustrated by Lear. Total of 320pp. 5⅜ × 8½. (USO) 20167-8 Pa. $6.95

VICTORIAN PARLOUR POETRY: An Annotated Anthology, Michael R. Turner. 117 gems by Longfellow, Tennyson, Browning, many lesser-known poets. "The Village Blacksmith," "Curfew Must Not Ring Tonight," "Only a Baby Small," dozens more, often difficult to find elsewhere. Index of poets, titles, first lines. xxiii + 325pp. 5⅜ × 8¼. 27044-0 Pa. $8.95

DUBLINERS, James Joyce. Fifteen stories offer vivid, tightly focused observations of the lives of Dublin's poorer classes. At least one, "The Dead," is considered a masterpiece. Reprinted complete and unabridged from standard edition. 160pp. 5³⁄₁₆ × 8¼. 26870-5 Pa. $1.00

THE HAUNTED MONASTERY and THE CHINESE MAZE MURDERS, Robert van Gulik. Two full novels by van Gulik, set in 7th-century China, continue adventures of Judge Dee and his companions. An evil Taoist monastery, seemingly supernatural events; overgrown topiary maze hides strange crimes. 27 illustrations. 328pp. 5⅜ × 8½. 23502-5 Pa. $7.95

THE BOOK OF THE SACRED MAGIC OF ABRAMELIN THE MAGE, translated by S. MacGregor Mathers. Medieval manuscript of ceremonial magic. Basic document in Aleister Crowley, Golden Dawn groups. 268pp. 5⅜ × 8½. 23211-5 Pa. $8.95

NEW RUSSIAN-ENGLISH AND ENGLISH-RUSSIAN DICTIONARY, M. A. O'Brien. This is a remarkably handy Russian dictionary, containing a surprising amount of information, including over 70,000 entries. 366pp. 4½ × 6⅛. 20208-9 Pa. $9.95

HISTORIC HOMES OF THE AMERICAN PRESIDENTS, Second, Revised Edition, Irvin Haas. A traveler's guide to American Presidential homes, most open to the public, depicting and describing homes occupied by every American President from George Washington to George Bush. With visiting hours, admission charges, travel routes. 175 photographs. Index. 160pp. 8¼ × 11. 26751-2 Pa. $10.95

NEW YORK IN THE FORTIES, Andreas Feininger. 162 brilliant photographs by the well-known photographer, formerly with *Life* magazine. Commuters, shoppers, Times Square at night, much else from city at its peak. Captions by John von Hartz. 181pp. 9¼ × 10¾. 23585-8 Pa. $12.95

INDIAN SIGN LANGUAGE, William Tomkins. Over 525 signs developed by Sioux and other tribes. Written instructions and diagrams. Also 290 pictographs. 111pp. 6⅛ × 9¼. 22029-X Pa. $3.50

ANATOMY: A Complete Guide for Artists, Joseph Sheppard. A master of figure drawing shows artists how to render human anatomy convincingly. Over 460 illustrations. 224pp. 8⅜ × 11¼. 27279-6 Pa. $10.95

MEDIEVAL CALLIGRAPHY: Its History and Technique, Marc Drogin. Spirited history, comprehensive instruction manual covers 13 styles (ca. 4th century thru 15th). Excellent photographs; directions for duplicating medieval techniques with modern tools. 224pp. 8⅜ × 11¼. 26142-5 Pa. $11.95

DRIED FLOWERS: How to Prepare Them, Sarah Whitlock and Martha Rankin. Complete instructions on how to use silica gel, meal and borax, perlite aggregate, sand and borax, glycerine and water to create attractive permanent flower arrangements. 12 illustrations. 32pp. 5⅜ × 8½. 21802-3 Pa. $1.00

EASY-TO-MAKE BIRD FEEDERS FOR WOODWORKERS, Scott D. Campbell. Detailed, simple-to-use guide for designing, constructing, caring for and using feeders. Text, illustrations for 12 classic and contemporary designs. 96pp. 5⅜ × 8½. 25847-5 Pa. $2.95

OLD-TIME CRAFTS AND TRADES, Peter Stockham. An 1807 book created to teach children about crafts and trades open to them as future careers. It describes in detailed, nontechnical terms 24 different occupations, among them coachmaker, gardener, hairdresser, lacemaker, shoemaker, wheelwright, copper-plate printer, milliner, trunkmaker, merchant and brewer. Finely detailed engravings illustrate each occupation. 192pp. 4⅝ × 6. 27398-9 Pa. $4.95

THE HISTORY OF UNDERCLOTHES, C. Willett Cunnington and Phyllis Cunnington. Fascinating, well-documented survey covering six centuries of English undergarments, enhanced with over 100 illustrations: 12th-century laced-up bodice, footed long drawers (1795), 19th-century bustles, 19th-century corsets for men, Victorian "bust improvers," much more. 272pp. 5⅜ × 8¼. 27124-2 Pa. $9.95

ARTS AND CRAFTS FURNITURE: The Complete Brooks Catalog of 1912, Brooks Manufacturing Co. Photos and detailed descriptions of more than 150 now very collectible furniture designs from the Arts and Crafts movement depict davenports, settees, buffets, desks, tables, chairs, bedsteads, dressers and more, all built of solid, quarter-sawed oak. Invaluable for students and enthusiasts of antiques, Americana and the decorative arts. 80pp. 6½ × 9¼. 27471-3 Pa. $7.95

HOW WE INVENTED THE AIRPLANE: An Illustrated History, Orville Wright. Fascinating firsthand account covers early experiments, construction of planes and motors, first flights, much more. Introduction and commentary by Fred C. Kelly. 76 photographs. 96pp. 8¼ × 11. 25662-6 Pa. $8.95

THE ARTS OF THE SAILOR: Knotting, Splicing and Ropework, Hervey Garrett Smith. Indispensable shipboard reference covers tools, basic knots and useful hitches; handsewing and canvas work, more. Over 100 illustrations. Delightful reading for sea lovers. 256pp. 5⅜ × 8½. 26440-8 Pa. $7.95

FRANK LLOYD WRIGHT'S FALLINGWATER: The House and Its History, Second, Revised Edition, Donald Hoffmann. A total revision—both in text and illustrations—of the standard document on Fallingwater, the boldest, most personal architectural statement of Wright's mature years, updated with valuable new material from the recently opened Frank Lloyd Wright Archives. "Fascinating"—*The New York Times.* 116 illustrations. 128pp. 9¼ × 10¾. 27430-6 Pa. $10.95

PHOTOGRAPHIC SKETCHBOOK OF THE CIVIL WAR, Alexander Gardner. 100 photos taken on field during the Civil War. Famous shots of Manassas, Harper's Ferry, Lincoln, Richmond, slave pens, etc. 244pp. 10⅝ × 8¼.
22731-6 Pa. $9.95

FIVE ACRES AND INDEPENDENCE, Maurice G. Kains. Great back-to-the-land classic explains basics of self-sufficient farming. The one book to get. 95 illustrations. 397pp. 5⅜ × 8½. 20974-1 Pa. $7.95

SONGS OF EASTERN BIRDS, Dr. Donald J. Borror. Songs and calls of 60 species most common to eastern U.S.: warblers, woodpeckers, flycatchers, thrushes, larks, many more in high-quality recording. Cassette and manual 99912-2 $8.95

A MODERN HERBAL, Margaret Grieve. Much the fullest, most exact, most useful compilation of herbal material. Gigantic alphabetical encyclopedia, from aconite to zedoary, gives botanical information, medical properties, folklore, economic uses, much else. Indispensable to serious reader. 161 illustrations. 888pp. 6½ × 9¼. 2-vol. set. (USO) Vol. I: 22798-7 Pa. $9.95
Vol. II: 22799-5 Pa. $9.95

HIDDEN TREASURE MAZE BOOK, Dave Phillips. Solve 34 challenging mazes accompanied by heroic tales of adventure. Evil dragons, people-eating plants, bloodthirsty giants, many more dangerous adversaries lurk at every twist and turn. 34 mazes, stories, solutions. 48pp. 8¼ × 11. 24566-7 Pa. $2.95

LETTERS OF W. A. MOZART, Wolfgang A. Mozart. Remarkable letters show bawdy wit, humor, imagination, musical insights, contemporary musical world; includes some letters from Leopold Mozart. 276pp. 5⅜ × 8½. 22859-2 Pa. $7.95

BASIC PRINCIPLES OF CLASSICAL BALLET, Agrippina Vaganova. Great Russian theoretician, teacher explains methods for teaching classical ballet. 118 illustrations. 175pp. 5⅜ × 8½. 22036-2 Pa. $4.95

THE JUMPING FROG, Mark Twain. Revenge edition. The original story of The Celebrated Jumping Frog of Calaveras County, a hapless French translation, and Twain's hilarious "retranslation" from the French. 12 illustrations. 66pp. 5⅜ × 8½.
22686-7 Pa. $3.95

BEST REMEMBERED POEMS, Martin Gardner (ed.). The 126 poems in this superb collection of 19th- and 20th-century British and American verse range from Shelley's "To a Skylark" to the impassioned "Renascence" of Edna St. Vincent Millay and to Edward Lear's whimsical "The Owl and the Pussycat." 224pp. 5⅜ × 8½.
27165-X Pa. $4.95

COMPLETE SONNETS, William Shakespeare. Over 150 exquisite poems deal with love, friendship, the tyranny of time, beauty's evanescence, death and other themes in language of remarkable power, precision and beauty. Glossary of archaic terms. 80pp. 5$^{3}/_{16}$ × 8¼. 26686-9 Pa. $1.00

BODIES IN A BOOKSHOP, R. T. Campbell. Challenging mystery of blackmail and murder with ingenious plot and superbly drawn characters. In the best tradition of British suspense fiction. 192pp. 5⅜ × 8½. 24720-1 Pa. $5.95

THE WIT AND HUMOR OF OSCAR WILDE, Alvin Redman (ed.). More than 1,000 ripostes, paradoxes, wisecracks: Work is the curse of the drinking classes; I can resist everything except temptation; etc. 258pp. 5⅜ × 8½. **20602-5 Pa. $5.95**

SHAKESPEARE LEXICON AND QUOTATION DICTIONARY, Alexander Schmidt. Full definitions, locations, shades of meaning in every word in plays and poems. More than 50,000 exact quotations. 1,485pp. 6½ × 9¼. 2-vol. set.
Vol. I: 22726-X Pa. $16.95
Vol. 2: 22727-8 Pa. $15.95

SELECTED POEMS, Emily Dickinson. Over 100 best-known, best-loved poems by one of America's foremost poets, reprinted from authoritative early editions. No comparable edition at this price. Index of first lines. 64pp. 5³⁄₁₆ × 8¼.
26466-1 Pa. $1.00

CELEBRATED CASES OF JUDGE DEE (DEE GOONG AN), translated by Robert van Gulik. Authentic 18th-century Chinese detective novel; Dee and associates solve three interlocked cases. Led to van Gulik's own stories with same characters. Extensive introduction. 9 illustrations. 237pp. 5⅜ × 8½.
23337-5 Pa. $6.95

THE MALLEUS MALEFICARUM OF KRAMER AND SPRENGER, translated by Montague Summers. Full text of most important witchhunter's "bible," used by both Catholics and Protestants. 278pp. 6⅝ × 10. **22802-9 Pa. $11.95**

SPANISH STORIES/CUENTOS ESPAÑOLES: A Dual-Language Book, Angel Flores (ed.). Unique format offers 13 great stories in Spanish by Cervantes, Borges, others. Faithful English translations on facing pages. 352pp. 5⅜ × 8½.
25399-6 Pa. $8.95

THE CHICAGO WORLD'S FAIR OF 1893: A Photographic Record, Stanley Appelbaum (ed.). 128 rare photos show 200 buildings, Beaux-Arts architecture, Midway, original Ferris Wheel, Edison's kinetoscope, more. Architectural emphasis; full text. 116pp. 8¼ × 11. **23990-X Pa. $9.95**

OLD QUEENS, N.Y., IN EARLY PHOTOGRAPHS, Vincent F. Seyfried and William Asadorian. Over 160 rare photographs of Maspeth, Jamaica, Jackson Heights, and other areas. Vintage views of DeWitt Clinton mansion, 1939 World's Fair and more. Captions. 192pp. 8⅞ × 11. **26358-4 Pa. $12.95**

CAPTURED BY THE INDIANS: 15 Firsthand Accounts, 1750–1870, Frederick Drimmer. Astounding true historical accounts of grisly torture, bloody conflicts, relentless pursuits, miraculous escapes and more, by people who lived to tell the tale. 384pp. 5⅜ × 8½. **24901-8 Pa. $8.95**

THE WORLD'S GREAT SPEECHES, Lewis Copeland and Lawrence W. Lamm (eds.). Vast collection of 278 speeches of Greeks to 1970. Powerful and effective models; unique look at history. 842pp. 5⅜ × 8½. **20468-5 Pa. $14.95**

THE BOOK OF THE SWORD, Sir Richard F. Burton. Great Victorian scholar/adventurer's eloquent, erudite history of the "queen of weapons"—from prehistory to early Roman Empire. Evolution and development of early swords, variations (sabre, broadsword, cutlass, scimitar, etc.), much more. 336pp. 6⅛ × 9¼. **25434-8 Pa. $8.95**

AUTOBIOGRAPHY: The Story of My Experiments with Truth, Mohandas K. Gandhi. Boyhood, legal studies, purification, the growth of the Satyagraha (nonviolent protest) movement. Critical, inspiring work of the man responsible for the freedom of India. 480pp. 5⅜ × 8½. (USO) 24593-4 Pa. $8.95

CELTIC MYTHS AND LEGENDS, T. W. Rolleston. Masterful retelling of Irish and Welsh stories and tales. Cuchulain, King Arthur, Deirdre, the Grail, many more. First paperback edition. 58 full-page illustrations. 512pp. 5⅜ × 8½. 26507-2 Pa. $9.95

THE PRINCIPLES OF PSYCHOLOGY, William James. Famous long course complete, unabridged. Stream of thought, time perception, memory, experimental methods; great work decades ahead of its time. 94 figures. 1,391pp. 5⅜×8½. 2-vol. set.
Vol. I: 20381-6 Pa. $12.95
Vol. II: 20382-4 Pa. $12.95

THE WORLD AS WILL AND REPRESENTATION, Arthur Schopenhauer. Definitive English translation of Schopenhauer's life work, correcting more than 1,000 errors, omissions in earlier translations. Translated by E. F. J. Payne. Total of 1,269pp. 5⅜ × 8½. 2-vol. set.
Vol. 1: 21761-2 Pa. $11.95
Vol. 2: 21762-0 Pa. $11.95

MAGIC AND MYSTERY IN TIBET, Madame Alexandra David-Neel. Experiences among lamas, magicians, sages, sorcerers, Bonpa wizards. A true psychic discovery. 32 illustrations. 321pp. 5⅜ × 8½. (USO) 22682-4 Pa. $8.95

THE EGYPTIAN BOOK OF THE DEAD, E. A. Wallis Budge. Complete reproduction of Ani's papyrus, finest ever found. Full hieroglyphic text, interlinear transliteration, word-for-word translation, smooth translation. 533pp. 6½ × 9¼. 21866-X Pa. $9.95

MATHEMATICS FOR THE NONMATHEMATICIAN, Morris Kline. Detailed, college-level treatment of mathematics in cultural and historical context, with numerous exercises. Recommended Reading Lists. Tables. Numerous figures. 641pp. 5⅜ × 8½. 24823-2 Pa. $11.95

THEORY OF WING SECTIONS: Including a Summary of Airfoil Data, Ira H. Abbott and A. E. von Doenhoff. Concise compilation of subsonic aerodynamic characteristics of NACA wing sections, plus description of theory. 350pp. of tables. 693pp. 5⅜ × 8½. 60586-8 Pa. $14.95

THE RIME OF THE ANCIENT MARINER, Gustave Doré, S. T. Coleridge. Doré's finest work; 34 plates capture moods, subtleties of poem. Flawless full-size reproductions printed on facing pages with authoritative text of poem. "Beautiful. Simply beautiful."—*Publisher's Weekly.* 77pp. 9¼ × 12. 22305-1 Pa. $6.95

NORTH AMERICAN INDIAN DESIGNS FOR ARTISTS AND CRAFTS-PEOPLE, Eva Wilson. Over 360 authentic copyright-free designs adapted from Navajo blankets, Hopi pottery, Sioux buffalo hides, more. Geometrics, symbolic figures, plant and animal motifs, etc. 128pp. 8⅜ × 11. (EUK) 25341-4 Pa. $7.95

SCULPTURE: Principles and Practice, Louis Slobodkin. Step-by-step approach to clay, plaster, metals, stone; classical and modern. 253 drawings, photos. 255pp. 8⅛ × 11. 22960-2 Pa. $10.95

CATALOG OF DOVER BOOKS

THE INFLUENCE OF SEA POWER UPON HISTORY, 1660–1783, A. T. Mahan. Influential classic of naval history and tactics still used as text in war colleges. First paperback edition. 4 maps. 24 battle plans. 640pp. 5⅜ × 8½.
25509-3 Pa. $12.95

THE STORY OF THE TITANIC AS TOLD BY ITS SURVIVORS, Jack Winocour (ed.). What it was really like. Panic, despair, shocking inefficiency, and a little heroism. More thrilling than any fictional account. 26 illustrations. 320pp. 5⅜ × 8½.
20610-6 Pa. $8.95

FAIRY AND FOLK TALES OF THE IRISH PEASANTRY, William Butler Yeats (ed.). Treasury of 64 tales from the twilight world of Celtic myth and legend: "The Soul Cages," "The Kildare Pooka," "King O'Toole and his Goose," many more. Introduction and Notes by W. B. Yeats. 352pp. 5⅜ × 8½.
26941-8 Pa. $8.95

BUDDHIST MAHAYANA TEXTS, E. B. Cowell and Others (eds.). Superb, accurate translations of basic documents in Mahayana Buddhism, highly important in history of religions. The Buddha-karita of Asvaghosha, Larger Sukhavativyuha, more. 448pp. 5⅜ × 8½.
25552-2 Pa. $9.95

ONE TWO THREE . . . INFINITY: Facts and Speculations of Science, George Gamow. Great physicist's fascinating, readable overview of contemporary science: number theory, relativity, fourth dimension, entropy, genes, atomic structure, much more. 128 illustrations. Index. 352pp. 5⅜ × 8½.
25664-2 Pa. $8.95

ENGINEERING IN HISTORY, Richard Shelton Kirby, et al. Broad, nontechnical survey of history's major technological advances: birth of Greek science, industrial revolution, electricity and applied science, 20th-century automation, much more. 181 illustrations. ". . . excellent . . ."—Isis. Bibliography. vii + 530pp. 5⅜ × 8¼.
26412-2 Pa. $14.95

Prices subject to change without notice.

Available at your book dealer or write for free catalog to Dept. GI, Dover Publications, Inc., 31 East 2nd St., Mineola, N.Y. 11501. Dover publishes more than 500 books each year on science, elementary and advanced mathematics, biology, music, art, literary history, social sciences and other areas.